DEVS

Double Dragon, Double Lion

The Official Biography of John Devereux

DEVS

Double Dragon, Double Lion

The Official Biography of John Devereux

Andy Howell

ST DAVID'S PRESS

Cardiff

Published in Wales by St. David's Press, an imprint of

Ashley Drake Publishing Ltd
PO Box 733
Cardiff
CF14 7ZY

www.st-davids-press.wales

First Impression – 2023

ISBN
Paperback 978-1-904609-05-6
eBook 978-1-904609-06-3

British Library Cataloguing-in-Publication Data.
A CIP catalogue for this book is available from the British Library.

Typeset by Prepress Plus Technologies (www.prepressplustechnologies.com)
Cover designed by the Welsh Books Council, Aberystwyth

Contents

To my mum and dad, Peter and Valerie, who gave me everything they could, Auntie Florrie who loved me like the son she never had, and to Alison and my two wonderful daughters, Jessica and Ellen, whose love and support have helped me achieve so much. I've been a lucky man to have had you all in my life.

Acknowledgements

When the idea of a book was first discussed with my publisher a few years ago I jumped at the chance to tell the story of my rugby career and my journey through life, and I'm very grateful to all those who have helped me gather my memories and clarify my recollections from decades ago. Rugby is a team game and publishing a book is no different. Many people have been involved over the past few years, and I'd like to thank everyone for their kindness and support.

I've been incredibly humbled that so many former teachers, teammates and coaches – John Lloyd, Dai Harris, Jonathan Davies, Rob Ackerman, Stuart Davies, Dai Rees, Paul Moriarty, David Bryant, Des Hasler, Shaun Edwards, Mark Jones, Tony Gray, Sir Ian McGeechan, Clive Griffiths, Derek Quinnell, Jim Mills and Dougie Laughton – agreed to be interviewed for the book and so generously contributed some very kind comments about my abilities as a rugby player. A special word also for the great Clive Rowlands who contributed to the book but sadly passed away before its publication. Without question one of the greats of the game we all love, who captained and then coached Wales before acting as team manager for the 1989 Lions, 'Top Cat' is hugely missed by us all. His passion for Wales and enthusiasm for rugby will never be forgotten.

I'd also like to thank those who have sent me photographs of events mentioned in the book, and some occasions that I'd long forgotten! Some were included while others didn't make the final cut, but I sincerely appreciate them all.

This book would not have been written without the incredible work of my biographer Andy Howell, who has done a great job of telling my story. Andy was also a student at Cyncoed back in the mid-1980s, where we shared many good times.

Thanks also to my publisher, Ashley Drake of St. David's Press, for his commitment and dedication to this project from the start, and for his guidance and positivity throughout the publishing process.

My wife, Alison, and my two daughters, Jessica and Ellen, deserve a special mention for their encouragement and patience while I've been working on this book. You mean the world to me, and I can't thank you enough.

A special thanks goes to Tina Phillips, Alisons mum, who I met when I was just 15, and who became a great support to me Alison and our girls, and still continues to offer unconditional support.

To my great friend, Lyndon Thomas, the former captain and chairman at Bridgend RFC who has been instrumental in helping me make the correct decisions and steering me in the right direction in my life outside of rugby. Also, a big *diolch yn fawr* to Gareth Milton-Jones for his support and generosity during this book project, and for many decades before that. Ultimately, none of this would have been possible without the love of my parents, Peter and Valerie, and my two sisters, Lynne & Ceri.

All sporting careers and life journeys are a mix of ups and downs and I've been extremely fortunate to have experienced far more ups than downs. Both of these aspects of my life are important as they helped shape the person I became and, right from the very start of the project, Andy, Ashley and I agreed that it was essential to recount the downs as well as the ups, and that is what we've tried to do.

The opinions I express in the book, on a number of issues, are mine and mine alone. I don't claim that my views are more important or more correct than those of others, they are just the way I've experienced life and rugby, in union and league.

John Devereux
Pen-y-fai, Bridgend
November 2023

Foreword

I first met John 'Devs' Devereux when he was named in the Wales team for his debut, against England at Twickenham in the 1986 Five Nations, and we immediately hit it off to become great friends.

Devs was only 19 but he was a great kid and already a big and powerful player with one of the strongest hand-offs in rugby, union or league. He was a guy you wanted alongside you in the trenches, a hard man who wouldn't take a backward step and who you knew you could rely on. I remember being on the receiving end during a mass brawl in Tonga. It was a fight like no other and Devs was the only Welsh player to get the better of his opponent.

He was devastating at the inaugural union World Cup of 1987 in Australia and New Zealand. We had some great footballers in our team and they were able to shine because he provided the power in the backs to get us going forward.

John set up an important try against Ireland in a vital pool match, scored against England when we rolled them over in the quarter-finals, got another in the semi-final defeat to New Zealand and ran amok against an outstanding Australia side in the third-place play-off. Wales still haven't bettered that finish and Devs remains one of Wales' most influential players in World Cup history.

Our friendship continued when he came north to join me in rugby league at Widnes. He certainly made a mark on his debut, getting yellow carded following a scrap with Darrel Williams when we faced the Kiwis. We shared some fantastic memories with club, Wales and Great Britain. It's not easy to make the transition from union to league but Devs did it and more. He was prepared to learn, was a diligent trainer, hated losing and was extremely popular with teammates and supporters.

There was also an absent-minded and accident-prone side to him, whether it was the mishaps he had with panes of glass or when he ran into a goal upright during a warm-up lap in training and sustained a bloody gash to his forehead.

When Devs was fit and firing, he was one of league's best wingers. He's the last Wales rugby union international to play in a league World Cup final, for Great Britain against Australia at Wembley in 1992.

I'll never forget when he went head-to-head with New Zealand All Blacks great Inga Tuigamala as Wales faced Samoa in the RL World Cup at Swansea City's Vetch Field ground in 1995. Devs squared up to him as Samoa did their pre-match *Haka* and wanted to rip Inga's head off. When the whistle sounded to start the match it all kicked off. It was one of the most brutal and memorable games I played in. We won and Devs was in the thick of it.

Not many British league players have made it in Australia's crack National Rugby League or, for that matter, been offered a contract, but Devs did with Manly and was a huge hit Down Under. That's a mark of John the player and man. He was special on and off the pitch!

Jonathan Davies
September 2023

1

'Is There a John Devereux Here?'

'You could sense something special was happening as Devs produced probably the single most overwhelming case I have ever witnessed for selection by Wales.'

Stuart Davies

On a cold winter's day in 1986, a biting crisp wind blew off the Bristol Channel and chilled shoppers walking along the streets of Cardiff in search of bargains in the January sales.

John Devereux was also in the centre of the Welsh capital, visiting the city's historic castle. He wasn't among the many tourists from across the world who were busy taking snapshots, though, but on a field visit with some of his student pals and a few college lecturers from South Glamorgan Institute of Higher Education, which is known now as Cardiff Metropolitan University, or Cardiff Met.

'It was a pretty typical college day,' he said. 'We were in one of the castle's beautifully ornate rooms studying its architecture when a chap appeared from nowhere, in a scene which could have been from the cartoon Mr Benn, and said: "Is there a John Devereux here? There's an urgent phone call for him".'

Devereux wasn't expecting a call and had no idea who knew he was at the castle, or why they had contacted him. His initial reaction was to panic, thinking something major had happened to his family in the Garw Valley, 30 miles away. Fearing the worst, he followed the member of staff through the castle to the office where the phone was located, then nervously picked up the phone: 'Hello. John Devereux speaking'. A voice at the other end responded: 'Good morning, John, it's John Dawes here.'

Dawes was the man who had captained Wales to glory in the early 1970s and led the 1971 British and Irish Lions to an historic first, and thus far only, Test series conquest over New Zealand. He was, like Devereux, a centre, and possessed one of the brightest and sharpest rugby brains in the game. After retiring as a player, Dawes then coached Wales to Grand Slam glory and took charge of the 1977 Lions in New Zealand. The rugby world mourned when he sadly passed away in 2021. In 1986, however, John 'Sid' Dawes was the Welsh Rugby Union's coaching organiser and, more importantly, one of the selectors of the national team. Without doubt, Dawes was rugby royalty in a rugby-obsessed nation.

Confused as to why he was supposedly being called by Dawes, the undergraduate wasn't sure whether to believe it was Dawes speaking to him, or if he was the victim of a student prank: 'I genuinely thought it was a wind-up. I don't think it could happen in this day and age. I was absolutely gobsmacked and found it hard to believe that the great John Dawes was on the other end of the telephone line.

'The penny dropped, and I knew it was definitely him on the telephone, when he congratulated me and told me I had been selected to play for Wales against England at Twickenham in the Five Nations Championship on 18 January. This was no wind up. I was going to play for Wales! I was 19 years old, had never played for my country at any level, and was 'only' playing for a college side. Even now, when I think back to that moment when John said those magic words, the hairs on the back of my neck stand up and it brings a smile to my face. It was just an incredible moment.'

As Devereux was digesting the news he'd just heard, his fellow students and their lecturers were anxiously waiting to find out who had tracked him to the castle, and urgently summoned him to the phone. Their fear that something terrible had happened quickly turned to joy when the young student returned to them with an obvious spring in his step and a huge grin across his face. Hardly believing it himself, Devereux recounted his conversation with Dawes, and that he'd been selected to play for Wales.

'That calls for a celebration,' said a lecturer, who immediately cancelled the field trip and directed the students out of the castle, across its drawbridge, and over the road to the Horse and Groom on Womanby Street, a popular pub with South Glamorgan Institute students. Of course, one thing led to another.

'It didn't take long for the jungle drums to beat, and word got back to college about my selection,' beamed Devereux. 'Pretty soon, the pub was crammed as students descended on it from the Institute's

Cyncoed Campus and other parts of Cardiff. Before long it seemed like half the college was either in or gathered outside the pub, and it quickly became an unofficial day off. It was a crazy day, and night, as the beers kept flowing. Crikey, looking back, we had heck of a session – I can't remember much that happened after 9.30pm that night!'

Journalists at *The Western Mail*, the national newspaper of Wales, and its evening counterpart, the *South Wales Echo* – headquartered a few hundred yards away in the city centre – soon heard of the student party on Womanby Street, probably due to the eagle-eyed freelancers at Hills Welsh Press agency which happened to be based a few doors down from the Horse and Groom. The reporters found Devereux somewhere inside the pub and were soon having photographs taken of the new rugby sensation pulling pints behind the bar. The festivities then spilled out into the street, where he was carried shoulder-high by his friends and fellow students: 'It was an occasion I will never forget and I feel privileged to have shared it with a wonderful group of people. Most of them are still firm friends.'

Devereux's student days had started in September 1984 when he enrolled on the Human Movement Studies course at South Glamorgan Institute, with the intention of becoming a secondary school PE teacher. 'That's where I saw my future,' he said, 'until Wales rugby came calling. Then things changed.'

Saturday, 16 November 1985 was the day Devereux's life changed forever and led to the phone call from John Dawes a few weeks later. On that cold mid-November day, a crowd of noisy students and nervous Cardiff RFC supporters stood around the Institute's rugby pitch in the leafy Cyncoed suburb of the Welsh capital to watch the college side play the famous Arms Park-based club in first round of the Schweppes Welsh Cup. It was a major competition back then, attracting big crowds and considerable media attention, with the final at the old National Stadium usually a sell-out affair.

Llanelli were the cup kings but Cardiff were a huge draw. The self-proclaimed greatest rugby union club in the world boasted a squad of Wales and Lions stars, and even had an England international in the ranks in gnarly No.8 John Scott. They were the team everybody wanted to shoot down.

Cardiff had been in a rich vein of form, and travelled the short distance across the Welsh capital on the back of five straight wins, over Harlequins, Newbridge, Leicester Tigers, Oxford University and Ebbw Vale. Anglo-Welsh matches were the norm in the days before the establishment of formal league rugby, and to defeat Harlequins at The Stoop then doing a hatchet job on the Tigers at Welford Road highlighted how well the 'Blue and Blacks' were playing, and the power and quality at their disposal.

Now in his second year at a college famed for the sporting stars it had produced, Devereux and his fellow student rugby players knew that the cup tie was not only a chance for them to measure themselves against a team packed with star players, it was also a huge opportunity to put themselves in the shop window, and that impressive performances would boost their individual chances of attracting offers from senior clubs after graduating from South Glamorgan Institute.

'Cardiff showed us enormous respect by fielding a near first-choice side,' recalls Devereux. 'Gareth Davies, their star outside-half who missed the game through injury, was the only major name not playing. We were undaunted, though, by the strength of their side and totally determined to take Cardiff on, with all guns blazing. Our coach, Leighton 'Nutty' Davies, didn't need to do much to get us all pumped up. The campus was absolutely buzzing with expectation in the days before the game and if we couldn't motivate ourselves to face the city slickers, we shouldn't have been playing rugby.'

In the days of the old Merit Table, first-class clubs had devised a practical and generally successful plan to overcome the fit and energetic college boys of Cyncoed. By deploying the superior experience, strength and power of their forwards to keep the ball tight, opposing teams relentlessly smashed and exhausted the Institute's front eight, which would ensure that the college's quick and inventive backs were starved of any decent possession.

Cardiff, with an all-Wales front-row of props Jeff Whitefoot and Ian Eidman packing down either side of hooker Alan Phillips, weren't in the mood to mess around with the upstart undergraduates. Eidman was a giant, Whitefoot a bruiser who knew all the tricks in the book, while 'Thumper' Phillips was a highly mobile hooker who seemed to spend much of his time, during broken play, lurking on or near the wing. He had a panache for scoring tries. If he was a footballer, Phillips would have been called a goal-hanger. He had played for the Lions and went on to coach Cardiff, spend 19 years as Wales team manager to six head coaches, and was Warren Gatland's fixer during his first, 'golden', spell which brought four Six Nations titles, three with Grand Slams and two appearances in the World Cup semi-finals.

That Cardiff front row was just the tip of the iceberg. The Blue and Blacks also boasted a man who would be up there with Alun Wyn Jones if it came to a debate over who would be the best lock pairing in Welsh rugby history. Robert Norster had captained his country and was a peerless line-out jumper and natural athlete. It was the days before lifting was allowed, and Norster had such a spring he soared above teammates and opponents.

Behind Norster at No.8 was John Scott who, with his drooped moustache, looked like a gunfighter from the Wild West, and played like one. He was menacing and ready to inflict pain and punishment at will.

Cardiff's backs weren't mugs either, with Adrian Hadley on the wing, another Wales international, Alun Donovan, at centre, while Paul 'Pablo' Rees, 'arguably one of the best Welsh players not be capped,' according to Devereux, 'was a fearless full-back.'

Apart from full-back Rees, an uncle of Wales' 2021 Six Nations Championship title winning wing sensation Louis Rees-Zammit, fly-half David Barry and scrum-half Steve Cannon, the entire Cardiff team were full internationals. However, that only served to stoke up the hungry students to double their efforts.

'The big names didn't deter us,' said a grinning Devereux. 'In fact, they inspired us. We had a steely determination to do ourselves, our families, the college and our student friends proud. We even stayed off the beer for a few days! I could sense the tension in the air. Some of the lads may have been nervous but they were fired up to give their all. We not only wanted to get stuck into Cardiff physically, but also to show what we could do. We knew the only chance we had of beating them was to move the ball and exhaust their old stagers like Eidman and Whitefoot.'

Being a student campus, the changing rooms at Cyncoed were situated well away from the pitch and meant that the players had to cross a road and walk down a path to take the field. 'That walk, on the tarmac,' winked Devereux, 'helped to sharpen up your studs nicely before kick-off.'

When the students got to the pitch and looked across at the star-studded opposition, Devereux realised there was another international player in the Cardiff ranks, one he'd overlooked. Rob Ackerman had just joined the Arms Park club from London Welsh and was making his Blue and Blacks debut. The press had devoted many articles that week about Cardiff's new recruit but Devereux admits that he had been 'blissfully unaware' Ackerman had joined the team he was playing that afternoon. 'However, I did know he'd been a Test Lion in New Zealand 18 months earlier and was the holder of the Wales No.13 jersey.

'I may have missed the news about the move, but the presence of Ackerman didn't faze or over-awe me because I had confidence in my ability and just concentrated on doing what I did best. I was pleased with how I played and happy with the number of breaks I managed to make, thanks to a few straight-arm handoffs on Rob that put him on the deck and me through the Cardiff defence. We lost the match 25-15 but outscored Cardiff on tries and I stole the headlines. Everyone wanted to know about the student who'd got the better of the current and highly-respected Welsh international centre. I was the talk of Wales and news of my performance was splashed over the Sunday and Monday newspapers, which in those days were influential and had big circulations.

'When the final whistle was blown and the players started shaking hands, I could clearly see my muddy finger marks and hand prints on Rob's shirt and face. He was generous in his praise and I knew I'd earned his respect. My good performance had been won at his expense, which must have been hard to take, but I soon discovered what a lovely man he was and we were soon to become firm friends.'

Accomplished journalist John Kennedy, who had been a scrum-half of note in his native Zimbabwe and a writer who was a fine judge of a player, had been covering the match for the *Western Mail*. 'JK nicknamed me 'Dalek' for the hand-off I was to become known for,' chuckled Devereux, as he cast his mind back. 'A newspaper mocked up a picture of me stood next to one of Doctor Who's Daleks and I suddenly became known. My career really took off from that point. I never looked back after that match.

'I'd gone from being a nobody to a somebody in the space of 80 minutes. It was an incredible feeling to read the positive articles about me but I was determined to keep my feet on the ground. I had been told by my coaches and teachers that no matter what happened, I had to keep working hard at my game and strive to improve as a player.'

Ironically, Devereux hadn't spent much time working on his deadly hand-off. 'It was just something I had picked up at a young age and it came to me naturally,' he explained. 'If an opposing player rushed in to tackle me and was stood upright, then I would free a hand to push him off. It was about timing and power and was to work well for me over the years. I don't think I'd get away with it these days because the hand-off to the face has been outlawed by World Rugby in its bid to make the game safer and reduce the number of concussions.'

Ackerman went on to become a school teacher in New Zealand and Australia, where he still lives, and has vivid memories of the tie. When he answered his 'phone and was told the purpose of the call, he laughed and said: 'That match! I clearly remember it. Devs had one hell of a game and I was below par. I was taken to a place no player wants to go. I haven't been the only one because John Devereux was no ordinary player, he was outstanding.

'I would like to think I was a pretty physical player but he was more so. I would liken him to Philippe Sella, the great French centre. The pair of them were super strong and both liked the hard stuff, the physical side of rugby, but they also possessed skill and finesse. It was just the way it was. Devs out-played me that day, he had a huge fend-off and he put me on my back. I went for him and he went for me, and he won. He was on fire, it's as simple as that.

'I didn't have a clue who he was before that match,' Ackerman added. 'I had never heard of him and I don't think many others had either, but his name was on everybody's lips afterwards because of the way he played. I take my hat off to him.'

Stuart Davies, another future Wales international of note who was also to become captain of Swansea RFC, played at No.8 for the student side that day when reputations were made and lost, and has nothing but the highest praise for his teammate and friend, John Devereux: 'It was David versus Goliath when it came to South Glamorgan Institute against Cardiff. The tie attracted a big crowd and we got well and truly stuck into them. It was one of those occasions where you could sense something special was happening as Devs produced probably the single most overwhelming case I have ever witnessed for selection by Wales.

'All of us at Cyncoed knew he was handy, but he wasn't on the national selectors' radar until he comprehensively destroyed Rob Ackerman in that game; the destructive job he did on him was just extraordinary. We left the pitch with our heads held high and with good memories. None more than Devs.'

Dai Rees, who played at outside-half for the Institute that day, is another with vivid memories of the match. 'I can see John's hand-offs of Rob as though it was yesterday. They spun John from nowhere into the Wales team. What were Devs' strengths? He just played without fear. He was physical, a big centre for his era, about 6ft 2in tall, weighing over 15st and he was fast. If I remember rightly, John had been injured and the match was supposed to be about Ackerman, the Wales incumbent who'd signed from London Welsh and was making his Cardiff debut.

'All the headlines before the game had been about Rob,' said Dai, who was capped by Wales B, and went on to coach through the Welsh age grades, Sevens and Women's teams before becoming high-performance manager at the Hong Kong Rugby Union, 'but John had other ideas and sat him on his backside numerous times with his big fend-off. Afterwards, the headlines were all about Devs. It was a day none of us who played for the college will forget. It was one of those "we were there" moments.'

Despite being on the losing side on that November day, Devereux's impact on the match, and on Welsh rugby was huge, a literal overnight sensation. 'After the Cardiff game we were buzzing and all went out and had a great night,' he recalls. 'The following morning, I was woken up by a load of friends banging on the front door of my Bangor Street digs in the Roath district of Cardiff. They threw the newspapers at me, which were full of journalists asking who was this John Devereux and where had I been hiding? My pals loved it.'

Cardiff went on to lift the cup that season, which said something about the quality of Devereux and South Glamorgan Institute's display, but the match had also ignited Devereux's career. It had taken off in an instant and was to lead to a career that allowed him to travel the rugby world, to play union for Wales and the British and Irish Lions and international rugby league for Wales and Great Britain.

2

Garw Valley Boy

'He set such high standards, he wanted to be the best he could and left no stone unturned.'

John Lloyd

Wednesday, 30 March 1966. Liverpool were striding towards their seventh Football League title to equal Arsenal's then record. It was a convincing triumph under the guidance of legendary manager Bill Shankly as they finished six points clear of Leeds United with Burnley in third. Liverpool also reached their first European final, going down 2-1 to German side Borussia Dortmund at Glasgow's Hampden Park. An all-red playing strip had been adopted for the season, and the colour and the club were to become a firm favourite of John Anthony Devereux after he entered the world at 9.30am in the morning at 81 Upper Adare Street, Pontycymer. It was same house where his father had been born 30 years earlier.

Devereux was an Aries, the British Prime Minister was the Labour party's Harold Wilson, Lyndon B Johnson, who had inherited the United States presidency when John F Kennedy had been assassinated, was wrestling with the war in Vietnam, while Pope St Paul VI was three years into his 15-year reign as head of the Catholic Church. The Walker Brothers were top of the UK singles pop chart with *The Sun Ain't Gonna Shine Anymore*, with The Hollies, The Beach Boys, The Kinks and Gene Pitney all in the top ten.

Devereux was one of Peter and Valerie Devereux's three children, and grew up in the village of Pontycymer in the Garw Valley with his sisters Lynne and Ceri. It was a mining village whose name – *pont* means bridge and *cymer* a confluence of two rivers or streams – pretty well sums up the place and, according to the 2021 census, had a population of around 2,500. Pontycymer may be a relatively

9

small place, but it can boast plenty of its people who have found fame, including broadcaster Huw Edwards, artist and journalist Molly Parkin, and professional snooker player Ryan Day. Another notable son of Pontycymer was Dr Dan Davies, a physician to the Queen of England and, during the establishment of the National Health Service, a chief advisor to Welsh royalty, Labour's post-war health secretary, Aneurin Bevan MP.

Like many mining valleys, the local rugby club played a major role in the life of the community and as the young John Devereux grew up, he would have been told of the Garw Valley's rugby sons, such as the great Ike Owens, who changed codes in 1943, went on to captain Leeds and tour Australia with the victorious Great Britain 'Indomitables' in 1946. There was also prop John 'Boyo' James who won a single cap for Wales against England in January 1968, Illtyd Williams the influential school teacher and rugby coach after whom a Bridgend and District schools cup competition was named, and future Wales union captains, John Lloyd and Jeff Young. As a physical education teacher at nearby Ynysawdre Comprehensive School, Lloyd was destined to play a highly influential role in the development of John Devereux, on and off the rugby field.

Unusually small for a coalfield community family, Devereux had a happy and carefree childhood. 'My dad was an only child while my mother's only sister had passed away when I was about three. I had three cousins, David, Gareth and Huw, who lived in Aberkenfig, and a lovely Aunt Florrie who treated me as if I was her son,' he recalled. 'Everyone knew everybody in the community. It may have been a deprived area but it was a safe village in which to live and people left their front and back doors open as there was little crime.'

It was quickly evident the young Devereux was very athletic and a natural across a range of different sports, from rugby, football and tennis to basketball, cricket and athletics. Give him a ball or a chance to show his physical prowess and he was in his element. 'I got my fast twitch fibres from my mother,' said Devereux, with a laugh. 'I'm told she was very good at school sports but she wasn't sporty as an adult, her time being occupied bringing up Lynne, Ceri and me, before returning to work.

'I was always out playing with my friends. We lived at the top of a hill and I can remember being exhausted and struggling to make it back up the steep slope at the end of long and balmy summer days after playing down in the village. We used to play 'kick the can', 'chase', 'tag' and loved climbing trees.

'If my mother needed me, she knew she'd find me playing with my friends on the mountain side or at Lawrence Park, the home of Pontycymer RFC. I was part of a little gang with Andrew 'Naco' Lewis, Gary Williams, Julian John and Paul Samuel. We were a mischievous bunch and would get into all sorts of trouble, like when we were, correctly, rapped over the knuckles for starting a brush fire on the common.

'Behind our house was farmland leading towards the top of the mountain. Everyone knew the farmer as 'Shinko', who used to ride a horse and carry a 12-bore shotgun. We used to wind him up and play in his barns but, if he caught us, he would have a right go at us – it was part of growing up.

'Another favourite was baiting the National Coal Board watchman at the Ffaldau Colliery in the village. We knew we were safe with him because he wasn't fast enough to catch us and we had plenty of escape routes mapped out. One of our favourite games was to climb on top of the coal-filled wagons then run along them, from one end to the other. We were always covered in thick black coal dust after that caper.'

John Devereux could have played for Ireland rather than Wales because his grandfather, Michael Devereux, had crossed the Irish Sea to take up work as a coal miner but, as he adamantly states: 'It never crossed my mind. I was Welsh, and back then there wasn't much player movement between countries. Rugby union was still amateur so the only people who played outside their home countries were those who had travelled for work, education or adventure. Back then, the rugby authorities didn't have people checking player heritage so when I was touted for my first cap the Irish were probably unaware that I was qualified for them. If they had asked me then, or now, the answer would have been the same: "Sorry but no, it's only Wales for me".

'I'm not a fan of players switching allegiance after they've already been capped. Once you've played international rugby for one country you shouldn't be allowed to flip to another. The residency rule has its place, in my view, for those who are uncapped, but it shouldn't be applied to those who've already won international honours. Football has very clear eligibility criteria – if you aren't born in that country, or have parents or grandparents who were born in that country, you are not eligible. I'm not saying that rugby should follow those stipulations, but it would certainly be transparent, applied equally across all nations, and prevent some unions from stretching the spirit of the game to breaking point.'

Nonetheless, playing Test rugby was far from Devereux's mind when, at the age of seven or eight, his father's half-sister took him under her wing: 'Aunt Florrie took me everywhere with her and Uncle Evan. She didn't have any children of her own after losing a son at childbirth, and I became her adopted son. We would travel on buses, visiting zoos and safari parks in England and, during the spring and autumn, when there were high tides, they would collect me from school and we'd take a bus ride to the lighthouse at Porthcawl to see the waves crashing over the top of it.

'My uncle and aunt had a great interest in, and love for, rugby and sometimes took me to games. I remember seeing my first live Barbarians match when they played, and lost, against Cardiff at the Arms Park in the annual Easter tour game, years before the introduction of leagues in Wales. I can vividly remember a very young Gareth Davies starring for Cardiff. He called the shots from outside-half and was among the best kickers of a ball I have ever seen. Better, I'd say, than many of those playing today. In my opinion, the tactical kicking – out of hand – was far more accurate during the amateur era and Gareth was a master of the art.'

Devereux regrets his Aunt Florrie never saw him play for Wales, saying: 'I was devastated that she passed away a year before my first cap as she would have been so proud. It was a real shame and left such a hole in my life.'

Another who provided him with valuable life lessons was Dai Harris, his school master at Ffaldau Primary School in Pontycymer. 'Dai told me the day I left for comprehensive school: "Remember John, you are a good rugby player but you must also work hard at school with your studies". I never forgot that advice and it has stood me in good stead.'

Harris later moved to the United States to teach, and now lives in Arizona. Although more of a football man, he taught rugby at Ffaldau, recalling: 'Arthur Thomas was the head teacher and if you were to do so much as bring a soccer ball into school, he would have disowned you! He was a rugby man so the oval ball dominated.'

Even as a schoolboy, it was clear to Harris that the young Devereux was something special. 'John was the outstanding player from the word go. He played scrum-half initially. The balls were leather back then and bounced about 20 feet high on a firm pitch in dry weather, but were as heavy as lead on a wet day when they'd absorbed moisture. If a wet ball hit you in the head, it could knock you out. Fixtures took place each Friday and John made a positive impression. He could also kick the ball a heck of a distance for a young lad.'

Reminiscing about his schoolboy rugby, Devereux commented: 'I got into the district team when I was nine, and Arthur Thomas used to give me a lift to the training sessions at Brynteg Comp in his Renault car. It was one of those vehicles where you pulled a lever on the dashboard to change gear.'

Harris then added: 'John had been moved to outside-half and I can remember us winning the Frowen Sevens competition at Ogmore Vale. You could already see he had the makings of being a special player. He had speed, was naturally strong, had a sporting brain, was extremely enthusiastic and detested losing. Throw in his wonderful skill and hand-to-eye co-ordination and you had a born sportsman. John would have been good at virtually any sport but chose rugby. Also, and I think this is most important, John also had the desire to learn and keep learning, a trait I believe he still possesses. He lived for his rugby, and basketball. We were fortunate in having a good team in both those sports, in no small measure thanks to John.'

Devereux left primary school aged 11, and headed for Ynysawdre School, a comprehensive, where he came under the tutelage of Lloyd, the ex-Wales prop and later coach of the national team. 'He was a bright-eyed lad, very popular and had a tremendous love of sport, which was coupled with a great sense of humour,' recalled Lloyd. 'He seemed to be able to turn his hand to any sport. Not only was he good at rugby but football, cricket, athletics and tennis, a true all-rounder with a mountain of talent.

'He was part of the rugby team from year seven right through to the senior team and played an important part in it. John played in a few positions and was a very gutsy player who always wanted to win. Winning was important to him – he had a good knowledge and understanding of sport, was a great team man and a very skilful ball player. I would say he was one of the best players to come through Ynysawdre because he went on to achieve so much.

'His competitiveness was unbelievable. If he was playing tiddlywinks he would want to win, and he set such high standards. John wanted to be the best he could and left no stone unturned. Only two boys in Ynysawdre did weight-training; John Devereux and Huw Bevan. That's why they were such powerful boys, the two best weight trainers the school ever had. John had a strong upper body and legs, and was ultra-disciplined with his nutrition.'

Lloyd's faith in his talented young pupil was illustrated when Ynysawdre's U16 and U18 teams travelled to Cowbridge Comprehensive for a double-header: 'I was 15 and playing for the U16s, but when a boy in the senior team got injured, John Lloyd called me off the field and told me I had to step up and play in the U18s match instead. It was a huge boost to my confidence that John thought I was good enough to compete against boys a couple of years older than me, particularly when I helped to set up the winning try with just ten minutes left.'

Devereux's fellow pupil and committed weight-trainer at Ynysawdre, Huw Bevan, went on to play hooker for Bridgend and Cardiff and was the England cricket team's fitness coach when they dominated the sport, as well as having similar roles in professional sport, including with the Ospreys and Dragons rugby squads before holding high performance roles with the United States and Welsh rugby unions.

'When I attended my first training session with Wales, I found I was stronger than the forwards, with the exception of Dai Young,' said Devereux. 'Dai used to do weight-training on the morning of a Wales game and was phenomenal when it came to lifting iron. I'd been weight-training since I was 14, and when I played for South Glamorgan Institute, against older men, a lot of them couldn't believe how strong I was – not just upper-body but my legs as well. A lot of players stop in contact but I kept moving through it and ran my weight. I was 15st with just 8% body fat, the fittest I ever was.'

Devereux was the only member of the group of friends that had grown up together in Pontycymer who went to higher education and graduated with a degree. 'Most of the gang left school at 16 and went to technical college or straight into work, as an apprentice or training for a trade. Me and Alun 'Maxi' Thomas were the only two who stayed on for A levels, in the sixth form at Ynysawdre. After a few months, Maxi decided to leave and got a job working for an insurance company in Bridgend town centre. He only did that for a year, before joining South Wales Police and went on to become a high-flying and very successful officer, retiring from the service as a Chief Superintendent at 49.

'I studied economics, geology and geography and worked my socks off to pass my A levels. It was great to be still in the school environment and play for the rugby team, but it was tough to see so many of my friends leave and progress to youth and senior rugby for their local clubs. I had the best of both worlds, playing with my friends for Blaengarw Youth RFC on Saturday afternoons, and representing Ynysawdre against other school teams every Wednesday and Saturday mornings. The only drawback being that I was knackered every Saturday night!

'The other down side was that schoolboys couldn't play in any of the youth cup competitions, so the likes of myself, Huw Bevan and Robert Jones were excluded. Watching the youth team progress and always seemingly fail at the final stages of the cup was agonising, particularly against sides I'm convinced we would have beaten with a full-strength team. I remember Maesteg Youth turning us over a few times in cup games. They had a strong pack but the stand-out player was a scrawny centre opposite me, by the name of Allan Bateman, who also went on to play for Wales in both codes, the Lions at union and GB at league.'

Although Devereux played at outside-half for Blaengarw Youth and Ynysawdre School, he was selected at centre for the Bridgend and District schools team because his talented contemporary, Sean McCarthy, was given the No. 10 jersey instead. McCarthy, who went on to have a successful career as a professional footballer with Swansea City, Plymouth Argyle, Oldham Athletic and Bradford City, impressed Devereux, who said: 'Sean had what it took to be a great rugby player and I firmly believe that if he'd concentrated on rugby he could have been capped.

'Frustratingly, WRU Schools honours eluded me while playing for Ynysawdre. It was a huge disappointment because I really believed I was good enough and had all the attributes required. An example of my frustration occurred when I was 18. With Sean McCarthy now fully focused on football, I was selected at outside-half for the Mid Glamorgan County team, ahead of David Evans, who would later play for Cardiff and Wales. However, when the Welsh Schools U18 team selection was announced, 'Dai' was selected to play at outside-half. It puzzled me but I had to accept the decison. I'd even had a few games for Bridgend RFC by this time but was still being overlooked.

'At that point, the powers-that-be at Bridgend and District decided to move me from outside-half to full-back. I was angry and frustrated at first but, after playing several games at No.15 for the county, I really enjoyed it and scored plenty of tries from my new position. Full-back gave me more room to run the ball, and the time to spot the gaps and defensive weaknesses, without their back line being just a few yards away, as happens when you're an outside-half or centre. Full-back also gave me more freedom to pop up in different places on the pitch. I often found myself out wide and was able to show my pace, which was something I was able to use to my advantage later in my career after switching to rugby league with Widnes.

'Finally, but rather unexpectedly, came another potential opportunity to play for Welsh Schools. Early one Sunday morning the phone rang at our house and my father took the call. It was someone from Welsh Schools asking if I would be available, that morning, to attend a training session for Welsh Schools U18's at the Brewery Field, Bridgend. The team were preparing to play Scotland and the incumbent full-back, Chris Bradshaw, had fallen out with selectors over something or other. They were apparently promoting Jonathan Callard to play full-back, and I was being asked to join the training session with the intention of me being named as a replacement for the international game. Both Bradshaw and Callard went on to have good senior rugby union careers, with Callard playing in the Rugby World Cup, not for Wales unfortunately, but for England. It was hard to forgive him for that!

'The big problem was that I'd been at a Bridgend RFC dinner the night before, and had quite a few drinks after being given some beer tokens by Glenn Webbe. Luckily, I had stayed the night at my sister's house which was close to the Brewery Field but it's fair to say that I wasn't primed and fully prepared for the chance. My father had driven into town, with my kit, to wake me and tell me a trial for Welsh Schools beckoned.

'The whole event was a bit of a blur. I remember running around the pitch and doing some training with the group, but my head was pounding, my mouth was as dry as sandpaper and my breath reeked of booze. Unsurprisingly, I wasn't selected. Instead, they put Bradshaw on the bench to teach him a lesson, and just maybe – now with hindsight – they were also sending a message to me as well. At the time though, I was oblivious to the rugby politics. What I did learn, though, was that running around a rugby field the morning after a heavy sesh was a great way to get rid of a hangover.'

Devereux put those disappointments behind him and focused on his studies. With two A levels to add to his eight O levels, he was offered a place at college in Cardiff and embarked on what he described as the best three years of his life.

However, a matter of weeks before enrolling at South Glamorgan Institute, injury struck while he was training at Blaengarw RFC: 'I did a forward roll and as I got to my feet I felt my right knee crunch. I knew immediately there was an issue. I was taken to hospital and was advised to have an operation to remove a piece of torn cartilage.'

Devereux therefore started college life on crutches and missed the chance to impress the rugby coaches at Cyncoed, for a while, but it didn't stop him and his new pal, Tim Gill, from doing the traditional three-legged pub crawl around Cardiff City centre during freshers' week: 'It was the start of a fantastic experience, one I have never forgotten, having fun, meeting some great people and making friends for life.'

3

The Welsh Rugby Academy

'I haven't got any regrets at losing my place to a player of Devs' ilk. He was strong – one of the strongest guys I ever played against.'

Rob Ackerman

South Glamorgan Institute of Higher Education in Cardiff was John Devereux's destination. He followed a long line of former Ynysawdre pupils who had previously been to the college, which was, and is, a highly regarded and widely acknowledged centre of sporting excellence that claims Olympic Games gold medallist long jumper Lynn 'the Leap' Davies as a much respected former student. Over 50 Wales rugby internationals studied at the former Cardiff College of Education at Cyncoed and the rugby team's Hall of Fame is full of household names, such as Gareth Edwards, JJ Williams, John Bevan, David Richards, Ryan Jones and Gareth Cooper, who all became British and Irish Lions.

Devereux was ambitious and focused: 'South Glam put out four to five teams on match days but I was only interested in the first team. Nothing else would do. Fortunately for me, there was an opportunity to play centre for the 1st XV because Kevin Hopkins, later of Swansea, Cardiff and Wales fame, had left the college the previous summer so his place in the team was up for grabs. I had recovered from my knee operation, was fit again and was relishing the prospect of playing rugby at a much higher level.'

Leighton Davies, a lecturer at the college who was nicknamed Nutty by students because of his unconventional methods and motivational techniques, was in charge of the 1st XV. He had an eye for talent and hard work and took the young Devereux under his wing. 'Nutty was an excellent coach and mentor to me, who had enjoyed a fine rugby career in his own right, playing for Bridgend, Maesteg and Newport. He worked us hard but was a massive influence on my career and that of others. Not everyone may have agreed with all his methods but I don't think you'll find anyone who came under his tutelage who doesn't speak fondly of him.' The assistant coach to Nutty was Don Llewellyn, who also had an excellent playing career as a prop forward, playing more than 93 games for Cardiff RFC before moving into coaching.

After a day of academic studies, the rugby squad would train during the evening on a Redgra pitch that was illuminated only by the street lights from the road that ran past the campus. Because the students relied totally on the street lights, their practice sessions tended to take place only on the side of the pitch nearest the road, which wasn't ideal.

'Training was tough and the coaches' expectations were high. If one of us dropped the ball during passing drills when we practised back moves, we had to lie on the floor while the forwards ran over us.' It was known as an 'Ashworth' after John Ashworth, the New Zealand prop who stamped on the face of legendary full-back JPR Williams, inflicting an horrific wound, when Bridgend had faced the All Blacks at the Brewery Field in 1978. 'After you'd had a shoeing from the Institute's forwards it certainly concentrated your mind and conditioned you to not drop the ball again, that's for sure,' said Devereux with a laugh.

Desperate to break into the side he threw himself into training and his hard work paid off when he was selected for the team, as a centre, and vowed never to be dropped. Rugby at Cyncoed involved more than just rugby, however, as new players were expected to immerse themselves socially with the other players. Devereux's initiation to South Glam rugby's social scene included an off-the-cuff trip to Porthcawl, and a new culinary experience. 'We'd decided on the spur of the moment to go to the resort for a few drinks and, as it turned out, I had my first experience of a proper Indian curry. Huw Bevan had borrowed his father's Ford Granada and a few of us, including Gareth Nicholas and myself, had crammed into the car and travelled to the seaside, parking at Coney Beach Caravan Park.' The plan was to have a bit of a session and then sleep it off in the car before travelling back the following day. Huw was a second-year student at the time, while Gareth was in his third year.

The two of them regaled Devereux with hilarious anecdotes and tales of student life, revolving around rugby, the Student's Union bar at the Cyncoed Campus, and living in digs in Roath or elsewhere in Cardiff. First year students had to stay in halls of residents at Cyncoed but, after that, were encouraged to pal up with other students and friends to rent a house somewhere close to college, preferably in the Albany Road and Wellfield Road area of Roath in order to be as near as possible to The Claude, a popular student pub, and the various curry houses in the locality.

'I thought I could handle drink until I went out with those two,' admitted Devereux, 'and the boozy night ended with us all in a curry house on the promenade. I had never tasted Indian food before, so 'Bevs' and 'Gar Nic' ordered me a nice hot number to top up the 20 or so pints of beer we'd downed earlier. It was my debut curry and I was very drunk. The food was a bit hot and I can remember having only a few mouthfuls before my stomach turned. I got up and ran out of the restaurant in some discomfort. A combination of beer and curry had caused me to need to find a toilet, and quickly.

'Stupidly, I had failed to realise there was a toilet in the curry house! Its staff may have thought I was attempting a runner without paying but then they would have heard the boys laughing at my predicament. I had one thing in my head, to get to the beach to, shall I say, lighten the load and get rid of the sharp pains in my stomach. Being very much worse for wear, I hadn't thought about the need for toilet paper, so I had to improvise and was a bit sheepish when I went back to rejoin my friends who were finishing off their meals, and mine, with cheeky smiles on their faces. It was mission accomplished for them, they had seen off me and my food.'

After leaving the curry house, Devereux soon discovered that his friends were nowhere to be seen. Somehow they'd got separated so he headed to where he thought the car had been parked. By now it was pitch black and he was hopelessly drunk and stumbling around trying to find the Granada. There were no mobile phones in those days and Bevan and Nicholas failed to respond when he shouted their names, with a few added expletives.

'I was fumbling around in a drunken stupor when I came across an abandoned car. There was grass growing around its wheels and it definitely wasn't the silver Ford I was searching for. I was desperate to find somewhere to sleep so tried the door, and it opened. I may have been drunk but I remember the car reeking of that musky, damp smell of neglect. It must have been there for months, or more, but all its windows were intact and it was dry inside. It seemed to be my best option for somewhere to sleep and, to be honest, I didn't have another option.'

'I lay down across its back seat and immediately fell into a deep sleep. I woke up a few hours later, at about 5am, with the first light of dawn breaking across Porthcawl. I was freezing cold and all the windows had steamed up with condensation. I was also dying for a pee so opened the door and stepped outside to find I was on a grassed area at the caravan park. Lo and behold, parked about 20m away was a silver Ford Granada just like Bevs' dad's car.

'I went over and, peering through the windows, I could just about make out two people fast sleep. It was Bevs and Gareth! They were cwtched up nice and warm in sleeping bags. I banged on a window and pleaded with the boys to let me in. Initially, they didn't stir, preferring to prolong my ordeal, but when I finally managed to wake them they very slowly began to move and eventually unlocked the door. I jumped in, slipped into my sleeping bag and began to tell my tale, but they just wanted to go back to sleep. Relieved to have survived the experience I assumed that would be the worst state I'd ever get into while at college. How wrong I would be!'

The Institute played all of the teams that competed in the Whitbread Merit Table, so facing the cream of Welsh first-class rugby gave the young talent at South Glamorgan a wonderful grounding and sporting education.

Apart from cup games, the lack of facilities at the college campus meant that all their matches were played away from home. 'We had some great battles against all the clubs and went toe-to-toe with the so-called big boys of Welsh rugby, and we won a few too. There was, though, a contrast in styles as we were extremely fit and liked to move the ball wide to our dangerous backs, but didn't have the power and weight up front. Opponents were terrified of our high tempo game, with most clubs keeping the ball as tight as possible. They wanted to out-muscle us in a wrestling match and our problem was getting the ball off them. When we did, our policy was to run from everywhere if it was on, so we were known for entertaining rugby and scoring spectacular tries,' said Devereux.

Not having the opportunity to play regularly on your home pitch made every game a tough prospect, so when South Glam were drawn at home in the Welsh Cup against Cardiff, the students were desperate to take their opportunity in front of a home crowd of hundreds who lived on the campus and in the nearby streets of Roath. They gave the

Arms Park club one hell of a fight and went down with honour. No one more than Devereux, whose deadly display and Dalek-like hand-off put him firmly on the radar of then Wales coach Tony Gray and his assistant Derek Quinnell, the former Lions and Wales forward, as well as the Welsh rugby media.

The following weekend, the Institute were playing Tredegar away at the Recreation Ground, which was situated on the side of the mountain overlooking the town and was renowned as one of the windiest and coldest venues on the first-class circuit. BBC Wales, fully aware of the dramatic headlines Devereux had generated a few days earlier, dispatched a cameraman to the game and asked the late Ray Gravell, a hard-hitting centre and legendary character, to cast an expert eye on this promising prospect.

'I idolised Grav as indeed I did the other great 1970s Welsh players and for him to be there was a real confidence booster,' admits Devereux, 'but in truth, the match was dire, played on a poor pitch in terrible conditions. Luckily for me, Grav and the BBC team did a great job of editing the footage and showed some good individual moments of play from me. My stock was still rising. I loved it but I remembered what Nutty had said and took it each game at a time. I never ever took selection for granted.

'By that time, having played a fair few games for the college, I felt I was playing well against some really good centres and not looking out of place. Pontypridd's Steele Lewis, Bridgend's John Apsee, Neath's Steve Powell, and Llanelli's Simon Davies were admired for their strength and power but I was holding my own against them, and I was competing well against the more silky footballers like Swansea's Kevin Hopkins, who I had succeeded at South Glam, and Alan Donovan at Cardiff.

'I was getting praise from different people for my performances and was named Man of the Match against Neath at The Gnoll receiving my award from Jonathan 'Jiffy' Davies who, unfortunately, was not available for Neath that day. It was the first time we'd met, and it was a great honour to receive the award from him as he was on the way to becoming a rugby legend. Little did we know that just a year later we would be lining up alongside each other for Wales and that we would play together many times for club and country throughout our careers, becoming great friends along the way.'

With the praise Devereux was now receiving there could have been a danger he would become over confident, but his coach,

Leighton Davies, kept his feet firmly on the ground: 'Leighton would say; "Yes, John Devereux (he always used my full name in these types of conversations), a good try today but you need to improve your (something or other) next week". I viewed his candid assessments as a challenge and always sought, all the way to the final whistle of the final match of my career, to improve as a player. Nutty's style of coaching and man management worked for me and many others.'

Cornishman Colin Laity played alongside Devereux at centre for South Glam and carved a reputation as a powerhouse runner. He later became a huge hit with Neath and faced the supreme New Zealand team of 1989 at The Gnoll. The Welsh All Blacks gave the New Zealand All Blacks a massive fright that day and Laity, who had played age-grade rugby for England but by then had settled in Wales, opted to play for his fellow Celts on residency grounds.

Laity was capped at B level but that was as far as it went, which surprised his former teammate, who commented: 'Wales never gave him a full cap, which I believed he deserved because he was a handful going forward and a strong reliable defender.'

Devereux was also full of praise for other former Cyncoed teammates: 'Our full-back Nathan Humphreys was regarded as potentially a great player. He oozed talent but it was an understatement to say he was laidback because he was fully horizontal. Nathan could turn it on when he wanted with his Christian Cullen-type gliding and he troubled Cardiff during the cup classic with his clever angles into space and speed.

'Huw Bevan, our no-nonsense hooker, was a livewire and went on to play for Bridgend before becoming a hugely successful fitness coach, in rugby and cricket. He got the England cricket team super-fit when it was the best in the world under its coach Duncan Fletcher. Then there was lock Tony Rees, who was to become the first Welsh player to lift the European Cup with French club Brive in 1997, when they ran amok against Leicester in the final in Cardiff. The rest of our team was pretty handy. We weren't mugs and certainly had the pedigree and know-how to score points against anybody if we could get enough ball.'

Stuart Davies was at No.8 for South Glam that day against Cardiff when reputations were made and destroyed. He recalled: 'We had all gone to the college for the same reason as it was a production line for first-class and international players during the amateur era. We had a great fixture list against Wales' Merit Table clubs and had settled into being a good side with a few of us, me included, already having had first-class experience.

'I was completely in awe of Devs at the time, with the confidence he had being justified by his ability. He backed it up. As soon as he had the chance to shine, he took it. Nobody could handle him that day – he was breaking the first line of defence nearly every time he ran with the ball and was a huge presence in midfield. Back then, I don't think Devs was a student of the game, he just went on the field without a second thought, did his stuff and got respect that way. He soon had it in buckets, though, and was very hard to handle. He was a great team man. We were all students and friends. In a college context the 1st XV was where a lot of the fun was, and Devs was part of it.'

North Walian Tony Gray was the Wales coach and had been impressed by what he had seen, explaining: 'We were developing a young group of players at the time and decided to pick John for the national squad after he had that pretty good game for South Glamorgan Institute against Cardiff in the Schweppes Cup. He was under the wing of Leighton, a former Maesteg flanker, at the college and we already knew about John and had spoken to Leighton about him. John Lloyd, who had taught him at school, had been the first to draw our attention to him and we liked what we saw. John Devereux had youth on his side, was very enthusiastic and committed, which were things we always looked for.

'He also offered us something different: raw power and an ability and willingness to blast his way over the gain-line. We had so many outstanding footballers in the squad, such as Mark Ring, Bleddyn Bowen, Jonathan Davies and others but we lacked a physical presence. John gave us that and enabled us to increase the number of opportunities we had to take advantage in attack. He could go back inside, straight, on the outside or create for others.'

Devereux's inclusion in the squad didn't find favour with everyone, with Gray recalling: 'I remember another centre, who I won't name, saying: "You can't pick JD, he can't pass". I had to say to that person that JD's presence would in fact benefit him because the opposition would be more worried about John and the physicality he possessed, whether in attack or defence, and that would give our skilled footballers more time and space in which to strut their stuff. Based on that belief, we picked John for his debut.'

Devs, and the man he would replace in the Wales XV, Robert Ackerman, soon came face-to-face when the pair were named in the Wales squad for the 1986 Five Nations, as it was in those days with Italy not yet having been admitted to the tournament.

Ackerman was determined to extract revenge for what had happened some two months earlier: 'Devs hadn't done me any favours, that's for sure, when we'd clashed at Cyncoed, so I had a bit of a crack at him at the Wales training session but I didn't get much change out of him and he was picked ahead of me for the tournament.'

Ever the gentleman and down-to-earth realist, Ackerman stressed: 'I haven't got any regrets at losing my place to a player of Devs' ilk. He was strong – one of the strongest guys I ever played against. They called him the Dalek because of the power of his fend-off, and I copped it from him. I've got the utmost respect for Devs. He's a top man, is dependable and epitomised what rugby was all about. John was a top-quality player, not just in union but also in rugby league. His success in both codes showed how good he was. You respect what he did in rugby, being a dual-code international and playing for Great Britain in the RL World Cup final against Australia at Wembley. To play for the Lions and GB is no mean feat because union and league are completely different games, the only thing similar about them is the shape of the ball. Virtually every union player who went to league found it tough going but it didn't take Devs long to crack it.'

The talk of Welsh rugby, Devs had burst onto the international game like a charging bull and he now set his sights on his first cap, against England at Twickenham.

4

Debut

*'John Devs was big, explosive, fit and full of enthusiasm. You could
see he could become something special.'*

Derek Quinnell

The inaugural World Cup, and its soon-to-be prestige as the pinnacle
of world rugby, was still over a year away as the 1986 Wales v
England clash at Twickenham approached. The Five Nations still
reigned supreme and, in the eyes of many supporters, the annual
match against England was then, and still is, the most important
in the calendar. To them, beating their neighbours and losing their
other Five (or Six) Nations matches was far preferable than winning
all of the other championship games but having a defeat inflicted on
them by the old enemy.

Devereux knew the importance of the annual encounter to the
Welsh team and the people of Wales. He was primed and ready to
do battle at the so-called 'headquarters' of the game, as the English
rugby fraternity like to call Twickenham. Facing England didn't faze
him at all. In fact, it was quite the contrary, the teenager couldn't
wait to get stuck into them, saying: 'All I wanted to do was get on the
field for kick-off and rip into them.'

Wales forwards coach Derek Quinnell, who had starred for the
British and Irish Lions as a player, had every confidence in the
ability of Devereux, stressing: 'John was a lovely kid and had a
huge impact. He had everything; strength, pace and was fearless.
He couldn't wait to go toe-to-toe and look the opposition straight in
the eye. He was big, explosive, fit and full of enthusiasm. You could
see he had every chance of becoming something special, which
he did, going on to play for Wales and the Lions during a superb
career.'

Devereux's performance against Cardiff for South Glamorgan Institute and his obvious potential saw him thrust into the limelight at a young age, yet he relished the big stage and it didn't come much bigger than a first cap at Twickenham. Even to this day, he can recall almost everything which happened that weekend: 'We didn't stay at a hotel but at some computer company's training headquarters. We even stopped on the way to London for some fish and chips, washed down with jugs of Coca Cola. Nutrition and eating healthy hadn't come in then! Some of the boys even had a couple of pints of beer or lager the night before a match to settle their nerves.'

Devereux, scrum-half Robert Jones – who was to later captain his country and starred during the Lions' Test series triumph over Australia in 1989 – and lock David 'Muddy' Waters were making their Wales debuts at Twickenham. Newport favourite Waters had been due to make his Test bow the previous year but the match against Ireland was postponed because of foul weather and he had missed out on selection when it had eventually taken place.

Swansea starlet Jones, who possessed one of the best passes in the business and was an astute tactical kicker off either foot, was paired with attacking sensation Jonathan Davies at half-back, Bleddyn Bowen and Devereux formed the centre partnership, while Adrian Hadley and Phil Lewis were on the wings with master goal-kicker Paul Thorburn at full-back. Jeff Whitefoot, Billy James and Ian Eidman formed the front-row, John Perkins and Waters were partnered in the second-row, with Mark Brown and captain David Pickering paired at flanker and Phil Davies at No.8.

England had Huw Davies at full-back. He had a Welsh sounding name and roots, but had been born in Eastbourne, Sussex and was brought up at Stourbridge in England's West Midlands. Davies had, though, attended Cardiff University and played for Cardiff RFC before going to Cambridge University and playing for Coventry, who were then a major club, and Wasps, who went sadly bust during the 2022-23 season. Davies had been an outside-half but was picked at full-back because of Rob Andrew's dominance at 10. He was only 5ft 9in and weighed just 11st 10lbs, which would be minuscule by today's standards, and was peppered with up-and-unders by Jonathan Davies as Wales launched an aerial assault at him.

England possessed a wonderful open-side flanker in Peter Winterbottom and giant second rows in the so-called 'Blackpool Tower', Wade Dooley, and the late Maurice Colclough, who played for Swansea and had a restaurant in the city. Ace finisher Rory Underwood was on one wing while Devereux was marking Haverfordwest-born Simon Halliday in midfield. Halliday tried to use his physical presence to dominate the rookie 19-year-old student but didn't get any change out of Devereux who, in the words of Quinnell: 'Held his own because he was a big, physical presence who always took the game to the opposition, in attack and defence. He knocked the wind out of the opposition, no matter who they were and for whom they played.'

For Devereux, the memories of that debut weekend remain vivid: 'After having fish and chips – prop Staff Jones, who had a huge appetite, had that much food on his plate he said he didn't know whether to "eat it or climb it" – we arrived at the facility where we were to spend the night before the game. Because it was a place used by the company's employees it also provided single rooms, which was unusual as players normally shared twin rooms. Perhaps there was a Welsh connection high up in the firm who had wrangled a good deal for the WRU, but more likely they were getting it on the cheap because they didn't like parting with money!

'I was never a drinker on the eve of a match and had got my head down pretty early. I had a reasonable night's sleep but was suffering from the usual nerves and anxiety when I woke in the morning. I managed to polish off the game-day breakfast and then it was on the bus for the journey to Twickenham, being escorted by police out-riders on powerful motorcycles. It was such a novelty for me and I sucked it all in.

'The closer we got to Twickenham the better the atmosphere became as we drove slowly past supporters of both countries making their way to the ground. The Welsh supporters gave us the thumbs up, a cheer and a clap but there were some hand gestures of a different nature from the English! I lapped it all up as we got off the bus and strode through the crowd and into our changing room deep underneath an ancient grandstand which used to adorn Twickenham before it was demolished and rebuilt with modern, state-of-the-art facilities. The atmosphere was already electric and the hairs on the back of my neck were standing up.

'As I entered our dressing-room I spotted my red No.13 jersey hanging from a peg. It was a proud moment and one I will never forget because I'd never experienced that emotion before, having never been capped as a schoolboy. But, hey, here I was, a complete unknown to most of the rugby world and those people back home who only followed rugby when Wales were playing, and particularly when England were the opposition because it was and still is the country we love to hate when it comes to sport, and the opposition we want to beat more than any other.

'Touching that jersey for the first time was something very special and added to the heady mix of emotion and tension that surrounded the occasion. If anything, I got a bit too wrapped up in the pre-match build up and spent too much time reading the telegrams and good luck cards that were on my seat in the changing room. There were some lovely messages from friends and family and I was mentally floating away on a cloud of sheer joy and disbelief that my dream had come true.

'Then someone eventually grabbed my attention and brought me back down to earth by saying it was time to switch on and get ready for battle. I always got ready for matches in a pretty quiet sort of way. I didn't say much and went through my routine, focusing on going through the ritual of superstitions I had developed during my career, from my earliest days as a schoolboy playing rugby.

'It's strange how so many sportsmen and sportswomen have these little routines or superstitions. I always used to wear the same swimming trunks. I had them for many years; they were old and battered but I didn't have any intention of changing them for a newer model. I also always put my left sock on first and then my left boot, but first I had to polish my boots in the changing room with my own polish and brushes, which I carried in a little case. I remember getting loads of stick for doing this at all the teams I played for through my career. It was something I had always done from when I was a kid starting at eight years of age in Ffaldau Primary School. The ritual had started all those years earlier, rubbing dubbin – a grease to soften leather – into the school rugby balls.

'Our schoolmaster would select a player after every game who he thought deserved to take the rugby ball home to clean it and put dubbin on to soften it ready for the following week's fixture. I always wanted to be that player and, when I had the honour, I first used to dry the ball in front of the coal fire in our house. It was an old ball and when it got wet, which was often, it would weigh a lot more and kicking or passing it any distance became difficult. The wetter it got the heavier it became. If it was pouring with rain and the pitch had puddles it was like playing with a heavy medicine ball. It also became slippery, more like a bar of soap than a ball.

'After seeing me cleaning my boots in the Twickenham changing rooms, Jonathan Davies said he wanted to clean his boots with my stuff too, and who was I to argue! That done, I had a quick rub down from our physio before the call came to go out on the pitch and warm-up ahead of the match. You didn't have a warm-up kit to wear those days and the pre-match workout was nothing like it is today, it was more like individuals doing what suited them.

'I had my full game kit on as I ran on to the Twickenham turf for the first time in my career. The ground was already pretty full and the buzz from the crowd was amazing. I looked around for family and friends and then it was back into the 'shed' for our final preparation.

'The captain's team talk from David Pickering was superb. He made me, along with other new caps in Rob Jones and Dai Waters feel so welcome. 'Dai Pick' talked about how we had a great record at Twickenham and the English didn't have the grit and heart like us Welsh. Running out for the game was incredible, the feeling and the adrenaline rush was unbelievable. The roar of the crowd and the lushness of the grass struck me. The pitch was like a brand-new carpet and there wasn't any chance of the ball being weighed down by water and mud. I don't think my kit got any mud on it, just grass stains.

'We all had to line up before the game to meet the dignitaries but I was so hyped up and in my own zone I didn't realise who they were at the time. The roar of the crowd and the anthems were so emotional. All I wanted now was for that whistle to blow for the start of the game.'

Bowen went over for a try after Jonathan Davies, in trademark fashion, wreaked havoc in the England defence by cutting back towards the inside before sending his teammate past Huw Davies as Wales inched into a 12-9 lead at the end of the first half. It was four points for a try in those days. Thorburn converted Bowen's effort and added a penalty to the drop-goal Jonathan Davies had landed.

Wales led 18-15 during the second half but England, with Colclough instrumental, took control of the line-out – there were far more in matches back then – and pushed Wales back. Andrew levelled the scores with his sixth successful penalty as they ramped up the pressure in pursuit of victory.

Drop goal attempts were more common back then and Andrew put England into a winning lead during injury time by turning on to his wrong foot – his left – and striking the ball perfectly between the uprights and over the crossbar for a three-pointer. It was nip and tuck with Australian referee Bob Fordham awarding a string of penalties and England happened to be on the right side of the scoreboard when he blew the final whistle. Andrew had scored all of England's points in a 21-18 victory, with Wales replying through Bowen's touchdown, Thorburn's conversion and three penalties, and Jonathan Davies' drop goal.

'I always remember the whistle being blown for kick-off' said Devereux, 'and the game being so fast. We spent a lot of it tackling. Bleddyn, who was best man at my wedding a few years later and who, to this day, is my best friend, scored in the corner and there was jubilation. I thought we were going to win but unfortunately Andrew broke our hearts with his kicks. I couldn't get over how quick the game went compared to a normal club match. It was frenetic and I didn't get much of the ball as we spent much of the day just tackling, something I relished and it was a big part of my game but I only had one opportunity to run with ball in hand. I threw a dummy as England thought I was going to kick the ball out from our 22 but I ran and beat a few defenders before off-loading the ball to Dai Pickering.

'Although we struggled to win much line-out ball and lived off scraps of possession, we did score the only try, from a quickly taken line-out. The high-pressure, high-volume, atmosphere in the stadium was relentless. I was conscious of it but, because I was in the zone, I didn't focus on it. It was like having a constant and loud roar in the background all the time, but was impossible to see individual faces in the crowd.'

After the game finished, Devereux wasn't going to part company with his first Wales jersey and none of the England players asked him to swap as they stuck with one of rugby's traditions, that debut makers get to keep their shirt.

'The England captain Nigel Melville gave his jersey to Robert and didn't expect Robert's in return,' recalled Devereux. 'We were all very deflated after the game in the changing room after losing so narrowly. It was a quiet time to reflect. Tony Gray and 'DQ' [Derek Quinnell] said some words of encouragement but nothing would take that pain of defeat away. For Robert, Muddy and me it was our first game for Wales and we had lost against the old enemy so we were inconsolable.

'When we arrived back at our team base we were told to change into our dinner jackets and meet in the team room, where Robert, Muddy and I were presented with our caps by John Dawes. It was the proudest moment of my career. Then it was off to the Hilton in central London for the post-match dinner and the speeches from the captains. We may have lost the game but we drowned our sorrows and took those English boys on the beer!'

Devereux retained his place in the Wales team for the rest of the 1986 Five Nations championship and played a role when Thorburn made history by hitting the target with the longest penalty in history to break Scottish hearts in Cardiff. Scotland had scored three tries, through full-back star Gavin Hastings – who captained the British and Irish Lions in New Zealand in 1993 – right-wing Matt Duncan and raging blond flanker John Jeffery, but never recovered from the shock of Thorburn signalling his intent to New Zealand referee Bob Francis that he would be attempting a shot at goal from 70 yards and eight inches (nearly 65m).

'It was my second cap and my first at home,' said Devereux, 'so it was a special match for me. Most people though will remember it for Paul 'Thorby' Thorburn's incredible penalty. My claim to fame is I told him to go for it when he was weighing up the options. I could kick a ball a long way and knew Paul had it in him so encouraged him to give it a blast. There was also a strong wind that afternoon and we both knew it was blowing from behind him as it gusted into the ground from over the old East Terrace.

'Thorby struck the ball perfectly and it hurtled towards the posts as the wind grabbed hold of it, and cleared the cross bar with ease. The crowd was shocked, then a huge roar went up around the stadium as people realised the enormity of what they had just witnessed. It wasn't just them whose mouths were open wide in disbelief but also those of the Scotland players. They had out-scored us three tries to one but you could see the shoulders of the Scots slump when the flags of the linesmen went up to signal Thorburn's kick was good.

'Psychologically, it was a massive blow and knocked the stuffing out of them. Jiffy had landed a drop-goal, while right wing Phil Lewis went over for our try after I had run hard at the Scotland defence on a crash ball from Jiffy before managing to spin when I was tackled and throw a pass over a shoulder in the direction of Phil. I knew he would be in support and, sure enough, he was and scored to secure the victory 22-15.

'The Scots couldn't believe it and probably thought it just wasn't to be for them, especially with Hastings only being successful with one of his shots at goal. His misses, and Thorby and Jiffy keeping the scoreboard ticking over for us before delivering the killer blow meant we came out on the right side of the ledger.

'My first Wales cap was unforgettable despite the loss to England, but appearing for my country at home for the first time, and winning, was just fantastic. I couldn't help but think that just a year earlier I had gone to Edinburgh to watch Scotland versus Wales with my student pals, 12 of us squeezed into a Ford Transit van. Wales had won on that occasion, at Murrayfield, and one of our drunken party had jumped into the freezing fountain on Princes Street in celebration and spent the next hour shivering as he sobered up a bit sharpish.'

Wales' next assignment was against Ireland at Dublin's Lansdowne Road and, for the second match in a row, there was seven points between the participants. The encounter was settled with a second-half burst from Wales, during which the visitors scored 12 points in 10 minutes to move into a decisive lead. Ireland had led 12-4 after Devereux, as he recalled, had come off second best to Trevor Ringland: 'I was covering and he wrong-footed me with a side step before scoring in the corner, but we showed character to battle back and Phil Lewis got a similar try to the one he had scored against the Scots after I'd thrown a pass to him over my shoulder as I was being tackled. Thorby, once again, had his kicking boots on and delivered a faultless display.'

Paul Moriarty, a powerful, athletic and fiery back-row forward who was very quick for such a big guy, had made his debut in the side which was captained by his elder brother, Richard. The younger Moriarty and Devereux were to become close friends and later both made the move to rugby league after signing deals with Widnes.

'We have been great pals ever since,' confirmed Devereux. "Muzzy' is a character and there's no nonsense with him – he's always been honest, blunt and straight to the point. He brought a physical edge on the pitch and took some shackling. His loss to rugby league was a big blow for the Wales union team because he was a dynamic ball-carrier who consistently put his side on the front foot.'

Devereux, though, had taken a bump during the clash with Ireland and didn't take part in the post-match celebrations, explaining: 'I had a terrible headache from the end of the game until I went to bed and fell asleep. I went to my room quite early because I was out of it. Who knows, I may have been suffering from concussion but we didn't have the rigorous checks back then they do these more safety-conscious days.'

Wales took the field for their final fixture of the campaign with a chance of being crowned European champions but were brought down to earth by a superior and vastly more experienced France at Cardiff Arms Park. The Welsh defence was given the run around by a French back line containing revered greats Philippe Sella and Serge Blanco, a Napoleonic type general in scrum-half Pierre Berbezier while outside-half Guy Laporte, Sella's centre partner Denis Charvet and wings Éric Bonneval and Jean-Baptiste Lafond oozed class.

'Sella and Charvet were fantastic,' stressed Devereux. 'It was the first time I had faced Sella and he was outstanding. I thought I had got hold of him in a tackle but he somehow wriggled his way out of it to score a try. It was unbelievable what he could do on a rugby pitch. Everybody who faced him in union would tell you he was a fabulous player. Pound for pound, he was one of the strongest players in the business, possessed great speed and had a superb rugby brain to match. If there was one opponent who I never got the upper hand against it was Philippe. I'd use one word to describe him: *Magnifique!*'

Lafond raced over for a brace of touchdowns while ghostly strike running full-back Blanco, who glided over the pitch and seemed as smooth as a Rolls-Royce, breezed through an all-at-sea home defence as France cruised to a 23-15 triumph and the Five Nations title with four unanswered tries to hammer home their dominance on a dismal St. David's Day for Welsh rugby.

'The French certainly taught us a lesson,' said Devereux.' I think, at that stage in our development, we didn't truly believe in ourselves and went on the pitch not convinced we could beat them. They were one of the best teams in the world at that time, with a giant and brilliant pack. They were the complete package, the real deal so to speak, and they didn't take any prisoners. It could be brutal facing them because they certainly put it about – boots, knees, fists, elbows, butting and gouging – they had that dirty and rough edge to them but you couldn't hide from the fact they were capable of producing delicious take-your-breath-away rugby. At their best they were a joy to watch from the grandstands but it wasn't much fun attempting to stop them when they were in full flow.'

5

The Brawl to End Them All

*'It was a fight like no other and Devs was the only Welsh player
to get the better of his opponent.'*

Jonathan Davies

Defeat against France meant Wales slipped to third in the final Five
Nations table, with Scotland overtaking them to take second place.
England finished fourth while Ireland were whitewashed to finish the
championship bottom and without a point to their name.

Nevertheless, as Devereux explains, the mood in Wales was quite
positive: 'Supporters had seen some promise. We were a young team
but had a future star in Robert Jones, while Jonathan Davies was
a huge talent and crowd pleaser, a classic Welsh outside-half who
could turn a match in an instant with his speed and skill. The feeling,
both in and outside the camp, was we could only get better.'

Wales had a perfect summer tour destination lined up to help them
continue their progress; a trip to the Pacific island nations of Fiji,
Tonga and Western Samoa, as it was known then. Those countries
were about the right level for the Welsh squad who knew the Tests
would be competitive but winnable. However, little did Devereux and
his teammates know when they boarded their aircraft in London,
how fiery those encounters would be, with the clash with Tonga
turning out to be one of the most violent Test matches of the modern
era: 'It was the icing on the cake for me to be touring with Wales.
What could be better than a month in the tropical paradise of the
South Pacific? I was still a student, though, and the only thing I had
to sort out was sitting my second-year exams while I was on tour.
Luckily for me, the University of Wales agreed for my exam papers to
be entrusted to Wales coach Tony Gray, who was a lecturer at Bangor
University in north Wales.

'When the day of departure arrived, Glenn Webbe turned up to catch the team bus to Heathrow Airport with two large suit cases and a Welsh kit bag around his shoulder. "Glenn," I said. "What's with all the gear?" He said he had brought all his best clobber for his night time "manoeuvres".

'The entertainment started in earnest when we got to Heathrow and Paul Moriarty couldn't find his passport. There he was, with all his bags open on the floor of the airport terminal, sweating and cursing profusely. Then he came out with the classic: "I can see it now on the mantlepiece in the living room of my mam and dad's house".'

While the younger Moriarty was ready to self-combust as he feared being left behind, Devereux recalled the elder brother, Richard 'Dickie' Moriarty, was quietly chuckling as his brother panicked: 'Little did Paul know that Dickie had lifted the passport from their parents' home to play a prank on him at the airport. He made Paul sweat a little bit more before presenting him with the passport as the rest of us watched, doubling up with laughter at Paul's expense. Muzzy was that hot under the collar the steam was coming off him.'

It was 36 hours before the squad touched down at Nandi Airport in Fiji after flying via Los Angeles and New Zealand, but not all the players' luggage had arrived. The unlucky tourist, chuckled Devereux, was Glenn Webbe: 'Both his suit cases had been 'misplaced', according to Air New Zealand – lost in transit in plain English – and we all had another laugh at a teammate's expense.

'Someone quipped that the baggage handlers had seen the dancing gear and come to the conclusion he wouldn't be needing it in Fiji! Glenn was kept in suspense and he didn't get the cases back until the day we were leaving Fiji. He spent that leg of the trip wearing our cast-offs!

'Our base, The Morecambo Hotel, was a stone's throw away from the airport. It was a sprawling, low level building that had everything we needed. Paul and I went straight out to investigate the new surroundings and its facilities. There was a golf driving range, swimming pool, tennis courts and a 24-hour restaurant.'

Although the squad had journeyed 9,827 miles and across 11 time zones, the younger members of the Wales party weren't in the mood to sleep off the effects of jet lag. Forwards coach Derek Quinnell recalled: 'It was the first trip Wales had been on for eight years, and we soon discovered that Paul, Robert Jones and some other youngsters, in particular John Devs, had boundless energy. We had arrived in Fiji in the early hours of the morning following a long flight and said to the squad: "Listen now, boys. Have a few hours kip, just relax and we will look at getting together after breakfast at about half past ten, for a little stretch or a game of football".'

Quinnell and head honcho Gray had a shock, though, when they arrived for breakfast in the hotel restaurant a few hours later, as Quinnell fondly recalled his conversation with the younger players: 'John Devs, Moriarty and Robert were already there!

"Have you had any kip boys?" I asked.

"A bit," they replied.

"It's a nice place," I said. "There's meant to be a tidy swimming pool here."

"Yes," they replied. "We've already had a swim."

"Oh, okay. Have you seen the tennis courts?"

"Yes. We've had a game of tennis, and table tennis."

"Oh, great. There's a pitch and putt golf course here too."

"We've already played," came the reply.

'It was nine o'clock in the morning, we'd only been in Fiji a few hours and they'd done everything at the hotel!'

Then Gray chipped in: 'When we went away Derek used to say he didn't miss his kids because the youngsters we had in the squad, like John, Paul, Robert and Rowland Phillips, were like children.'

Devereux and his side-kicks eventually heeded the advice of the team management and lounged around the swimming pool as the hot sun beat down, but it wasn't too long before they started getting bored and were ready for some playful antics.

No groups of Wales fans had made the trip, the only supporter they had was Brian Kempson, a member of the Welsh Rugby Union's general committee who had forked out of his own pocket to pay for the pleasure of travelling and staying with the squad.

'He was a character and reminded me of the comic actor Arthur Askey,' said Devereux. 'You could always find Brian at the bar or at the hotel pool and he used to stand out as the archetypal British tourist with a white handkerchief, knotted in each of its four corners, just about covering his balding head. He also wore a leisure vest he'd bought at the airport with a 'Fiji Bitter' logo on its front.'

The young brigade initially left him alone for fear that winding up a WRU committeeman the wrong way could backfire on them and damage their chances of being selected should he take any prank aimed at him the wrong way. That state of affairs didn't last long, for Kempson was too inviting a target for the restless youngsters, with Devereux to the fore: 'We were sunning ourselves by the pool and Brian was sprawled out on his lounger. We had been dying to throw him in the pool but no one had plucked up enough courage to do it. Brian sensed what was going on and decided to ease the tension, so to speak, by taking the initiative.

'He just got up off his lounger and said; "Go on, throw me in, you won't shut up until you do." With that, Jiffy, Webby and a few others picked him up and lobbed him into the pool and retreated, giggling, to their loungers.'

Job done, the players left the committee man splashing around in the water but their frolics almost, according to Devereux, turned into a tragedy: 'No-one had bothered to check that Brian was ok. He wasn't, and was lying at the bottom of the pool.'

Only the prompt action of experienced lock forward Robert 'Bob' Norster, who had been watching events unfold from his sunbed, averted a potential drowning, recounted a thankful Devereux: 'Bobby was the only person to notice Brian had not resurfaced so he jumped off his lounger, sprinted to the side of the pool, dived in, swam to the bottom and fished him out. Brian was coughing and spluttering. It was only then that Brian confessed he could not swim. I dread to think of the consequences had the worst happened. That was the end of our throwing Brian in the pool antics and we had to find other forms of entertainment to amuse us.'

Alternative activities, such as a game of golf with a difference, was then devised. The players decided to see if anyone could drive a golf ball over the fence at the bottom of the driving range. With a few real golfers in the squad, in the shape of Bleddyn Bowen, Malcolm Dacey and Mark Wyatt, joined by the Devereux and Moriarty hit-and-hope brigade, the players gave it everything they had: 'We made up for our lack of skill with brute force! We did indeed get a few over the perimeter fence at the bottom of the range, much to the annoyance of some local inhabitants who were walking there and suddenly found they were dodging golf balls.'

Wales held their first training session the following day but it certainly wasn't like those of today in the professional world, where a host of coaches, medical staff, nutritionists and scientific boffins are on hand to measure every effort and wade through the extensive data provided by the GPS devices modern day players wear.

'Our session was just a bit of a light workout,' said Devereux. 'We were all dressed in our own T-shirts and shorts because there wasn't any proper tour training kit provided, so we looked like a bit of a rabble. It was the amateur era and was a world away from today where players are provided with a mountain of kit and everything they do is synchronised, and every last detail, never mind how minor, taken care of by an assortment of staff.'

Although it was supposed to be a light session, Devereux remembered that Kevin Hopkins tore a hamstring: 'The session ended up as a bit of a damp squib, but Kevin stayed on tour and spent the rest of the trip as duty boy. He was at our beck and call day and night and answered to the name Tour Dogsbody. We took pleasure in winding him up as often as possible.'

'The following day, after training, we received an invitation from the captain of a British Merchant Navy ship docked in Nandi, to visit for curry, tea and a few drinks. After a bus journey of about an hour, we arrived at the dock then boarded the ship, which was laying telecommunications cables in the Pacific Ocean. The officers were dressed in their formal uniform of white shirt, white shorts and long white socks, and had kitted out the top deck of the ship with bunting, flower garlands and canopies so we could keep out of the sun.

'It looked fabulous but most of the forwards in the squad were more interested in knowing where the beer was stored and whether it was ice-cold. They were rubbing their hands together in delight when they found the "treasure" as there appeared to be enough Fiji Bitter to sink the ship. After the formal speeches and the polishing off of the bumper buffet, we started to get a little bored. Glenn, the party animal that he was, suggested we start some drinking games. We started with the usual game of Buzz, and then Glenn introduced a game which was new to me, Hello Harry. It involved a cork from a bottle, a lighter, and a bottle of Tipp-Ex correction fluid.

'Glenn explained the rules and the game got underway. I must admit I was not very good and you had to drink a half pint glass of bitter as a forfeit when you got the Hello Harry sequence of words wrong. Glenn, being the game's master, would grab the cork and, with the lighter, burn one end to create some soot. He'd then then press the blackened end on your forehead, so after being hauled over the coals for repeatedly answering incorrectly, your face was covered in black dots and resembled something out of a film about the Plague.

The only problem was it didn't work for Glenn, being black, so we used a bottle of Tipp-Ex on him instead. The game, with the Tipp-Ex, was actually Glenn's idea and we should have realised he'd be an expert player. In fact, he was so good at it that he ended up with only one white dot on his face.

'Rob Jones wasn't getting the hang of the game and was soon covered in black dots. He found drinking the half pint fines hard going so I started drinking them for him. When the beer was all gone the crew, how can I say, encouraged us to leave, and we clambered in a drunken state back on to the bus to head back to the hotel. I was sat right behind the bus driver and was smashed. About five minutes into the journey, I started to feel extremely unwell but I didn't have time to shout "stop the bus". Before I could utter a word, I had thrown up all over the back of the driver's seat. It was a mess and smelt horrible. The driver was very kind and didn't complain although I'm certain he cursed me after we got back to the hotel and headed straight to bed.

'There was an early start to training the following day and I was, unsurprisingly, feeling under the weather. My spirits lifted when Rob walked into the hotel restaurant still dressed as he was the day before and with his face still covered in black dots. He said he hadn't been feeling well and decided to find one of the ship's toilets, where he'd promptly fallen asleep, waking up about 6am to the sound of the roar of its diesel engines. Running out of the toilet, fearing he was heading out to sea as a stowaway, a sheepish Rob raised the alarm and was put ashore before getting a taxi back from the dock to the team hotel. We were in stitches at missing him in the roll call on the bus, and at the thought of him waking up out at sea and needing more than a taxi to get him back to the hotel.'

The opening match of the tour was against a Western XV at Lautoka, on a firm pitch and in sweltering conditions. Wales were narrow winners 19-14, with Webbe the star attraction having quickly become a favourite of female spectators in the packed crowd: 'When Glenn ran with the ball it sounded like most of the women began to scream and shout loudly.'

Wales came off distinctly second best in their next fixture, at the National Stadium in Suva, where a big and physical Eastern XV defeated the tourists 29-13. It was hardly an ideal preparation for the Test against Fiji but Wales turned it around in another physical battle to emerge 22-15 victors in the match that really counted.

'While Fiji was fantastic fun,' said Devereux, 'the Tongan leg of the tour will always be remembered for just two things, the biggest fight you will have seen in a Test match other than the Lions against South Africa in 1974, and a rat running across a shelf while we were eating dinner in a restaurant.

'I knew I wasn't playing in our first game in Tonga because I had to sit my second-year university exam, so was doing some last-minute revision in my sweat box of a room at the aptly named International Dateline Hotel, while the boys larked about at the pool building human pyramids. At 2pm, Tony knocked on the door and entered with my exam paper. I sat at a little desk and he sat on a chair on the balcony with the door open. Tony was a great guy and great coach who had a calmness about him and spoke ever so softly. He and DQ were the type of guys who would never let you down. It must have been pretty boring for him, and during the three hours I spent sitting the paper, Tony must have puffed his way through a packet of cigarettes. I could have done more preparation but I did have quite a lot to distract me. Thankfully, I later found out that I'd done well enough to progress to the third year at Cyncoed.

'We stayed at the hotel for ten days and the evening meal was the same every day, with French onion soup as a starter, a pork chop dinner and apple pie and ice cream for dessert. Don't get me wrong, the meals were cooked well and tasted great, but it did become a bit wearing towards the end of our stay.'

While the Tongans were passionate, welcoming and friendly off the pitch there was an altogether nastier edge when it came to the matches themselves.

'It started with our game against a President's XV at Teufaiva Stadium in Nuku'alofa,' said Devereux. 'Malcolm was injured so Jiffy had to play, and hopefully stay fit for the Test against Tonga three days later. Jiffy was our playmaker and he was targeted during a bad-tempered ordeal. It started even before a ball had been kicked when a huge prop forward sporting a black beard looked at Jiffy and gestured at slitting his throat. For 80 minutes, Jiffy did a fantastic job of passing the ball and running in the opposite direction to get away from the prop who seemed to spend most of the game chasing him around the pitch. There were fights breaking out every few minutes and the officials were dreadful, ignoring lots of cheap shots as we scraped home 13-9 winners.

'We had torrential rain for a few hours each day, which turned the pitch for the Test into a paddy field. It was surrounded by large palm trees, with the spectators lined up 10-deep, apart from one side which had a stand constructed from an old steel frame covered in a corrugated sheet roof and with wooden seats. Our changing room was tiny and had two small windows, through which the spectators tried to peer at us. Our giant prop, Stuart Evans, got peeved and slammed shut one of the windows. Unfortunately, it smashed, showering broken glass down into our changing room. Events turned sour when the police got involved. They came to the changing room door and tried to arrest big Stu. It was farcical and we told the Tongan Rozzers where to go, in no uncertain terms.

'After leaving the changing room we had to go up into the main stand to meet the King of Tonga before the match started. He was a huge man of about 25 stone and was sitting in the royal box on the halfway line. I followed Jiffy up the steps so we could all, individually, shake his hand. Oddly, the King wasn't wearing anything traditional. He had Dr. Marten boots and a long black leather coat like those worn by Nazi SS officers. He was also wearing a pair of ski goggles and, to put it mildly, it was bizarre.'

The term 'game', in retrospect, may be the wrong word to use under the circumstances because within five minutes it had become a war after Wales No.8 Phil Davies, who is now World Rugby's director of rugby, was smacked in the face during an off-the-ball assault and, according to Devereux, was sparked out: 'There was a big scrap, round one if you like, between the forwards. Us backs, as per normal, just watched.'

Referee Brian Kinsey temporarily restored order and called the captains in for a chat. Dickie Moriarty was skipper that day as Dai Pickering had picked up an injury against Fiji, and Kinsey instructed both captains to tell their teams he would not tolerate any further foul play, and any offenders would, from now on, be sent off. Dickie relayed the message but, as Devereux recalled, had an extra one of his own, telling the Welsh team: 'When it kicks off again, and it will, I don't care who you are standing next to, just twat them. Understood!'

The Wales captain didn't have to wait very long for his instructions to be carried out, as Devereux recalled: 'Boy did it erupt! It was like when players throw off their gloves in an ice hockey match and start punching the nearest opponent.' The Tongans didn't take a step back, however, they took two steps forward. To put it bluntly, Wales were beaten up with one notable exception, as Jonathan Davies recounted: 'Devs was a guy you wanted alongside you in the trenches, a hard man who wouldn't take a backward step and who you knew you could rely on. That mass brawl was a fight like no other and I have to say Devs was the only Welsh player to get the better of his opponent.'

Bowen concurred and went further, saying: 'That was the only game where I was actually afraid on the field. There was fighting everywhere and I was scared, but John Devereux seemed to enjoy it and was the only one to win his individual battle.' Jiffy added: 'We were backed up against the crowd, who were pushing us back on to the pitch so the Tonga team could get stuck into us.'

The Garw Valley boy stood his ground, though, admitting: 'I was probably the only Welshman who won his fight. We watched the replay of the brawling back at the hotel on a VHS video tape that was entrusted to us by Huw Llewelyn Davies of the BBC. It was the only copy of the game and everyone was keen to see the action. Some were sitting there with ice packs on swollen eyes, as we had been in a real battle.

'As the fight erupted, we watched in awe as Tevita Bloomfield, the Tongan tight-head, set upon the Welsh team single-handedly. He was a huge guy. He went through us like a tornado ripping up trees in a forest. He floored hooker Billy James with one punch, boom! Then smashed Stuart Evans with another, and down he went as well. Then he smacked Adrian 'Adolf' Hadley square on the jaw. Adrian was snoring before he hit the turf.

'Bleddyn bravely followed Dickie's orders and came in from the blind side, clouting Bloomfield as hard as he could on the jaw, but the giant just turned, smiled menacingly at Bleddyn then started chasing him. Bleddyn was doing a figure of eight around the posts then tried to run off the field, only for the spectators to push him back on. He eventually found a gap in the crowd and ended up in someone's back garden with the pigs and chickens.

'When Bleddyn had plucked up enough courage to return to the carnage, the fighting had ceased but Adrian was still unconscious, lying face down in the mud. Then they drove an estate car with a Red Cross painted on a door on to the field, opened its back door and threw him in the back, but it got stuck in the mud and a number of players from both teams had to give it push off the pitch, leaving big ruts in the turf.

'None of our medical staff or management went with Adolf to the hospital so duty boy for the day, Mark Titley, jumped in the ambulance instead. Afterwards, we found out from Adrian and Mark, that when the ambulance got to the hospital there were no doctors present as they were all at the game. The two of them even had to thumb a lift back to the hotel from the hospital as there were no taxis there either.'

Wales managed a 15-7 win and, remarkably, there wasn't a single sending off. To say there was a bad atmosphere when the two teams renewed acquaintances at the post-match dinner, though, was an understatement, as Devereux recalled: 'Jiffy was asked to reply in Welsh to the Tongan captain's speech, because Dickie Moriarty was not a Welsh speaker. Jiffy wasn't very complimentary as he stated how the Tongans' overly aggressive on-field behaviour wouldn't see him wanting to return in a hurry. The Tongan dignitaries, assuming he was saying lovely things about them and their country, warmly applauded the speech as the jaws of the Welsh speakers in the tour party dropped in silent astonishment. Once the rest of us were briefed as to what he'd said, we all laughed and patted him on the back. Jiffy was spot-on.'

Gray commented: 'That was a vicious game. It was the only place I have seen an ambulance being driven across the pitch to retrieve a player. Adrian was kicked from behind the dead ball line to the 22.'

Any chance of World Rugby [the International Rugby Board as it was then] getting hold of the footage of the sorry affair and taking disciplinary action against Tonga quickly evaporated, as Devereux explained: 'Broadcaster Huw Llewelyn Davies came to the hotel to collect the VHS video tape of the game but it had disappeared. To this day there is no record of that game. There are a few conspiracy theories but the most feasible was that someone from the Tongan party took it so the crimes of the game would never see the light of day outside of the country. All I know is that it would have gone to No.1 in the video nasty charts if it hadn't gone missing.'

After departing Tonga, Wales then rounded off the eye-opener of a tour by beating Western Samoa 32-14 in Apia, with Devereux touching down for his first Wales try.

'Samoa had Michael Jones and John Schuster in their team, who would both go on to play for New Zealand,' said Devereux. 'Jones was a key figure, a brilliant player for the All Blacks who lifted the inaugural World Cup the following year. Looking back, the eligibility rules were pathetic, a joke, how could you play for the country of your birth and then move to another in the space of a year and come away with a winners' medal from the biggest tournament in the sport?'

6

Accidents Will Happen

*'There was an almighty sound of breaking glass and John was
screaming. He was standing in a pile of broken glass and blood was
pouring out of him.'*

Paul Moriarty

There wasn't any denying 1986 being a wonderful year for Devereux,
and he had gone far in his quest to cement a regular place in the
Wales team. Much was expected of him the following season as
Wales prepared for the inaugural Rugby World Cup in New Zealand
and Australia, but he nearly didn't make it after suffering a serious
hand injury in a household accident.

Already addled with a reputation with his college pals for being
accident prone, some compared him to Frank Spencer in the popular
television comedy series *Some Mothers Do 'Ave 'Em*, starring Michael
Crawford. Everything Spencer did turned to near disaster as he
wreaked havoc with his comic antics and frequently ended up in
hospital.

While Spencer's accidents were fictional, Devereux's were of the
real variety and it took the skill and expertise of surgeons to repair
the injuries he suffered, some so serious, as Devereux recalled, they
threatened his playing career and perhaps worse: 'It began while I
was at college at South Glamorgan Institute. I was living with a group
of lads near the Claude Hotel in Roath, the Cardiff pub which was
a magnet for students. You knew you could always find somebody
familiar in The Claude if you popped out for a pint in the afternoon
or evening.'

Unfortunately for Devereux, he was unaware that his room in
the house he shared with fellow students had a dangerous window:
'Our digs were in Claude Road. It was a three-story house and my

room was on the top floor. As far as I knew there weren't any hidden dangers. How wrong was I!'

As a grimacing Devereux recalled, one of his house-mates and pals, Geraint Jones – known as 'Mr Magoo' – was knocking furiously at the front door desperately trying to get the attention of his house mates because he had forgotten his key and couldn't get in: 'Being a typical lazy student, I couldn't be bothered to walk down two flights of stairs to let him in. Neither could anyone else. It was a case of who caved in first to Magoo's knocking, which was getting louder and louder by the second and in danger of annoying our neighbours. In the end I cracked but, rather than take to the stairs, I decided to open the window of my bedroom and throw a key down to him. Not that he was likely to catch it because his eye sight wasn't the sharpest, hence his nickname.

'There wasn't, however, anything untoward with Magoo's hearing and he could soon hear the painful shouts coming from my room. I'd pushed open the catch so I could lift up the bottom section of the window, which I expected to stay in place, but as soon as I released the catch the top section of the window came crashing down like a guillotine. Instinctively, I stuck out a hand to try and stop it falling any further, but I didn't know or realise someone had cut the ropes that held the counter-weights inside the sash window frame.

'I feared the glass would smash when the sash dropped on the frame so attempted to prevent that from happening. It turned out to be the wrong move and the consequences were to cost me a number of Wales caps. However, it could have been worse for me and my career. As I tried to stop it falling, my hand went through the glass and a piece of knuckle on my left hand was sliced off. There was blood everywhere and I was in great pain. It was immediately clear to me, Magoo and the rest of the lads, I needed to get to hospital.

'Back then, the city's Accident and Emergency Unit was located at the Royal Infirmary on Newport Road. It wasn't far from our house and I was soon being assessed. I was told I had to have an operation to graft the knuckle back on.'

However, in true Frank Spencer style, it wasn't the end of the matter as the drama continued: 'I think the consultant there used me as a guinea pig for a junior doctor to practise inserting an anaesthetic nerve block under one of my armpits. The young doctor failed on several occasions and, in the end, I lost count of the number of times he tried. I reckon it took him about a dozen attempts before I said to him, "Enough is enough". So, it was a general anaesthetic for me and the surgeon used all his skill to graft the knuckle back on. I was relieved to be told the operation was successful because all sort of crazy thoughts had been going through my mind.'

Devereux was detained in hospital overnight before being discharged the following day with his left hand heavily bandaged and his arm black and blue from bruising caused by the number of attempts to administer the nerve block. Going home was the last thing on his mind, though. Instead, he headed straight to watch South Glamorgan College face Tredegar in the Schweppes Cup. It was the competition in which Devereux had burst into the minds of the public the previous campaign and he had been expected to star in the encounter with the Gwent club.

Tredegar were certainly relieved he wasn't playing, and did a job on the college with their heavier and more experienced pack: 'I was gutted to miss the game and watching us go out of the cup. I'd been so looking forward to it and felt we could progress after how close we came to beating Cardiff the previous season but it wasn't to be.'

Devereux missed some Wales fixtures as a result and it was the start of a recuring theme as he suffered more serious and dangerous off-field mishaps. Thankfully, he had been fit and firing on all cylinders for the 1987 World Cup, terrorising the opposition with his piston pump hand-off and being a key strike weapon in Wales finishing third, but the good times didn't last as he had what can only be described as a brush with death soon after returning from New Zealand.

'I came home from the high of the World Cup play-off triumph over Australia in Rotorua and graduated from college. I had been offered a chance to spend two weeks doing some rugby coaching with my good friend, and fellow Garw boy Huw Bevan, at the posh Stowe private school in Buckingham. It had been arranged by Simon Cohen, who was another pal who went on to have a long stint as chief executive of Leicester Tigers during the club's golden years in England and Europe.

'At that time Simon was running a rugby summer school for boys. We had great fun coaching the boys during the day and getting rather sloshed at night in the teachers' private bar, hidden away in the school's cellars.'

Devereux, though, had an important date in his diary for he was to be a guest at the wedding of his Wales teammate, Robert Jones, and Megan Rowlands, the daughter of Wales team manager, former coach and ex-captain, Clive 'Top Cat' Rowlands, in Swansea: 'Rob and Meg were getting hitched halfway through the fortnight I was coaching at Stowe so Simon kindly loaned me his racy black Ford Fiesta XR2i car so I could drive back to Wales for their big day. The journey passed without any problem and everyone had a wonderful time celebrating the marriage.'

The Sunday afternoon trip back to Stowe the day after the wedding was uneventful until Devereux made a miscalculation that could have had catastrophic consequences: 'I made one of the most rash and crazy decisions of my life. The thing that made it even more needless was that it happened only four miles away from the school. I had come up behind a slow-moving car and decided to overtake it. As I pulled out and started the manoeuvre I spotted a Ford Capri in the distance coming around a bend. Instead of slowing down and pulling back in, however, I put my foot down on the accelerator, thinking I had enough time to get past the car. How wrong I was.

'It was a mistake which could have cost my life and that of the driver of the Capri. I realised too late that I wasn't going to make the pass so slammed on the brakes, but with no ABS braking in those days I couldn't evade the oncoming car. The XR2i slid uncontrollably towards the Capri at high speed and my life went into slow motion for those split seconds. My life did flash in front of me but, luckily for me and the driver of the Capri, the man upstairs wasn't quite ready for us.

'A high-speed head on smash in any car, let alone a small car like a XR2i, isn't advisable. The fact I was physically strong in my upper body may have saved my life as the car was a write-off. The other driver had the benefit of a bigger crumple zone as the Capri had a long bonnet and fortunately also survived. We were taken to hospital in the same ambulance but there wasn't much chat between us. I spent the next five hours in Accident and Emergency at Oxford's John Radcliffe Hospital suffering from a broken right foot, severe whiplash, a broken nose, and cuts and bruises. The other guy needed attention for the damage I'd caused to his nose.

'Simon collected me later that evening and drove me back to Wales in one of the school's minibuses. I was so remorseful and apologetic about his car. I couldn't believe how stupid I'd been, and how I'd totalled his lovely XR2i. Fair play to Simon, though, all he was concerned about was my well-being, saying: "Jesus, John don't worry about the car, it's just piece of metal, your health is more important." Simon had been to see the wreckage and was amazed I'd got out alive. I often wonder myself how the hell I got out of that crash with just a broken foot and some cuts and bruises.

'It was my fault and I put up my hand and said so when the police came calling. I was prosecuted for dangerous driving and pleaded guilty. I was fined and given five points on my driving licence but there were no complaints from me. I was just grateful to still be alive.'

A fortnight after the accident, and with his right foot in plaster, Devereux and his Wales teammate Paul Moriarty, decided a break was in order and booked a two-week summer holiday with their then girlfriends, now their wives, in Majorca. 'My mother didn't think going on holiday to a place with swimming pools and the sea while sporting a plaster cast was a sensible idea but we went anyway,' said Devereux.

'We arrived at Cala Ratjarda in Majorca and were having a great time. The only drag was that I had to wrap plastic bags around my plaster cast to shower or go on an air bed in the pool or sea.'

'I pulled John's air bed around the pool or took him out to sea and swam alongside him,' recalled Moriarty. 'We were doing everything to make sure his plaster didn't get wet, but common-sense went out of the window when we started drinking heavily one night. We were at one of those Spanish bars where the waiters used to put the receipts on a metal spike with a wooden base on your table to keep a record of what you had drank. I don't know how many drinks we had but there was a load of receipts and we were drunk.'

Devereux remembered the incident: 'We were five days into the holiday and were in a bar drinking what seemed like a gallon of sangria like it was pop. It was a really hot night and Muzzy and I stripped off down to our boxer shorts as we walked back to the hotel. It was about 2.30am when we reached the hotel and there was a gang of youngsters by the pool. They had been quite noisy and annoying during the day so me and Muzz grabbed a few of them and slung them into the pool for a laugh. Then I pushed some others in, and Muzz as well.

'After I'd pushed Paul in, he shouted: "You're going in next". There was no way I was going in wearing a plaster cast so I turned and started hobbling away as fast as I could. It was dark as I approached the hotel reception and there were two options in front of me – the staircase or an illuminated doorway in the distance towards the back of the hotel.'

Both Devereux and Moriarty are clear about what happened next: 'I chose the doorway, still thinking Muzz was in hot pursuit, and believing it was open, but it wasn't. There was a huge smash and all the air in my lungs was forced out, just like being smashed by Mal Meninga on the rugby field. I was stood there, dazed and ankle-deep in a pile of glass. As the shock wore off, I noticed my left leg was dangling and, as I looked down, I could see it had a deep cut across it, just below my knee cap. I knew our summer holiday was over.'

Moriarty added: 'Devs didn't realise the door was closed because it had smoked glass and was difficult to see in the light. I first heard the almighty smash as the glass door shattered and then him screaming in shock and horror. I ran to him and he was standing in the broken glass with nothing on his feet. Blood was pouring out of the wound in his good leg. There was blood everywhere. He was lucky he hadn't severed a main artery or it could have been worse.'

As Devereux recalled: 'The hotel's duty manager must have heard the commotion and quickly appeared. I was screaming Muzzy's name with blood seeping from my leg but he just stood there impersonating a raging bull with his hands, like horns, either side of his head. The cheeky fucker!'

There was an on-call doctor nearby who was quickly summoned by the hotel manager. A wound on Devereux's shoulder was stitched and his leg was wrapped in bandages to stem the bleeding. Then an ambulance was summoned: 'They threw me in the back and I had Alison for company during an hour-long trip to Palma Hospital with a driver who thought he was Formula One legend Ayrton Senna by the speed at which he threw the ambulance around the bends in the road.'

Devereux passed out after half an hour but wasn't sure whether it was from drink, tiredness or blood loss. As he recalled, he woke to find himself in a room at Palma Hospital: 'It was a lovely place, very clean and modern with good medical advice. I had a private room with a sea view of the bay. They advised I needed an emergency operation to repair the patella tendon in my knee as it had been completely severed. I didn't have any hard feelings to the medical team at the hospital but I was determined to have the operation back home.

'Alison made some phone calls and my good friend Lyndon Thomas contacted the WRU via Rod Morgan, a neighbour of his and chairman of the 'Big Five' Wales selectors, who sorted everything out. I was put on the first available flight out of Majorca to, of all places, Glasgow. I arrived in Scotland at midnight and a taxi was waiting to drive me the seven hours to the Princess of Wales Hospital in Bridgend. I arrived there at 7.30am to be met by Alison, who had travelled back on a different flight.

'The surgeon did a good job on repairing the patella and I spent 10 weeks in plaster plus another month to recuperate, but was able to make a full recovery. I also had a cut that started at my shoulder that stretched across my chest around to the other shoulder, missing my carotid artery by less than an inch. The scars are still there to remind me how lucky I was. If that artery had been cut, I may have bled to death.'

Moriarty also mentioned another incident, when they were playing for Widnes, which highlighted the accident-prone nature of his friend: 'The day before a match we used to have a team run-out in a public park opposite Naughton Park, called Leigh Rec,' he said. 'We were playing Wigan the following day in a huge match and were going through a few drills and tactics. We started by running around the pitch in pairs, passing a ball to each other as we ran, but somehow or other Devs managed to run straight into an upright. The posts were greased so kids couldn't climb them and John had a dollop of grease on his forehead. When he wiped away the grease, blood came spurting out of a cut. I, and I'm sure everyone else who was there that day, still can't believe how he managed to run into a post. You had to be there to believe it, but that was Devs, things seemed to happen to him. He played against Wigan the next day with black tape on his head to protect the wound. I wouldn't say he was jinxed but he was certainly accident prone.'

Wales' one-man accident magnet, Devereux appeared hell-bent on causing mayhem and chaos wherever he went. A few years later, on a sunny September afternoon in 2005, he drove from his home in Bridgend, with his eldest daughter Jessica coming along for the ride, to pick up a new leather settee from a warehouse in Nantgarw, just north of Cardiff.

Taking up the story, Devereux winces as he recalls the next few hours: 'The M4 was very quiet, apart from a few rally cars coming from Port Talbot, where they had been racing one of the forest stages of the Great Britain Rally.

'We got to the warehouse at about 10am and loaded up the trailer. It took two men to carry the settee and place it on the trailer. I had brought ropes with me and asked, "Shall I tie it down"? But when one replied, "That's going nowhere son," I didn't bother. What a mistake that was.

'After re-joining the M4 at junction 32, I noticed that the plastic wrapped around the settee had puffed up, and as we were passing junction 34, I looked in my mirror again only to see that the settee was now moving very slightly sideways. I was now very concerned so touched the brake while keeping an eye on the settee in my rear-view mirror. To my horror, the settee took off from the trailer and flipped end-over-end before crashing down onto the middle lane of the motorway.

'A car behind me had to take evasive action to avoid the settee as it landed on the tarmac and slid across the road into the central reservation before coming to a stop against the crash barrier. It ended right-way-up in a position where you could have sat on it and watched the traffic passing. I pulled over on to the hard shoulder and put my head in my hands before quickly phoning Alison with the bad news.

'I was panicking a bit by now and contemplated running across the three lanes of the motorway, grabbing the settee – which was very heavy – and dragging it across to the hard shoulder. Luckily, before I did anything daft, an unmarked police car pulled up behind me and a police officer walked up to the car: "What's up?" he asked. I sheepishly replied, "You're not going to believe this" and gestured towards the settee in the central reservation. "How the hell did you do that?" he asked.

'As I explained what had happened another police car turned up and a plan was hatched to recover the settee. However, to carry out the operation, the traffic had to be stopped by one of the police cars doing a rolling block, allowing an officer and me to run to the settee, pick it up and carry it safely across the M4 to the hard shoulder before placing it back on to my trailer. This time I made sure it was tied down safely, but it was ruined and heading for only one place when I got home, the tip!

Devereux expected to get the book thrown at him but the police officer said: "On your way, I wouldn't want to be you when you get home to the wife. You are very lucky as that could have been a lot worse." He then said he'd just come from Port Talbot, where a rally car navigator called Michael Park, had been killed in the GB Rally that morning. I vividly remember the silence in the car on the way home as me and my daughter contemplated what had just happened and how the rally driver's death had put our lucky escape into perspective. Life is too precious to take careless risks.'

7

The Inaugural Rugby World Cup

'John made a big impact at the 1987 World Cup. He's right up there
when it comes to Welsh players making a mark on the competition.'

Tony Gray

The promise Wales had shown during 1986 seemed to have disappeared during the following year's Five Nations when they finished joint bottom of the table alongside England, with their sole success having come against the old enemy.

Devereux was still recovering from his sash window hand injury when Wales picked their team for the opening match of the tournament, against Ireland in Cardiff, with Pontypool's Roger Bidgood pencilled in to make his international debut. Fortuitously for the injured student, a heavy fall of snow in Cardiff saw the game postponed until later in the season and the talented Pontypool man had to wait a number of years before getting to wear the cherished red jersey.

By the time Wales faced France in Paris in 1987, Devereux was fit and went straight back into the team at the expense of the unlucky Bidgood, partnered in the centre by Kevin Hopkins. France were Europe's best team and, although Wales defended well, they went down 16-9 having lost the goal-kicking expertise of Paul Thorburn, who had broken his collarbone in a challenge.

Thorburn was replaced by Mark Wyatt at full-back for the clash with England in Cardiff and had the best view of an almighty punch-up as the teams, who had both been fired up during a heated pre-match build-up that week in the media, slugged it out.

The apparent dislike between the sides erupted in the sixth minute when England lock Wade Dooley flattened Phil Davies with a punch. Davies suffered a fractured cheekbone and was replaced by Richie

'With my lovely gran, Hannah Taylor (top left), my mother's mother. Sadly, I never knew my other three grandparents. Two died before I was born and one past away when I was still a young child.'

'On the mountain above our house with my sisters, Lynne and Ceri (top right). The mountain, and Lawrence Park below, were the two places I loved most when growing up in Pontycymer.'

'Being photo-bombed by Ceri while having a cwtsh with my father, Peter (bottom left).'

'The blonde hair didn't last long.'

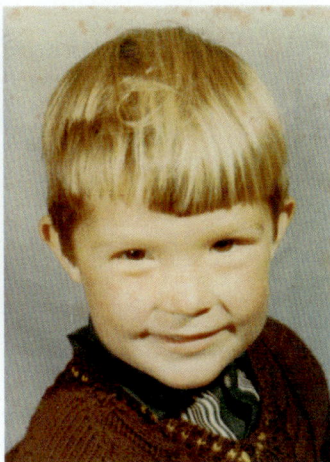

'I loved going on holiday with my parents. We always had a great time together and had so much fun.'

'My Auntie Florrie (bottom left) had a huge influence on my life as I grew up. Here we are at Clifton, on a trip to Bristol Zoo when I was around eight years of age. She took me to so many places to learn about the world and widen my horizons.'

'With my wonderful mum, Valerie, on one of our Spanish holidays (bottom right). Our hotel is in the background.'

'At Ffaldau Primary School we were very lucky to have a headmaster like Arthur Thomas (left) and Dai Harris (right) as a PE teacher. My good friend Huw Bevan was captain for the 1975-76 season when we were very successful and I (front, second from right) led the team the following season.'

'When we won the Fronwen 7s (below) I was voted Player of the Tournament and was photographed in action for the first time by the local paper.'

'The Bridgend & District U12 team won the DC Thomas Cup two years running, and for one of those victories I was a year younger than my teammates (back row, fourth from right). I had to play centre because Sean McCarthy (with the ball), who became a professional footballer, got the nod at outside-half. It was quite a team, that also featured future international Mike Hall (back row, far left) and Gary Reffell, (crouching, second from left) the father of current international Tommy.

'A few years later, the Bridgend & District U18s played New Zealand tourists from Kelston Boys High School. We drew 3-3 and I kicked our penalty.'

'I was fortunate to be an all-round athlete. In my 5th year at Ynysawdre Comprehensive I won the Victor Ludorum award at our annual sports day, winning most of the events, including the Long Jump, with our PE teacher and former Welsh international, John Lloyd, checking my progress.

'Captaining Ynysawdre School's 1st XV at every age level from the first form to the sixth form was a great honour.'

'I've always loved football and it was a proud day when I took the field at Ton Pentre FC in the Rhondda to represent the Boys' Club of Wales U16s (bottom left). I played centre forward against a Scottish Schools XI but we lost 5-1 to a team of skillful boys, most of whom has already signed for the top clubs in Scotland. My club, Garw 33 (bottom right, I'm wearing the iconic 1970s Wales kit), established by Dick Smiles, played to a good standard and we won several trophies.'

'I loved my time at South Glam Institute and made many friends for life including Nathan Humphreys (top right, to my left) and Geraint John (to my right).'

'We were a very decent side and won a few awards, including the 1986-87 Bridgend 7s, when I captained the team (top left)'

'We also knew how to party as Geraint "Magoo" Jones (left, with red hat), Andrew Thomas (with moustache, and now a senior figure in Welsh education) and Tim Gill (in straw hat) can testify.'

First Round — Schweppes Cup

South Glam Institute
v
Cardiff

Saturday, 16th Nov. 1985

at CYNCOED – K.O. 2.30 p.m.

Official Programme 50p
This is a donation to
South Glam. Institute

SOUTH GLAM. INSTITUTE	v	CARDIFF	
15	Nathan Humphreys	15	Mike Rayer
14	Kevin Morgan	14	Alan Glasson
13	John Devereux	13	Robert Ackerman
12	Colin Laity	12	Alan Donovan
11	Michael Holding	11	Adrian Hadley
10	David Rees	10	David Barry
9	Carwyn Lewis	9	Steve Cannon
1	Steven Hodnett	1	Jeff Whitefoot
2	Huw Bevan	2	Alan Phillips (Capt.)
3	Alan Cleverly	3	Ian Eidman
4	Sean Turner	4	Kevin Edwards
5	Anthony Rees	5	Robert Norster
6	Andrew Coughlin (Capt.)	6	Mike Teague
8	Stuart Davies	8	John Scott
7	Steffan Phillips	7	Tim Crothers

Replacements:	Replacements:
Andrew Norman, Nigel Gibson, Steven Phillips, Gareth Phillips, David Harries, Gareth Nicholas	Chris Webber, Neil O'Brien, Chris Collins, Robert Lakin, Owen Golding, Peter Crane

Referee:	D. O. Hughes
Match Balls donated by:	Balan Sports (Cardiff) Qui Qui Wine Bar (Cardiff)

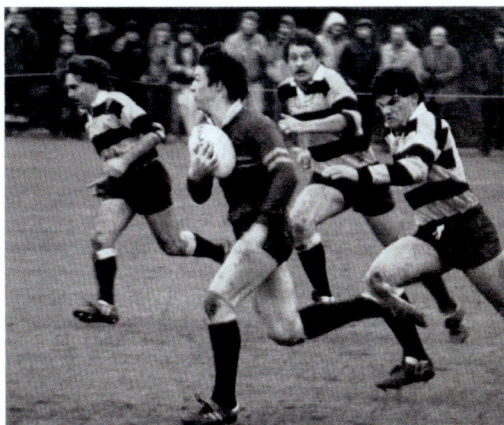

'My life changed when a star studied Cardiff RFC side came to Cyncoed in 1985 for a Welsh Cup 1st Round tie. We lost 25-16 but the whole team played well and definitely gave the Blue & Blacks a real fright.'

'Both Colin Laity and me formed a solid partnership at centre (top right), and I left my mark on Rob Ackerman, the Wales centre at the time. I was an unknown student before the game, but that had all changed 80 minutes later after several charging breaks that had then panicking (top left).'

'Colin went on to have a fantastic career with Neath and was capped by Wales B, while my performance was noticed by the Welsh media, and the WRU's Big Five selectors.'

Student power rocks Cardiff

S Glam Inst 16, Cardiff 25

IT was sad to see the students disappear after the first round of the Schweppes Cup because they played much better football than Cardiff in appalling conditions, writes **Wilfred Wooller.**

John Devereux, at centre made the newly-arrived Cardiff international Ackerman look like a leaden-footed selling plater. David Bees at fly-half and Nathan Humphreys from full.

Devereux is top material

S Glam Inst 16pts, Cardiff 23   By PAUL REES

ROBERT ACKERMAN has cause to feel hard done by in the rush to get him into the Cardiff first team. He had the misfortune to be up against the best centre threequarter seen in Wales this season.

John Devereux, who has not played for a first class club, is just the latest player to roll off Leighton Davies's conveyor belt of talent at South Glamorgan Institute. Anybody who thinks the college produces backs and not forwards should have been at Cyncoed on Saturday — Cardiff's forwards soon found they were not in for a jolly day trip.

But above everyone and everything stood Devereux, a tall, strong centre, he breaks with modern tradition by running fast and straight, handing-off and timing his pass. Twice a burst of his through Ackerman led to tries, from wing Michael Holding and centre Colin Laity.

At Newbridge recently, against arguably the best pair of centres in Wales, Steven Crandon and Chris Manley, Devereux and his colleagues reduced the home side to nervous tatters by refusing to play rugby by the manual.

The students had the man of the match in centre John Devereux, a 20-year-old former Ynysawdre Comprehensive pupil from Blaengarw, whose strong, straight running — and devastating hand-off — created the openings for the first two tries.

The magnificent centre play of the institute's John Devereux that shone like a beacon through the gloomy afternoon.

Twice his incisive running and powerful hand-off split the Cardiff defence and produced tries, while his all-round play revealed him without doubt as a potential international.

'Being called up for the national team was a dream come true, but to celebrate that occasion with my great friend Huw Bevan (holding me aloft) and my college mates was unreal. What an amazing afternoon we had at the Horse & Groom on Womanby Street.'

'Blaengarw RFC organised a special event to mark my first cap and invited some of the coaches without whom I wouldn't have succeeded: (l-r) Leighton Davies, Dick Smiles, Arthur Thomas and John Lloyd. My sisters, Ceri and Lynne, and my father also joined in the celebrations.'

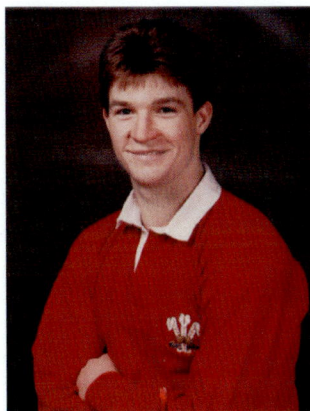

'Three of us made our Wales debuts that day in Twickenham, and it was a proud moment when Robert Jones, David Waters and me were presented with our caps.'

'It was a tight game that flew by, but I did manage to make a break or two and show the rugby world that this 19-year-old student wasn't out of his depth. The selectors must have liked what they saw, and picked me for the rest of the tournament.'

'The Wales tour to Tonga, Fiji and Western Samoa in 1986 was a wonderful experience, well, apart from the game against Tonga which was mainly a fist-fight.'

'Those were definitely the pre-professional days (top) as we had to wear our own clothes for training.'

'Glenn Webbe's drinking game on the ship in Fiji left its mark on our faces, and Robert Jones got left behind for the night.'

'Touring is fun, but it also builds team unity and the Wales team was getting stronger by the match.'

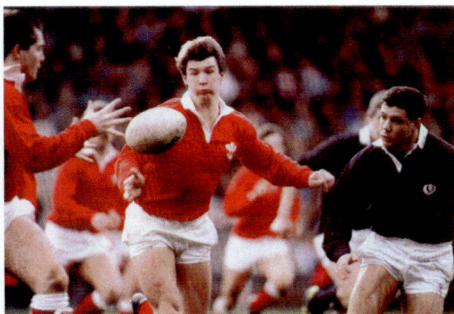

'Not only was I now a regular for Wales (above), but invitations from the Barbarians and the Lions began to arrive.'

'Wearing my Cyncoed socks (left), I played in the Mobbs Memorial match at Northampton, and for the 1986 British & Irish Lions match in Cardiff against a Rest of the World team to celebrate the centenary of the International Rugby Board (now World Rugby).'

'To have been capped by Wales, invited to play for the Barbarians and selected for the Lion, all while still a student, was unbelievable. Life was good, and getting better.'

'Playing in the inaugural Rugby World Cup in 1987 was a learning curve for us all, but Tony Gray, Derek Quinnell and the inspirational Clive Rowlands were a brilliant management team, and so well supported by Richard Moriarty as captain.'

'First up were Ireland (below, left), who we beat 13-6 at Wellington, then our old sparing partners Tonga were seen off 29-16 at Palmerston North, before a 40-9 victory against Canada at Invercargill (below, right) saw us qualify for the quarter-finals, and a mouth-watering tie against England.

'Our confidence grew from game to game and it still remains the best Welsh performance in the tournament.'

'As soon as the great Bill McLaren was spotted we all headed over to say hello and have a photo to mark the occasion. He was rugby royalty and is still missed by all who love our game.'

'A memorable moment, scoring my first try of the World Cup and my first against the Old Enemy, at the end of the quarter-final which secured our 16-3 victory over England in Brisbane. We now looked ahead to the semi-final against the All Blacks.'

'The semi-final against New Zealand was a wake-up call to how far ahead they were in every facet of the game - on and off the pitch. We had already despatched Ireland, Canada and Tonga in our group before beating England fairly easily in the quarter-final, but this was a totally different challenge - they were brilliant.'

'The scoreboard rarely lies, and our 49-6 defeat said it all. The only highlight was my try, when I cut through the All Blacks' back line after a fantastic flat pass from Jiffy. 'Smokin' Joe Stanley' was given the Dalek hand-off (above, © Getty Images) and I dived over. The television commentator Nigel Starmer-Smith called it "fully deserved" and a "try of great courage". Paul Thorburn slotted over the conversion but we didn't bother the scoreboard again.

'Written off as a "bunch of bums" by the Australians, we were fired-up for the 3rd & 4th play-off game in Rotorua.

'Every single player stepped up and we went toe-to-toe with the Aussies, roared on by the local Kiwis who had joined with the Welsh fans who were still on tour.

'My trademark hand-off made a memorable appearance in a quick-fire triple fend that started with Aussie captain Andrew Slack (top right), followed seconds later by Michael Lynagh (left) who were both given a taste of Pontycymer.'

'A last minute try from Adrian "Adolf" Hadley, who brilliantly found space by the corner flag, left Paul Thorburn with a touchline conversion to win the match with just seconds remaining. With nerves of steel, and reminiscent of John Taylor's famous "greatest conversion since St. Paul" at Murrayfield in 1971, "Thorby" slotted over the kick to secure the 22-21 victory.

'The celebrations in that changing room (above) will stay with me forever. We were all mates and playing for each other. Our spirit was plain to see and we believed this side could dominate European rugby for a decade. Within a year, that dream would turn into a nightmare.'

'Following the success of finishing third at the Rugby World Cup, Wales won the Triple Crown in 1988 (I missed the tournament through injury) and were just a couple of points away from a Grand Slam. Now fully fit and back in the squad, I headed to New Zealand for the two-Test series - a tour that would have a dramatic impact on Welsh rugby for a generation.'

'We knew it would be tough and worked to close the gap, but the All Blacks had improved even more. The two heavy losses, 52-3 and 54-9, saw the coaches sacked. The WRU refused to listen to the players who urged them to adopt a more professional approach, and keep Tony Gray and Derek Quinnell, and the side that promised so much began to fall apart when so many players went north to rugby league.'

Collins, as Scottish referee Ray Megson, who was making his Test debut, failed to curb the constant niggle between the teams. Dooley somehow stayed on the field as the rain poured, with the only try of an unsavoury affair occurring when giant Wales prop Stuart Evans emerged from a pile of bodies to burrow his way over in the corner. That touchdown, and three penalties from Wyatt, gave Wales a 19-12 victory in a game that also saw lock Steve Sutton suffer a broken nose after accidentally being clouted by teammate Bob Norster.

Following defeats against Scotland and Ireland, the victory against England was Wales' sole success, in what Devereux agrees was a dismal campaign: 'It was an unexpected Five Nations because we had hoped to build on the previous season and the tour of Tonga, Fiji and Samoa. Things simply didn't go our way. The loss of Stuart cost us dearly in Scotland as we spent much of that game going backwards while Mark, who was normally an ultra-reliable goal-kicker, struggled against the Irish.

'However, we still believed we had a promising squad and believed we could make a mark at the upcoming World Cup. We remained confident although our poor results in the Five Nation title race meant some players were very concerned about not being picked for the trip to Australia and New Zealand. When the squad was announced, I think there was more than a sense of relief among those of us who were selected.

'I was in my third and final year at college and was finishing off my dissertation for my degree. Once I was selected in the squad for the World Cup, the dilemma I faced was whether or not the University of Wales would allow me to take my exams in New Zealand, as they clashed with the pool stages of the tournament. Fortunately for me, it was agreed I could sit two papers in Wellington and my final exam in Dunedin. I was very relieved to get clearance from the university to go to the first World Cup, as I hate to think what I would have done if the examination board had declined my request to sit them in New Zealand.

'The Scotland and Ireland squads were on the same flight as us for the journey to Auckland, and we happily combined to drink the plane dry of booze. When we arrived, I had to immediately depart for Wellington with the late Ray Williams, the then secretary of the WRU, as I had to sit the first of my exams at the Kiwi capital's university the following day. It meant we both missed the World Cup gala dinner in Auckland.'

Devereux and Williams were sweating, however, when their connecting flight touched down following a bumpy descent and heavy landing on the airport's short runway: 'Flying into Wellington can be a pretty traumatic event and it's not called the world's windiest city for nothing,' said Devereux. 'As we approached the airport, I could see nothing but white water below me as the sea raged. The plane was being thrown around by strong gusts of wind and I swear its wings were flapping like those of a bird. I looked at the air stewardesses for some reassurance but there wasn't any as their faces were also a picture of fear. We landed with a big bump but we had made it.'

Pleased their feet were back on the ground, Williams hired a car for the short journey into the city and, as Devereux recounted, the pair popped into an off-licence where Ray bought a bottle of wine: 'We were staying at a bed and breakfast hotel so Ray took me out for a Chinese meal at a bring-your-own-bottle restaurant and the wine came in handy. When we got back, I did some last-minute revision but must have fallen asleep as I woke up the next morning with my books spread out across the bed. Ray dropped me off at Wellington University for my 9am exam and gave me ten New Zealand dollars, saying: "Good luck, and catch a taxi to the team hotel when you're finished".'

The rest of the Wales squad were arriving later that day but reuniting with them was the last thing on Devereux's mind as he sat his exam: 'It went okay and, after leaving the university, and being a skint student, I thought I'd keep the $10 Ray had given to me by walking to the team hotel instead. I had a good idea where it was but finally arrived feeling quite ill from the petrol and diesel fumes after wandering through a long and busy tunnel. Ray asked if everything was all right but I didn't dare tell him about walking to the hotel in case he wanted the money back. When the rest of the squad arrived that afternoon, Tony Gray took me to one side and handed me my navy blue Rugby World Cup cap. What an amazing feeling that was.

'The hotel, though, was rougher than a crow's nest. It had a central garden area with an outside swimming pool, which was freezing, and the only thing it had going for it was a hot tub, which proved popular with the boys after training sessions.'

Devereux sat the second of his exams then turned his focus to facing Ireland, in Wales' World Cup opener: 'It was just eight weeks after our Five Nations defeat to the Irish but training went well. We were all positive and confident we could avenge that loss.'

The day before the Ireland game the Welsh squad watched the game between the other two teams in their pool, when Canada beat Tonga 37-4, then saw England lose 19-6 to Australia, but what had transfixed them was the opening game of the tournament when New Zealand destroyed Italy 70-6. The All Black machine easily steamrolled Italy with John Kirwan, a new superstar in the making, scoring a spectacular 90m try.

Wales were marginal underdogs against Ireland but were on top for large parts of the match with Devereux playing a prominent part in the build-up to co-centre Mark Ring's vital try – the only one of the match – with a trademark burst and overhead pass during a 13-6 triumph.

'It was a dry day with not a cloud in the sky,' remembers Devereux, 'but there was a howling gale battering Athletic Park. The stadium was situated on a hill so it was really exposed. The wind blew so hard it flattened the grass. We played against the wind in the first half of what was a cagey affair, with Ireland using the elements to their advantage with lots of up-and-unders that forced us to defend resolutely for long periods.

'Michael Kiernan gave Ireland a 6-0 lead with two first-half injury-time penalties when big Stuart Evans was penalised for picking up the ball in an offside position, while I caught their winger Keith Crossan a bit high with a tackle. Only conceding six points after playing into the wind boosted our confidence and we knew we had a superb tactician and out-of-hand kicker of the ball in Jonathan Davies.

'Early in the second half Paul Thorburn put over a penalty to open our account, but the turning point came when I brought down Hugo McNeil in midfield. We stole the ball and turned defence into attack with some good interplay. We moved the ball across the line and Adrian Hadley came off the left wing and into the line to create the overlap. He passed the ball out of the tackle to Thorby, who handed it on to me. I stepped inside a defender and passed to 'Ringo' who scored our first try of the tournament. Thorby surprisingly missed the conversion, and a penalty, before Jiffy put over two drop goals to give us the victory.

'The game gave us a huge confidence boost because we knew we were expected to beat Tonga and Canada so it had been a probable group decider, with the victors advancing to the quarter-finals. The signs were good and we were able to put together some nice passages of rugby. When you have players like we had in the back line anything was possible.

'We then travelled by bus to Palmerston North to play Tonga. It was rural New Zealand and there were sheep everywhere, a bit like driving through mid-Wales. We had an official welcome from the mayor of Palmerston North and were driven around its streets perched on vintage vehicles. I was with Bob Norster on the back of an old fire engine. It was one of those moments you had to be there to believe.

'I was rested and missed our next mass brawl with Tonga which included the craziest tackle I have seen. Glenn Webbe caught a pass and the Tongan full-back launched himself head first into Glenn's chest. There was a massive impact and Glenn hit the deck, but then bounced straight back up and started running with the ball, in completely the wrong direction. He had no idea where he was. Glenn was superb that day and scored a hat-trick of tries in a 29-16 victory but couldn't remember any of them after being substituted, suffering from a suspected concussion. In modern day rugby's Head Injury Assessment protocols, he would have been hauled off within seconds.

'The next stop for us was Invercargill, the most southerly city in New Zealand. It was bloody freezing and even the penguins huddled together for warmth. The training ground was basic and there was ice everywhere.

'Les, who had been assigned to us by the New Zealand Rugby Union as our baggage man, soon showed he had other key skills. We quickly discovered he was an amazing masseur, which upset the WRU's physio, Tudor Jones, because most of us we were going to Les to have our legs massaged. Les was short but built like a battleship, and also introduced us to giant green lipped mussels. They can grow to eight inches in length but the ones Les had us eating were about four inches. Then he brought us oysters, which were already deshelled, in large Tupperware containers and covered in brine. Les said they were great for "the pecker" and he had us eat them, uncooked, starting with a whole one. They were horrible. Rob Jones, Anthony Buchanan and I just couldn't keep them down.'

Devereux avoided more possible stomach strife the following day when he was up early to fly to Dunedin on 'a crop sprayer' of an aeroplane to sit his final exam: 'I landed at Dunedin Airport and waited for my liaison officer to pick me up, but he was nowhere to be seen. I was there for ages and getting concerned as time was knocking on but, thankfully, he appeared before panic really set in. It was a big relief to get my final exam out of the way and, from then on, I could fully concentrate on the World Cup and producing my best.

'I returned to Invercargill on the twin propeller plane for the following day's match with Canada which took place on a lovely but cold day and the old stadium was rammed with a crowd of 12,000. We won the game 40-9. I scored my second try for Wales, Ieuan Evans bagged four and we were through to a quarter-final with England, in the sunnier climes of Brisbane, Australia.'

The squad had picked up some injuries so the team management sent for some replacements. Prop John Rawlins arrived after a 30-hour flight and, as Devereux explained, was brought straight from the airport to the training ground: 'We were doing some sprints and someone asked John to join in. It was daft thing to do, and surely enough he pulled his hamstring. I felt his pain, one sprint and his World Cup was over.'

It would have taken a couple of days to get another replacement prop from Wales so it was decided to bring Dai Young into the squad. He was a young, up and coming prop with Swansea and had a good pedigree, who was playing a season of rugby in Australia, along with Swansea flanker Richard Webster, to widen his experience.

When the Wales party arrived at the Mayfair Crest Hotel in Brisbane, they discovered that Webster had also travelled to the hotel with Young, and slept on the floor in Young's room. Dai was kitted out in Welsh gear but Webster had travelled light, so members of the squad gave him some bits and pieces to tide him over. He also attended training sessions and voluntarily joined in as proverbial cannon fodder.

Young impressed during workouts but it was still a massive shock to Devereux when the uncapped forward was picked at tight-head prop to face England at Ballymore: 'The weather in Brisbane was so much nicer than the grim weather we had just experienced in New Zealand. The sun shone, it was warm and we were able to train in shorts and T-shirts. We had a great time. Most afternoons were free so we used them to play golf and see the sights.

'No Welsh person needs any motivation when playing England but just to add some spice we heard the Rugby Football Union had already booked a hotel for the semi-final in the expectation they would get through, which certainly added a bit more edge.

'Ballymore, the home of the Queensland Rugby Union, was rammed for the match and we had the majority of the crowd shouting for us. There were loads of 'Mad Taffs' and most of the Australians watching were right behind us because they like nothing better than Pom-bashing and seeing England being beaten at anything.

'We were pumped up for the game anyway, but there were a few old scores to settle from the battle in Cardiff a few months earlier. The match itself was a typical Wales versus England tussle. Not for the first time, or the last, England were supremely over-confident which just played into our hands. At no time during that quarter-final did I think we'd lose. We played well and totally commanded the game.

'Dai, or 'Ted' as we named him, had an outstanding game against the hugely experienced Paul Rendall. Rob Jones shone and scored his first try for Wales before the moment I had practised for over and over as a young boy on Lawrence Park in Pontycymer occurred, scoring a try against the English. I anticipated a stray pass from their outside-half Peter Williams, intercepted the ball and sprinted 40m for a try between the sticks. It was the final nail in England's coffin as we ran out 16-3 winners and I couldn't hide my emotions. I was so, so happy. I'd scored two tries in as many matches and we were through to the semi-finals of the World Cup at the expense of the old enemy. It was brilliant.

'We had a great party back at the Crest Hotel with plenty of Aussie lager being consumed by the squad, the management and our supporters. The following morning we set off for Surfers Paradise on the Gold Coast after inheriting England's now unrequired hotel booking. Paul Moriarty and I liked to be active and by the time the clock had chimed for noon we had visited the sights, been in the sea for a dip and had a game of tennis on the third floor of our hotel.'

Awaiting Wales for a place in the final were co-hosts New Zealand, who had already crossed for 30 tries and amassed 190 points – conceding just 34 – after victories over Italy, Argentina and Fiji. It didn't come any harder than facing the All Blacks machine but rugby was amateur back then and this was illustrated when news reached Wales prop forward Steve 'Wally' Blackmore that he had become a father. The Wales management team, Tony Gray and Derek Quinnell, agreed that the squad could celebrate the safe arrival of Wallys first child, but Devereux recalled how the celebrations got out of hand and lasted a few days.

'We weren't being disrespectful to the Welsh people or our coaches,' he said, 'but I guess we knew we were up against it, playing against New Zealand, who Wales had last beaten in 1953. Even if our drinking session had been confined to a day. I don't think anything would have changed against the All Blacks. We knew how good they were: they had prepared for two years for the tournament, having special arrangements with their employers to be allowed to be physically and tactically ready for it. They were semi-professional, at least, in an amateur game while we were a team of players with great ability but with nowhere near the strength and fitness levels of that Kiwi team.

'They had one of the best back-row players in the world, Michael Jones, at openside flanker. 'Buck' Shelford was at No.8, Alan Whetton was at blindside flanker with his twin brother Gary in the second row and a young Sean Fitzpatrick at hooker. Fitzpatrick had only got his chance because Andy Dalton, who had been due to captain New Zealand, had picked up an injury before the tournament but, boy, did he take it. Their backs were no slouches either, and their new sensation, Kirwan, was a beast of a winger.'

The Wales squad sobered up, though, when skipper Richard Moriarty called a training session: 'Dickie took us for a bare foot blowout run along the beach. It was brutal. The beach at Surfers Paradise just keeps on going, and Dickie kept on running and running. We were all suffering, not just with the run but also the thought that the further we went the further we would have to run back to the hotel when Dickie eventually decided to turn around.'

After blowing away the cobwebs, the squad went for a dip in the Pacific Ocean but it almost ended in tragedy as the adventurous few, who obviously included Devereux, were out of their depth when they were caught in a dangerous rip tide: 'The sea was a little rough and the weather was cloudy and windy. A few of us found we were unable to get back to the shoreline which was getting further and further away as the current took us out to sea.

'I was never a strong swimmer and, putting it mildly, it was very nervy. We knew we shouldn't panic and attempt to swim against the current because of the danger of becoming exhausted and drowning. We knew we had to tread water and swim parallel to the beach until the rip arced around and took us back to the shore, which it did. We were all knackered as we lay on the beach, and so relieved because there were no lifeguards on duty at the time. I'm not afraid to say it could have turned out much worse as our lives were in danger.'

Wales lined up against New Zealand on 14 June 1987. Devereux was just 21 with 14 caps to his name: 'I was about to play in a semi-final of the inaugural Rugby World Cup. It was also my first game against the All Blacks and the first time I'd faced the *Haka*. What struck me was that they all looked so much bigger than us. You could also sense the pressure they were under. It was palpable. The All Blacks knew they were expected to get to the World Cup final, while we knew that we were expected to take them on, and to perform.

'I never felt intimidated by the *Haka* but soon found out how good that New Zealand side was. The black wave hit us right from the kick-off. We piled into them but were pushed aside with ease. They were relentless and, even in the scrum where we thought we could dominate, they pushed us off our ball and set up attack upon attack with quick ball for their backs to exploit,

'We tried valiantly to defend everything they threw at us but it was a matter of time before we cracked and for them to score the first of their eight tries. Fox missed only one conversation as they racked up a record 49-6 win against Wales. We were thankful it was only four points for a try in those days.

'We played really well at that World Cup but had come up against a supreme All Blacks machine. It was an absolute battering – boys against men. They just took us apart with wave after wave of pressure. They were a special side – the best union team I have seen to this day.'

New Zealand's bid to stop Wales scoring any points was scuppered when, as he recounts, Devereux powered over for a consolation score: 'We had a rare attacking opportunity from a scrum and Jiffy called one of the back moves we had practised many times in training. He threw a pass to me, missing out Bleddyn Bowen at inside centre. Jiffy and Bleddyn were supposed to loop around me and I would then pop Jiffy a pass over my left shoulder. But I noticed my marker, 'Smokin' Joe Stanley, coming up slower than the rest of the New Zealand defence so I ditched the move and had a go.

'I went outside him and pinned my ears back. The rest of it seemed to take place in slow motion. Within a second or two I knew I'd got the beating of him. It was about 15m to the line and I saw Kirwan racing across from the wing to make a cover tackle. I remember thinking: "I'm nearly there. Just get that dive for the line right and hold on to the ball." Then, boom! I was over. I know we were getting hammered but, for a moment, I knew how proud my mum and dad would be back home in Wales, watching the match on television.

'I walked back carrying my right boot. It had come off in Kirwan's tackle and I looked at the main stand at Ballymore where our replacements, the non-playing members of the squad and our supporters were celebrating the score. Not many Welshmen had scored tries against the All Blacks so to have that privilege was something special and something I will always cherish.'

The All Blacks have always hated teams scoring against them and the backlash came, not just on the scoresheet but, as Devereux recalled, when a brawl broke out: 'We had lock Huw Richards sent off for punching one of the Whetton brothers. I'll rephrase that, Huw was actually carried off because Shelford had retaliated and laid him out with a hammer punch. He was lying there, dazed, and having the magic sponge treatment from Tudor when Australian referee Kerry Fitzgerald gave him his marching orders. It was an outrageous, harsh and shocking decision. Shelford should have gone for retaliation but Fitzgerald didn't even say a word to him. It was difficult enough playing New Zealand with 15 men, but impossible with 14.'

Following the heavy defeat, a dejected Wales squad retreated to their hotel to drown their sorrows. A surprise guest who joined them was the former England and Manchester United football captain Bryan Robson who was in Australia doing some promotional work for the Sydney Olympic committee. By all accounts, Robson was good company who enjoyed the drinking games and could put the booze away well for a relatively small bloke.

Wales then headed back to New Zealand for their third-place play-off against an Australia team that had lost a crackerjack of a semi-final against France. After flying into Auckland and taking a bus to Rotorua, the Welsh squad stopped off at the beautiful Lake Taupo for food and a stretch of the legs, the perfect setting for mischief makers Webbe and Ring to play a prank on Webster.

'We were outside a café and nearby was a telephone box,' said Devereux. 'Glenn quickly got the number of the public phone, then he and Ringo sneaked off to the café and waited for Webster to be close to the phone box then phoned it from the phone in the café. One of the boys went to the phone box, picked up the receiver and heard a voice saying: "Hi, it's the *Western Mail* back in Wales, can I speak to Richard Webster please?"

'A startled Webster was summoned to the phone and was then interviewed by the bogus reporter. He was caught hook, line and sinker! It was one of the funniest pranks I've seen. Webster was convinced he was being interviewed by a Welsh reporter but couldn't understand how they knew he was at Lake Taupo at that particular moment and how they had the number of the telephone box.

'Still chuckling, we got back on the bus and completed the journey to Rotorua. It's famous for its hot water geysers, springs and mud baths but the sulphur escaping from below the surface smelt of rotten eggs.

'We had been totally written-off by the Wallabies in the newspapers. They didn't want to play against us and their coach, Alan Jones, and motormouth winger, David Campese, were slating us in the media saying, in effect: "What's the point in playing against a team of bums?"

'That only fuelled the fire burning inside us and Campese would have those words rammed down his throat. We were really down to the bare bones with the number of players sidelined by injury and Webster's persistence in being in the right place at the right time paid off as he was selected to play at openside flanker. He was a real dog of a player who put his body on the line every time he went on the park. He'd do the really dirty work when no one else fancied it and was kicked and stamped on in virtually every game he played.'

Australia thought they should have been in the final and didn't have any respect for the Welsh. 'We didn't need a team talk because they had handed one to us on a plate with their big mouths,' said Devereux. 'We were so pumped up for the chance to show them what a "bunch of bums" could do.'

There was a heated start to the game with Australia flanker David Codey being sent off by English referee Fred Howard for 'mountaineering' at a ruck after stamping on Wales back-rower Gareth 'Ming' Roberts.

'So much for a nothing game. There was a real edge to it. We played out of our skins and I happened to have a top game. Everything I did seemed to come off. The Dalek hand-off was my trademark and in that encounter it really came to the fore.

'We also scored one of the greatest Welsh tries that never was. As Jiffy was preparing to take a drop-out he said to me: "Have a look on the blindside, I'm going to take a quick drop-out." Jiffy faked to kick left then dropped the ball on to the outside of his right boot and took a quick drop-out. He gathered the ball and shot off before finding me and Ringo. Ieuan Evans crossed for the try, only for it to be brought back for an alleged forward pass. Never, in a million years, was it a forward pass.

'Paul Moriarty and Ming did get tries before one of my favourite moments on a rugby pitch occurred. I was so fired up by Campese & Co, I let loose after taking a pass from Ringo. I straightened up and handed off Australia captain Andrew Slack then Michael Lynagh before choosing 6ft 7in lock Steve Cutler as my third victim. It certainly got the team, and the crowd, going.

'Lynagh dropped a goal to make it 21-16 to Australia with only five minutes remaining when Jiffy put up a towering 'Garryowen'. I tracked the ball and didn't take my eyes off for even a split second. I then out-jumped the defence and caught the ball before hitting the turf. Ieuan acted as scrum half to send the ball to Ringo. He found Thorby, who put in a great hand off, before passing to Hadley for a try in the corner.

'Thorby had been kicking poorly, by his standards, all tournament but he slotted the most important one and then mayhem erupted with a pitch invasion. Our supporters thought it was all over, but there were a few minutes left. Australia still had a chance to win it but Campese turned left to pass when his support runner was on his right, enabling us to stifle the attack and win an incredible clash 22-21.

'We had a fabulous booze-up, one of the best of my career, after the match but the Wallabies didn't want any part of it. We went to the Aussie hotel for the post-match dinner, but Alan Jones kept the Aussie team in the back room and they didn't join us for the speeches, food or drinks. They were sore losers and it was poor sportsmanship, which is a rarity in rugby.

'Playing in that first World Cup was, and still is, special to me. That third-place finish still remains Wales' best at a World Cup, which is amazing and a bit disappointing when you consider how many Grand Slams and Six Nations we have won since 2005.'

Devereux had certainly made an impression with Gray reckoning his former charge deserved all the plaudits which came his way then and, subsequently, saying: 'John made a big impact at the 1987 World Cup. He's right up there when it comes to Welsh players making a mark on the competition.'

Former Wales captain and coach Lloyd, who taught him at Ynysawdre School, was adamant: 'When you analyse the performances of Welsh players at union World Cups, John Devereux's at the 1987 tournament highlight that he has been one of our most influential players in the history of the competition. One of the reasons we did so well was because of John being so dynamic. Factor in he also played in the final of the Rugby League World Cup for Great Britain against Australia and you realise what a special talent he was.'

8

The Talk of Wales

*'I think Devereux can pose more problems at international level than
Jonathan Davies.'*

David Watkins

John Devereux laughed when asked if he had more impact on the
playing field than Jonathan Davies, replying: 'It's subjective. If
anybody says I was, I'll take it, but Jiffy was a fantastic talent.'

However, Devereux is ahead of Davies when it comes to his
curriculum vitae with a listing that would make a taxing quiz question.
Ask people the name of the last Welshman to play in rugby league's
World Cup final and most reply: 'Davies'. Some are surprised when
told it was Devereux, when he was a half-time substitute for Great
Britain against Australia in the 1992 final at Wembley.

Not that outside-half and stand-off great David Watkins, who was
the first Welshman – and first player – to captain the British and Irish
Lions at union and Great Britain in league, had any doubts about
his ability. He was gushing in his praise of Devereux following the
1987 union World Cup, declaring: 'His performances made people
who were sceptical about him, which included me, sit up. Before the
tournament I didn't think he was in the same class as the legendary
Bleddyn Williams but that changed. He was quick for a big man, a
very good tackler and put himself about a bit. I think Devereux can
pose more problems at international level than Jonathan. If Jonathan
learns when to pass the ball, and if Devereux can stay clear of injury,
who knows how far he can go.'

Cliff Jones, another Wales outside-half great, put it in simple
terms: 'I played with four outstanding centres in Claude Davey, Wilf
Wooller, Jack Matthews and Bleddyn Williams, but Devereux was
superb at the World Cup, never more so than against the All Blacks.

His display against them put him on the same level as those four. He is one of the best all-round centres we have seen since the Second World War. You could even argue he is the best. To be an all-round footballer, you need attacking and defensive qualities, and he has both. Imagine how good Devereux would have been behind the All Blacks pack which ran amok at the World Cup.'

With such praise ringing in his ears, much was expected of Devereux, and Wales' other young guns, in the 1988 Five Nations Championship, but after sustaining multiple injuries in a car smash and suffering a serious gash and tendon damage to a knee after running into a glass door while on holiday in Majorca, he had been constantly in the headlines, for the wrong reasons. Almost on a weekly basis there were fitness bulletins and updates as the media focused on his recovery and whether he would be fit for the big European title race opener at Twickenham, against an England team thirsting to avenge their World Cup capitulation to the Welsh. For the battle ahead, Devereux was seen by the media as vital to the cause.

Things seemed to be on an upward curve when he returned to action for Bridgend with an impressive display during a hard-fought 12-6 success over Llanelli at the Brewery Field, but his injury curse struck again in a local derby against Maesteg at the Old Parish when he was involved in another freak incident.

'Back in those days you were allowed to play – in fact, it was the norm – the week before an international,' said Devereux. 'I was in need of minutes on the pitch to hone my match fitness following my recovery from what was a pretty horrific knee injury, but the jinx struck again when I got injured after getting cleaned out of a ruck. I can only assume I fell over and landed on my left hand.

'I didn't notice there was a problem at first as I'd also taken a knock to the face, but my hand began to throb. Bridgend's team doctor Phil Williams, the brother of the great JPR Williams, examined it and, as he did, we heard a bone crack. "I think you should go to the casualty department at the local hospital and get it X-rayed," he said. I asked, "Is it broken?" But he was non-committal, repeating what he'd said about getting it checked out at the hospital in Bridgend.

'With my injury record at the time I feared the worst and, sure enough, the X-ray revealed I had a spiral fracture from my little finger that ran up my hand. They put the damaged hand and arm in a sling and told me to see the Welsh Rugby Union's doctor.'

Devereux retained hopes of being allowed to face England with the hand strapped up but it quickly became apparent the injury was serious enough to rule him out of the Five Nations. 'It was a huge blow because, on the back of the World Cup, we all had high hopes and were optimistic we could make a run at the European title,' he said.

With his physical presence unavailable to Wales' Big Five selection panel, they took a different approach by picking four outside-halves in their back division with Jonathan Davies at 10, captain Bleddyn Bowen (12) and the mercurial Mark Ring (13) at centre, with Anthony Clement at full-back.

Devereux could only watch as the fab four conjured a double-strike for left-wing Adrian Hadley as Wales conquered Twickenham 11-3, and followed it up with Davies and right wing Ieuan Evans scoring sizzling tries in the win over Scotland in Cardiff before grinding their way to glory against Ireland in Dublin to clinch a first Triple Crown in nine years. A Grand Slam should have followed in wet and slippery conditions at the National Stadium in Cardiff, but Wales failed to take their chances and were pipped by France as the rain poured down and made the going treacherous.

Resigned to missing the Five Nations tournament, Devereux had his eyes fixed on returning to fitness for the upcoming tour to New Zealand and began experimenting with an unorthodox treatment used on greyhounds, as he explained: 'While I was waiting for the fracture to heal I got talking to Dai Richards, one of the regulars in my local pub, The Royal Hotel in Pontycymer, who had a greyhound he used to race and kept in a shed at the bottom of his garden in Alexandra Road. Dai told me he had an electric pulse machine to treat his dog's feet and legs whenever it had an injury and said that it was really effective in increasing blood flow levels. He invited me to his house to have a go on the machine, so I did, and few times a week I'd be sitting in his garden shed, watched by a curious greyhound, with my hand in the machine that emitted an electrical pulse to stimulate the blood flow. I have absolutely no idea what good it did and whether it assisted in the healing process, but I was so determined to make that summer's tour I would have tried virtually anything. By the end of the Five Nations, Wales had won the Triple Crown and my hand was healing. It was all systems go for the tour to the land of the long white cloud but, in hindsight, perhaps I should have ignored Dai and had another pint.'

Despite the final day defeat to France, Wales seemed, at least to their supporters, to be the coming team as they packed their bags a few months later for a return to New Zealand to face a supreme All Blacks team that was arguably better than it had been a year earlier. The squad, having been on the receiving end at the World Cup, feared what could happen during a traumatic trip which perhaps caused more damage to Welsh rugby than anything before and since.

'Nobody was that keen to go,' claimed Devereux. 'We went with trepidation because we knew what the All Blacks were capable of and it turned into a harrowing and humiliating experience.'

Wales' opening opponents were a Waikato provincial team captained by a hooker named Warren Gatland, who went on to coach Wales and the Lions to glory, and a back-five forward in John Mitchell, who was to coach the All Blacks at the 2003 World Cup.

'Our coaches, Tony Gray and Derek Quinnell, should have picked our strongest team for our first game in an effort to make a mark and raise morale but they didn't because Waikato were perceived as easier opposition and we went down 28-19,' said Devereux. 'That meant we were on a slippery slope and under intense pressure to open our account. Wellington was our next match and they had Hika Reid, John Schuster and John Gallagher in their ranks. Suffice to say, they put us away with ease, 38-22 and it was downhill and damage limitation more or less all the way from then.'

Wales narrowly beat Otago 15-13 in Dunedin but it wasn't the result which was the talk of the squad, it was the bitter weather in the deep south of New Zealand's South Island and the standard of the hotel accommodation with members of the touring party wearing layers of clothing to bed in an attempt to stay warm.

The itinerary was bruising, with New Zealand coach Alex Wyllie going as far as to state he wouldn't have accepted a similar fixture list for the All Blacks. The injury toll continued to mount with captain Bleddyn Bowen breaking a wrist in Wellington. His replacement as skipper, Robert Norster, who had become Wales' 100th captain following Bowen's exit, suffered a badly gashed knee, which resulted in Jonathan Davies taking over leadership duty for the second Test.

Wales had conceded 10 tries, with John Kirwan touching down four times, as they lost the opening Test by a record 52-3 at Christchurch's Lancaster Park, while there was a popular score for New Zealand scrum-half Bruce Deans, 83 years after his great uncle

Bob was famously denied during a controversial match in Cardiff in 1905. A second half penalty from Mark Ring was all Wales could muster during one of Welsh rugby's darkest days, and there have been a number!

A 54-9 loss, with Kirwan only getting two of the eight tries, followed in Auckland a week later and it said it all that the biggest cheer came when Davies, who had led by example and given his all, sprinted to a breakaway try. Mark Ring started the play deep in Welsh territory and it featured a scarred Jonathan Mason with Davies scrambling over the line to ground the ball despite the attention of chasing winger Terry Wright.

Devereux summed up the carnage which had occurred on the pitch: 'The All Blacks were an unbelievable side. They were fitter, faster, stronger and played a simple game. Their forwards provided a glut of front-foot ball and the momentum they generated enabled them to roll us over with absolute impunity.

'We thought we would have parity in the forwards but they had worked on their scrum from a year earlier at the World Cup and pushed us back. I don't think I ever ran as fast backwards as I did in that game. They live and breathe rugby in New Zealand and little old women would come out of shops and tell us we were going to get hammered. They proved to be right in their assessment of the two teams!'

Wales faced North Auckland between the Tests, and full-back Mason, who had been summoned to New Zealand from a family beach holiday in Ibiza, had his jersey ripped to shreds after being given a fearsome going over at a ruck. It was as if he had been thrown around inside a tumble-dryer. Back then, no-holds barred rucking was permitted, with intimidation and physical violence an accepted part of the game. It was a case of almost anything went and Wales were on the receiving end of it in spades.

Devereux can graphically remember the Mason incident, saying: 'The rest of us were milk bottle white and freezing because it was so cold in New Zealand. Jonathan stood out because he'd turned up with his bleached blond hair, sun tan and a guitar.

'It was like a red rag to a bull to the Kiwis as they honed in on him with an introduction to New Zealand trampling. North Harbour put a bomb up, Jonathan caught it but the whole of their pack seemed to arrive with the ball, hammered him into the ground and ran over the top of him. When he finally got to his feet, it looked like he had emerged from a threshing machine. It looked like 'Freddie Krueger' had had a pop at him. His bed clothes stuck to him for days afterwards because of the scabs he had on his back from the numerous stud marks.'

Flanker David Bryant, who like Devereux had been a student at South Glamorgan Institute, made his Wales Test debut against the All Blacks at the tender age of 21 and was a rarity in that he emerged from the tour with his reputation enhanced and bravery acknowledged. But his memory of it is as clear as that of his teammates: 'Painful would be the word I would use to describe it,' he said. 'My lasting memory of the tour was I would come off at the end of the game and they would take out the stitches I'd had the week before and put stitches in the new wounds. I had 28 stitches in the head during the course of that tour. New Zealand used to wear rugby league studs which ripped your skin and I had scars on my back which didn't heal properly for about a year.

'All round it wasn't the most salubrious of places to tour all those years ago. We seemed to spend a lot of time staying in Travelodges and in one place we all slept in our tracksuits because it was so cold. It was like sleeping in a car park.

'Wales had won the Triple Crown and come close to winning the Five Nations but we weren't prepared for the intensity we would encounter in New Zealand. It wasn't like traditional tackling, it was just throwing your body in the way to try and stop them. There was a painting of me in the old Kiwis bar in Cardiff, supposedly tackling John Kirwan but the truth was that he was running over the top of me.

'I remember chasing the kick-off in the opening Test, hitting the maul and thinking: "Oh heck, what have we let ourselves in for?" We smashed into them as hard as we could and the All Blacks didn't move at all. It was like running into a black brick wall. They were just a stronger and a more physically solid type of person. They were also able to do things quicker and maintain their skill level throughout a game because they were fitter. Our fitness lasted about half an hour.'

Such was the battering the tourists took, six players went home early. Some allegedly didn't need too much persuading to depart either. 'After the first Test, people were queuing up to go home. A few jacked it in there and then,' claimed Ieuan Evans, in his autobiography *Bread of Heaven*. 'Some of those who went home early were relieved to the point of being light-hearted, as if they had escaped from the front of a war zone. There was a queue outside the doctor's room every morning and we had an open ticket for players going home on the first available London-bound plane. I had not seen such a defeatist attitude. If ever a team was beaten before the match started, it was Wales on that trip.'

Dai Young, who went on to captain Wales in union and league before becoming a coach with Cardiff and Wasps, coined it 'the tour of death' because it resulted in 'the lost generation'. The tour effectively prompted a mass exodus of talent, headed by Jonathan Davies, Devereux and Paul Moriarty, to rugby league's paid ranks and ensured years in the doldrums for the national team until union went open, allowing the payment of players and the advent of professionalism, which ended the raids on Welsh rugby by league clubs.

'We had arrived believing ourselves to be the best team in Europe,' said Evans, 'but even those with supreme self-confidence, like Jonathan, were shaken to their foundations by the experience. The crushing defeats shook us to the very core.'

Wales were that poor, a bugler sounded *The Last Post* following the defeat to North Auckland as if he'd witnessed the death of Welsh rugby, and as far as Wales' losing streak against the All Blacks, which stretches back to 1953, nothing much seems to have changed, so what happened when Devereux and company headed Down Under has to be put in context.

'They were professional in all but name,' he said. 'We'd be watching television and an advert for an airline would come on featuring Kirwan and the great Australian cricket captain Allan Border. Mike Brewer was promoting chocolate bars and Andy Dalton was advertising quad bikes for farmers. The Kiwi newspapers were full of adverts that featured All Black players endorsing all kinds of products.

'It was a different world on and off the field to Wales. Jiffy said we had to cash in. When the WRU turned a blind ear to his plea for his voice to be heard at its annual general meeting, it was another nail in the coffin and pushed him and others towards the exit door and the road north to rugby league's heartlands of Lancashire and Yorkshire.'

Davies signed a big money deal with Widnes just a few months later, on the back of an abysmal home defeat to Romania in Cardiff. Wales had a new coach in John Ryan after Gray had been given the boot by the WRU, and Devereux was dropped for the first time in his career. Their only success in the Five Nations came against England but it was clear that Welsh rugby, not for the only time, was unravelling at the seams.

The repercussions were huge. Wales possessed a squad which, if it had stayed together and the services of Gray had been retained, had an age profile which suggests it could have become Europe's best team.

Quinnell doesn't have any doubts about its potential, saying: 'The All Blacks were world champions. They had easily beaten the French in the final and were one of the best sides I have ever seen. We had a tonking in New Zealand but we learnt a lot.

'We still had a great bunch of young players who we thought were going to serve Wales for a long time but the WRU, in its wisdom, decided not to invite Tony and me to continue coaching the team. We felt it was a knee-jerk reaction and a number of outstanding players, John Devereux among them, went north.

'It culminated in Wales having a great Rugby League World Cup in 1995, and that match against Samoa in Swansea was something else. When you look at the Wales team that electric night at The Vetch Field, the majority of it consisted of union boys who had played for us in '86, '87 and '88. They had come through the system but had been lost to league.

'Stuart Evans, Dai Young, Jonathan Davies, John Devereux, Jonathan Griffiths, Paul Moriarty, Rowland Phillips and Adrian Hadley went and were later followed by, among others, Mark Jones, Allan Bateman, Scott Gibbs and Scott Quinnell.

'There was a lost generation and most of the top of the pyramid had gone. Wales would have been one of the best union sides in the world if those players, who were exceptional, had stayed in union and the coaching group been allowed to continue. Tony was ahead of his time as a coach but the WRU couldn't see it.

'So, we went from a Triple Crown in March to not having coaches the following August. Not only was it unpleasant for Tony and me but it was also, in my opinion, a backward step, not because of the people who were coming in but because they were starting from scratch and didn't have the experiences of touring we could draw upon during trips to Fiji, Tonga, Samoa and New Zealand.'

9

Lion

'Ahead of a Lions tour you always look for players you would like to coach, and John was one of them. He was a player you didn't just play to, you also played off him.'

Sir Ian McGeechan

Devereux had been dropped from the Wales team by John Ryan during the 1989 Five Nations which had preceded the best of British and Irish rugby's bid for a conquest of Australia, and was never to play union again for his country.

'I had played in the first two games, against Scotland and Ireland in Cardiff. We had gone to Murrayfield as favourites but were well beaten and we were equally poor against Ireland. When I left the field of play against Ireland I didn't have any inkling it would be for the last time in the 15-a-side code.'

He had suffered a mouth injury and departed for repairs, expecting to return to the fray, but after having the wound stitched by WRU doctor Malcolm Downes, Devereux discovered Ryan had already substituted him with Mike Hall switching to centre and Carwyn Davies coming on at wing: 'There weren't temporary blood substitutions then, even so I thought they may give me a couple of minutes to be stitched up but "Buck" Ryan didn't hang around waiting for me to appear from the players' tunnel.'

Wales went on to lose a match after a kick from Bleddyn Bowen lodged itself in the midriff of Noel Mannion close to a touchline near the halfway line. It stuck to the big No.8 like Velcro and he was able to grab it before keeping the desperately chasing David Bryant at bay during a seemingly slow-motion sprint for a decisive score.

Devereux was on a real downer, saying: 'Neither I, or Bleddyn, were to be picked again. It turned out to be a sad way for both of us to go. I must admit I had given up all hope of selection for the Lions tour as both Wales and I had not had a great Five Nations, only winning one match.

'There were two fixtures remaining in the championship, against title chasing England in Cardiff and France in Paris, but Bleddyn and I got the chop. The England game was another dour affair with Mike, who had taken my place in the centre, scoring a disputed try after Rob Jones had lofted a box-kick. Rory Underwood caught it but his wild pass failed to find England full-back Jonathan Webb, and Mike pounced. Mike actually failed to ground the ball so it should have been disallowed but, fortunately, there wasn't a television match official in those days and Australian referee Kerry Fitzgerald failed to spot what had really happened so the score stood and Wales were able to edge it. I guess it was a form of retribution because Fitzgerald was the ref who had sent off a concussed Huw Richards at the 1987 World Cup and failed to punish All Black hardman Wayne Shelford for the punch which had knocked Huw out.'

Ironically, Devereux was in Australia, where the Lions were to tour a few months later, when Ian McGeechan named his squad for the mission and there was a sting in the tail when he was given the news by Ryan.

Whether or not Ryan, who died in 2022, was embarrassed by the twist, Devereux doesn't know or care, as he explained: 'I was playing for Wales at the World Sevens in Sydney, my third trip there in four years, when I found out 'Geech' had picked me for the Lions. Rob Jones, Ieuan Evans, Mike Hall and I were in the bar of the Camperdown Travelodge Hotel in a suburb of Sydney having a soft drink when Buck Ryan appeared with Tudor Jones, the Welsh team's physiotherapist. Both had big smiles on their faces. Buck told us we were in and proceeded to shake our hands and congratulate us. I was over the proverbial moon, so to speak, but inside I was smug and thanking McGeehan for showing faith in me where others, specifically Ryan, had failed to do the same. Geech knew what I could do for the Lions and all he had to do was give me some confidence.'

McGeechan, who was knighted after serving the Lions as head coach during four tours between 1989-2009, explained the criteria he used to select players: 'Ahead of a Lions tour you always look for players you would like to coach, and John was one of them. He was a big man who had always impressed me with the power of his running, the way he read a game and his support lines. John was a player who you, as a coach, knew that if he had an involvement in a game he was going to get you across the gain-line. Devs was quite exciting as a runner but there was far more to him than going down just one channel. He was clever where he put himself and, if he had some space to work in, he would take defenders on and off-load. He was a player you didn't just play to, you also played off him.'

So how did Devereux compare to fellow Wales centres Scott Gibbs, who was player of the series when McGeechan's Lions conquered South Africa over three Tests in 1997, and Rolls-Royce runner Allan Bateman?

'I had 'Gibbsy' as a young player in New Zealand in 1993 and he got into the Test team ahead of Will Carling. His work-rate and all round game was so good. In 1997 in South Africa, Scott had come back from a stint in rugby league with St. Helens and was, again, brilliant. League had made him a great professional and he was a superb communicator on the pitch,' said McGeechan.

'Allan Bateman was also on the '97 tour of South Africa and was probably one of the most under-estimated players around. He had played very well against Natal the week before the opening Test with the Springboks and was in contention for a place but suffered a hamstring injury. He was fit enough to be on the bench for the final Test with the series already decided in our favour and came off it to make a big impression in the second half.'

After a pause, McGeechan stressed: 'But John Devereux would have held his corner with those two because he was more than just a power runner. He had an awareness about how to bring others into the game and was a good defender who would certainly put in some big hits.

'In the World Cup, he gave Wales confidence because he took players on and wasn't afraid of reputations. He was the catalyst of the Welsh backs with others reacting to the way he was playing, and he was mainly responsible for the Welsh revival, particularly in the third-place play-off with Australia. Even against New Zealand, who aren't the easiest opponents to face, he adjusted to the greater physical demands of their game. He learnt from it and put it to good use against Australia.'

Coming from one of world rugby's most illustrious and knowledgeable figures – McGeechan was a Lions centre during the invincible tour of South Africa in 1974 – it's a genuine assessment of how highly rated Devereux was in the rugby world.

'I couldn't wait for the tour to come around,' said Devereux. 'We were sent training programmes and the seven Welsh picks met up in Cardiff to do a number of fitness modules at Sophia Gardens. The bleep test was one of these new fitness assessment tools that was used to compare the aerobic fitness of different players in different positions. Like with the lactic acid test, you always seem to do your best score the first time you do it. From then on, it's more mind over matter as it is so hard. Mentally you know what's coming and to push yourself to the limit you really have to put your body through the pain barrier. I did 13.8 first time around and that was my baseline. I always said I was built for power and my abundance of fast twitch fibres were no good for this test as the lactic acidosis build-up in my legs was unbelievable.'

When the time came for the squad to gather in London to prepare for departure to Australia, Devereux said his goodbyes to then girlfriend Alison and his family back in Pontycymer. His latest adventure had begun!

'Bob Norster, Ieuan Evans, Rob Jones, Mike Griffiths, Mike Hall, Dai Young and I walked into the foyer of the plush hotel on the bank of the River Thames dressed in shorts and T-shirts, carrying our kit bags and suitcases. It was a hot day. Walking towards us was Roger Uttley, assistant coach of the Lions. Uttley greeted us in turn, shaking hands: "Hiya Bob, Ieuan, Dai, Rob, Mikey, Mike". Then, when he got to me, he said: "Sorry, you are?" I was gobsmacked and laughed out of embarrassment for him. I said my name and was just glad he didn't call me Adrian Hadley, as most people seemed to get the two of us mixed up, even to this day! I'd played for the Lions in a one-off match to celebrate the centenary of the IRB in 1986, and been capped 21 times for my country, yet Uttley didn't recognise me. Wow! I suppose, in his defence, he was a forward and all they seem to care about are scrums and lineouts. Uttley clearly didn't give a shit who the backs were. What's the saying? Forwards win matches, the backs decide by how many points.'

The squad were told to gather on the croquet lawn at the rear of the hotel, which had been marked out with cones. Geech told them they had to do the bleep test one more time. It was a hot day but he clearly wanted to gauge his squad's fitness levels before departure.

Things then took a turn for the better as jugs of lagers were brought out for the bonding process to begin. The players sat in the sunshine sipping the amber nectar as they awaited the arrival of giant England lock forward Wade Dooley. The so-called 'Blackpool Tower' was late as he was a police officer and had to finish a shift.

'Wade arrived and was told to join us on the lawn in his kit. He was totally unaware of what he had to do and no-one let on,' said Devereux. 'To make things even more entertaining, he was brought a pint of lager on a tray, which he duly dispatched in one. Then he was told to do a bleep test. Fair play, for a giant of a man, he recorded 13.4. We were in awe of his achievement as it showed a fabulous athlete at the top of his game. Just imagine doing a bleep test with each stage getting faster and faster while having that gas-filled pint of lager sloshing around inside you?'

Legendary Wales captain, coach, team manager, WRU committeeman and president, Clive Top Cat Rowlands, was the Lions tour manager. He told the squad it would be the best Lions tour ever with stays at top hotels across Australia. 'The Burswood in Perth was a fabulous start, a five-star hotel situated out of the city and surrounded by lakes and golf courses,' said Devereux.

It was a Lions tradition that no two players from the same nation could share a room on tour. It also traditional to pair a back and a forward: 'I always gave my roomies marks out of ten after each stay,' said Devereux, 'and as there were 14 Englishmen on the trip, I had a few English forwards as roomies. 'Iron' Mike Teague was a genuinely funny guy, while there was the more reserved second-row pair of Paul Ackford and Dooley, who were both coppers at the time and early-night-cocoa kind of guys. Then there was the 'Pitbull', Brian Moore, who talked extremely posh for a man from up north but we got on very well, and Dean Richards who, like Ackford and Dooley, was a police officer, and always reminded me of a Shaun Edwards type character with an air of shyness about him. Flanker Andy Robinson was a nice guy and so professional, even in those amateur days. Then you had the Scots and the Irish, with captain Finlay Calder top of the list. He was quietly spoken but, when he talked, you listened. I scored them all nines and tens.'

Devereux sat out the opening match, an easy 44-0 win over Western Australia with England winger Chris Oti getting a bag of tries. There was also disappointment for the tour party as the Lions lost Ireland No.10 Paul Dean to a knee injury: 'It was so sad to see a member of the squad going home at such an early stage,' said Devereux. 'It was a warning to all of us that our involvement in the tour could end in the blink of an eye.

'The show, of course, went on with a team meeting before we left Perth. Tour captain Finlay Calder told us that 'JJ' – John Jeffrey, who was in charge of the social committee – had an idea on how to raise some cash for our beer kitty. At this point JJ spoke: "Lads, what we need is 20 Aussie dollars off you all. I was thinking of buying a few hundred white t-shirts and getting us all to autograph one of them and then have the signatures transferred on to the others with the words British & Irish Lions 1989 above our names on the back, and a picture of Lion and a Wallaby having a beer at a bar on the front. We can sell them at every location we stay in Australia".

'It was a brilliant idea and I bought several for myself. More importantly, we made about $500AU for our beer kitty, which was a decent amount back in 1989, and came in very handy as we were going to play hard off, as well as on, the field. We were determined to be successful but have some fun along the way.

'A five-hour flight took us to Melbourne which has an autumn climate similar to southern Britain. It was cool, wet and we faced stiff opposition in the shape of Australia B. During a hard-fought 23-28 victory in damp conditions, I set up a try for JJ – a farmer from Kelso – and felt I'd had a pretty good game. You may wonder where I get all this information, so I'll let you in on a secret. In 1989, a good friend told me to keep a diary of my time in the game. He said it may come in handy one day or be just nice to help jog the memory of what happened and where, from down memory lane.'

Devereux had been hooked on golf since playing the game for the first time with the Lions in 1986 at Radyr Golf Club, just outside Cardiff, when he had formed a trio with Gavin Hastings and Colin Deans.

'I assumed all Scots were natural golfers,' laughed Devereux, 'but I quickly learnt that wasn't the case. Big 'Gav' teed the ball up on the first and smacked it down the middle of the fairway of the par-four hole. Deans stepped up, with a cameraman crouched to his side, at right angles to the ball, but Colin accidentally sliced the shot and the ball headed straight towards the now terrified cameraman who had no time to move. Luckily, the ball missed his head by millimetres, only ruffling his hair. It was one hell of a near miss, but once we'd all got over the shock, we fell about laughing.'

Brisbane was the Lions' next stop, which held good and bad World Cup memories for the Welsh contingent. The Ballymore Stadium was the venue where Wales had beaten England in the quarter-final, and where they were hammered by New Zealand in the semi-final.

The Lions beat Queensland Reds 19-15 after a big battle. It had been another solid team performance and Devereux had hopes, having played in the match, that the team Geech had fielded was starting to resemble the Test XV.

The tour party then headed for Cairns in the far north of Australia. 'For winter, it was hot and humid,' said Devereux. 'Cairns is a big outdoor pursuits type of place, a tropical jungle and home to the biggest bats you have ever seen. After training on our first day there, we decided to go white-water rafting. It was a long minibus trek up into the mountains and the river was at the bottom of a large hydro-electric dam. The river was like nothing back in the UK with huge boulders the size of houses littering the river bed, with tropical jungle either side. When they released the water up at the dam, the river was transformed into a raging white-water torrent. I was on a boat with Dai Young, Bob Norster, Gareth 'Coochie Bear' Chilcott and Craig Chalmers, with one of the instructors at the back steering us down the river.'

Tragedy almost struck as the raft careered down the river. 'We set off and straight away we went over a ridge and into a torrent of white water breaking all around us,' explained Devereux. 'Brad, the instructor, was steering the boat between the huge boulders and, as we went over a big rock it ripped a hole in the bottom of our boat. Then we were immediately hit by a wave and Dai fell through the hole. He was under the water for a while before popping up alongside us. All we could see was his red safety helmet and were trying to get hold of him but we were getting buffeted and smashed around. Dai managed to stop himself by a boulder, but then started to slip down the side and back under the water. It was a desperate, life-threatening situation and we knew we had to get hold of him before it was too late. I managed to grab Dai's crash helmet with one hand and hauled him towards the boat by his head. Then a few of us managed to pull him onboard, which was tough as he wasn't the lightest bloke in the group. We were looking at him and thinking: "Oh my god, you were nearly brown bread". If he'd been sucked under that boulder I have no doubt he would have been toast.

'We eventually reached calmer waters and had to row about half a mile to where the minibus was parked on the river bank. Back on dry land, Brad told us they'd lost a Japanese tourist a few months earlier who had drowned in the river after being sucked under a boulder.

In order to retrieve his body, the hydro-electric power station had to stop generating power and stop pumping water. It certainly gave us something to talk about when we arrived back at our hotel.'

Rugby league clubs were already chasing the services of Devereux, with one going to great lengths for his signature as he made his way around Australia with the Lions. He found he wasn't the only Lion on the 13-a-side code's radar because England star Jerry Guscott, who was to become a key figure during the Test series with the Wallabies, was also in demand.

'Jerry Guscott and I got on well,' said Devereux. 'He was always talking to me about rugby league and how he'd had lots of offers to switch codes. He predicted we would be both playing league sooner rather than later. I always said: "Yeh, some of us have had meetings with league scouts but I had always said no, not interested." In fact, Chris Caisley, the chairman of Bradford Northern, had seemingly chased me across Australia during the Lions tour. At each hotel, I would find a message in my pigeon hole at reception, asking me to ring him. In the end I did call him to say I was happy in union and looking forward to playing many more games as the Lions had given me my spark back.'

McGeechan confirmed Devereux had been within reach of a starting place after performing strongly in a 23-21 triumph over a crack New South Wales Waratahs at North Sydney Oval, saying: 'He would have been a contender to play in the opening Test with the Wallabies if he hadn't been injured.'

Disaster had struck with five minutes of the game remaining, as Devereux explained: 'I took a pass in the middle of the park and, as I was passing the ball, I ran from the softer outfield on to the much harder cricket wicket. It was like concrete and I went over on my right ankle. I knew immediately that it was a bad one.

'I had to go off and feared the worst. My ankle was swollen and bruised, and I had to use crutches, so I knew my chances of making the first Test were remote. All the effort I had put in and all the talk about who was going to play alongside me in the centre against Australia were extinguished. I was distraught and not sure if I would be sent home. I was receiving intense physio from Kevin Murphy, England's physio, as I watched the others training ahead of the opening Test.'

Mike Hall got the nod over Scott Hastings at No.13, partnering Brendan Mullin, who had been Devereux's centre partner when the Lions played the Rest of the World in Cardiff in 1986. It was a surprise as Hall had been playing as a winger on tour.

When the Test series kicked off at the Sydney Football Stadium, Devereux and Mike Teague, who was also on the injured list, were captivated: 'We played every pass and made every tackle as we sat in our seats.' However, they couldn't do anything about the Lions being stuffed in most facets during a 30-12 drubbing.

'It came down to a failure in the execution of the game plan, individual errors and a few individuals freezing on the day as we suffered a battering. The dressing room was a sombre place as it's never good to start any Test series with a defeat. Geech was positive, and he and Top Cat Rowlands attempted to lift spirits, but nothing could hide the disappointment in the way we played. Something had to change before the second Test. The next day's Sydney newspaper headlines mocked us, calling us "Toothless Lions" and "Toothless Pussycats". In the cold light of day you really couldn't disagree with them and the tour looked doomed to fail,' admitted Devereux.

His damaged ankle was improving but it wasn't strong enough for him to be considered for selection for the second Test. McGeechan made changes, with Scotland's Craig Chalmers being replaced at outside-half by England's Rob Andrew, who had been summoned to Australia when Dean got injured, while Hall and Mullin were also dropped with Guscott and Scott Hastings forming a new centre partnership. There were changes too in the forwards with Dooley ousting Norster from the second-row and Iron Mike Teague recovering from a shoulder injury to replace Derek White in the back-row.

With the Lions knowing they had to win it was a feisty affair from the very start, as Devereux recalled: 'Early in the match hell broke out when Rob Jones stamped on Nick Farr-Jones' foot as the Wallaby scrum-half and captain was putting the ball into the scrum. Farr-Jones immediately smacked Rob and they started scrapping. It was hilarious because Rob was a hopeless scrapper. Clive, Geech and Uttley had told him: "Be brave, give him a smack back and when you start fighting the cavalry will arrive to help you." Fair play to Rob, the secret instructions he had been given to put NFJ off his game worked to a treat as the Lions' forwards tore into a startled Australian pack.'

Farr-Jones' focus, and that of the Australian team, was gone and the Lions capitalised. The tide started turning in their favour and they won 19-12 in what was to become known as the Battle of Ballymore.

Skipper Calder's pre-match speech had certainly wound his men up, including Rob Jones, who said: 'Finlay emphasised that we were not to take a backward step, that we would tackle hard, put on physical pressure up front, ruck hard and drive the line-out. I knew that if there was any trouble, four men would come instantly to my assistance: Teague, Ackford, Dooley and Richards.'

Dai Young was fortunate to stay on the field after an ugly stamping incident in the first half, which incurred the wrath of Farr-Jones, who claimed: 'To say the violence wasn't premeditated is absolute nonsense. Robert and I may have instigated it but the Lions forwards piled in straight off. They knew what they were up to and we couldn't match them.'

Teague, who was named player of the series, had said: 'We can't be seen to condone what went on, but needs must. There were some hard players on that tour; hard men and they all came together and sorted the job out.' An ebullient Calder also chipped in: 'They just looked at us and thought to themselves: "I don't fancy this lot".'

The Lions celebrated in the Toucan Bar in Brisbane, with Big Gav Hastings introducing a willing Devereux to Bundaberg Rum, 'and I'm still drinking it today,' he said.

With his ankle now strong enough for him to be considered for the third Test, Devereux knew it was going to be difficult to make the team because most coaches rarely change a winning side: 'I trained my heart out all week and was named on the replacements bench. It was a great honour to get selected for the Test side, having lost my Wales place a few months earlier and then getting injured a week before the opening Test.

'The decider, back at Sydney Football Stadium, resembled a game of chess with each side being extra cautious. Even though I was on the bench, the game seemed to go so quickly. Halfway through the second half, I'd thought I may get on when Jerry went down injured. I stripped off my tracksuit as Jerry received treatment but he got up and played on. Then came the moment that changed our fortunes for the series, David Campese was pinned back in a corner following a kick from Scott Hastings and threw a wild pass in the direction of Wallaby full-back Greg Martin, but it ended up bouncing over the try-line and was pounced on by Ieuan Evans for the winning try in a 19-18 victory. We were Test series winners, all of us, because it was a squad effort.

'It was party time. The celebrations on the pitch at the end were amazing and they carried on in the tunnel and in our changing room. Cans of lager were popping open everywhere. We had lots of photos taken and the emotion of winning took away my disappointment at not getting on the park.'

Most tours nowadays would be over after the final Test, but the Lions still had two games to play. In Newcastle, they hammered NSW Country 72-13. The team made famous for inventing the up-the-jumper ploy had another surprise tactic for the Lions that day, when a player took the ball and ran over the top of a scrum. In the final match of the tour the Lions faced the Anzacs, a combined team of Australians and New Zealanders playing their first match as a combined Barbarians-type team. Sadly, the Kiwis didn't enter into the spirit of things and failed to send a full contingent of players, with only Frano Botica, Kieran Crowley and Andy McDowell representing the land of the long white cloud.

'The Anzacs did have Australia's stars and it was a great game,' said Devereux. 'It was my big match and a few of us had points to prove, for one reason or another. 'Mikey Griff' stuck his head on Farr-Jones in front of the main stand and I made a try-saving tackle, right by the corner flag, on winger Ian Williams. I also managed to score a try as a Lion as we rounded off a magnificent adventure 19-15, in what transpired to be my last game of rugby union for a number of years. We had a few post-match drinks and visited a number of bars and clubs. Rob and I hitched a lift back to the hotel in a police car and, a few hours later, we were packing our bags for the long journey home. I was getting married four weeks later and had a wedding to prepare for!'

10

Going North

'Not many players were capable of scoring some of the tries he did, when he knocked two or three guys out of the way to get over. The only other player I have seen who could do that was Billy Boston, and Billy was the best player I have seen.'

Dougie Laughton

Rugby league clubs had begun their pursuit of Devereux even before his exploits at the 1987 union World Cup, but the interest had stepped up a level following his devastating display during the third-place play-off victory over Australia.

He was on St. Helens' shopping list, with their then chairman Lawrie Prescott admitting: 'We have been interested in Devereux for some time. Our Welsh scouts reported on him when he was at college. Dealings with rugby union players are always strictly confidential and we must observe this secrecy.'

Wakefield and Whitehaven had also shown a keen interest in him, but Devereux decided his immediate future remained in union. Nevertheless, rumours continued to swirl about his future, with interest ramping up following the big-money move of Wales captain Jonathan Davies to Widnes for a record fee of £230,000 in January 1989. The eye-watering money on offer made Devereux and other players sit up, take notice and consider their futures.

The stream of messages he received from Bradford's Chris Caisley during the Lions tour of Australia were impossible to ignore and he eventually spoke to the Yorkshire club's chairman. Devereux was the prey, and rival teams from the league's northern strongholds were ready to fight and pay heavily for his services.

There was a comical twist of sorts when Andy Gregory and Steve Hampson, two of Britain's top league stars who were on a playing sabbatical from Wigan with Australia club Illawarra, had managed to get past security and into the Lions' changing room following the tourists' Test series clinching triumph over the Wallabies. So much for union's strict procedures on amateur players mixing with professionals.

'It's quite laughable really,' beamed Devereux. 'Nobody gave two hoots, they had managed to get access to our dressing room and were celebrating with us. Everyone knew who they were. It never crossed my mind I would be lining up against them both a few months later. Who would have thought it?'

In fact, it wasn't switching codes to rugby league that was on his mind as the Lions tour reached a conclusion, it was a bombshell message from the South African Rugby Football Union (SARFU), which had been ostracised because of *apartheid*.

'Before we faced the Anzacs, our captain Finlay Calder said he needed a word with me and some other players,' explained Devereux. 'He ordered us to gather in a room and we were wondering what the heck was going on. Finlay closed the door and said: "The South Africans had requested us, along with some top French players, including Pierre Berbizier, Philippe Sella, Serge Blanco and Laurent Rodriguez, to play two Tests against the Springboks, in Cape Town and Johannesburg."

'Someone asked what they were paying for us because, if it was not a sanctioned tour, we could lose our amateur status. One player said he wanted £100,000 to take part. We were told there was money on offer and we each were to receive an official fax from the SARFU inviting us to take part.'

Devereux was delighted to be on the list alongside such an illustrious list of names but it was clear that negotiations and arrangements wouldn't be finalised before the Lions got home from Australia.

The Welsh players involved agreed that Paul Thorburn would negotiate on their behalf, as Devereux explained: 'Those of us who had been invited to South Africa agreed to meet after attending an informal, post-Lions, meeting with Welsh Rugby Union officials in a lounge overlooking Cardiff Arms Park. The union wanted feedback from us on what had made the Lions tour a success. Having the best players from Britain and Ireland in the squad wasn't a bad place to start, but we told the WRU the schedule, hotels, training facilities, food, free time and other facets all contributed to a good atmosphere and successful tour. When the debrief finished, we trooped off to meet with Thorburn and discuss the offer on the table from South Africa. The SARFU, or another party, would pay £35,000 to every player who accepted the invite. In 1989 that was a life-changing amount. It wasn't far short of three times my annual salary or, put another way, it would have enabled me to buy a family home. As I was about to get married, it would have come in extremely handy.'

Devereux, though, had failed to take into consideration the dates of the potential trip to South Africa, explaining: 'It would have clashed with my wedding to Alison a month later. She quite understandably wasn't keen on the idea of our wedding day being delayed. The timing couldn't have been any worse so, after much agonising, I pulled out of the trip with Mark Ring replacing me.

'Mike Teague was getting married just before the tour and he ended up taking his wife out to South Africa for a nice all-expenses-paid honeymoon. I had never been there and was told not to worry as there would be plenty of other opportunities in the future. Sadly, there would not be, as they didn't play professional rugby league in South Africa. The tour went ahead without me and the Rest of the World team lost both Tests but the players who went came back with bigger bank balances.'

Devereux may have missed out on that hefty windfall but a bigger pot of cash would soon be heading in his direction.

'A week and a half before my wedding I had a phone call from two of my former teammates who were now playing league for Widnes, having signed with them before the Lions tour. It was Jiffy and Paul Moriarty. They said Widnes were keen to sign me and asked whether I would be interested in talking?

'I told them both I was flattered but I was really looking forward to playing rugby union in the coming season. Out of courtesy, however, I agreed to chat with the club's coach, Dougie Laughton. He called me soon afterward and we spoke very briefly, just long enough for him to get me to agree to meet him face-to-face. I don't really know why but I did. Dougie is a very likeable man and he certainly had the gift of the gab.'

The former Widnes boss gave his side of the story, saying: 'Jonathan Davies was already up here and I was having a chat with him over a beer after a game about John Devereux. I asked him what Devs' strong points were and Jonathan said: "He's big, powerful, fast, scores tries and his defence is strong – he'd be a good man to have around the building". I then went to see Paul Moriarty and said: "I was looking for an Elgan Rees." Paul laughed at that and said Devs had it all and was quick too. I canvassed other opinions as well and had a good feeling about signing him. I met him as well and went to watch him play. I could see he was special. I spoke to our chairman and got the go-ahead to make a move for him.'

It was agreed Laughton and Devereux would hold talks but the latter's attempt to keep the meeting hush-hush, out of fear of the WRU getting wind of it and taking action against him, didn't go to plan.

'Dougie arranged to come down a week before my wedding,' said Devereux. 'I asked him: "Can we meet at a quiet hotel close to where I live please? We need be discreet because I want nothing linking me to you and Widnes Rugby League Club."

'I took my dad with me for moral support, and soon discovered that Dougie clearly hadn't taken any notice of what I'd said because he turned up with a Widnes committeeman. They were dressed head to toe in Widnes' colours, each wearing a club blazer. Their car was parked outside and had the words Sponsored by Widnes Car Centre emblazoned all over it. Discreet my arse! I knew word would soon get around that I'd been spotted meeting some big cheeses from Widnes.

'I noticed straight away that Dougie was a chain smoker and, one after another, he would puff away at his cigarettes. Dougie did all the talking and spoke a lot about his team, that he was looking for a certain type of player, and all his team must be fast. He looked me in the eye and said: "You are fast, aren't you?" I thought to myself: "Shouldn't you know that yourself? Have you ever seen me play?" I wondered if he was going by what he had been told by the likes of Paul, Jonathan and Alan Tait, the former Scotland union centre who was also at Widnes, along with other converts from union, Emosi Koloto from Tonga/New Zealand and Martin Offiah, the flying winger who moved to league before he had a chance of being capped in the 15-a-side code.'

Laughton recalled the conversation: 'Devereux seemed startled that we wanted him, saying: "You've come for me?" I replied: "That's why I'm here, we're not chasing Elgan Rees, we have come for you. We want someone big who can play, and Jiffy Davies said you can play".'

Devereux said: 'Dougie then got on the subject of money and claimed converts from rugby union didn't have to pay tax on their signing-on fee as it was part of giving up their amateur status. He said he had a letter from a QC telling him that. I reckoned he was just trying it on in the hope I would accept less if I thought a deal would be tax free. What he didn't realise was I knew what Jiffy and Muzzy had signed for, so I pitched my value around the same mark. He agreed on giving me a five-year deal worth around £350,000. There were a few other perks, a sponsored car, relocation money, as well as bonuses for winning cups and the league with Widnes, and playing for Wales and Great Britain.'

Laughton chipped in: 'The deal was done quickly. It was a certainty John was going to be a hit – you only had to give him an inch and he was gone. He got better and better, had a big step and was quick for a big fella. I can remember him beating Martin Offiah in a 50m sprint. He turned out to be a tremendous signing.'

Devereux laughed before saying: 'Fair play, Dougie was a great salesman. He knew how to close a deal; it was a culmination of his sweet talking and knowing which cards to play. He said to me: "You'll be a legend in our game, kid." I was extremely aware my dad was listening intently to what was being said. While he sat there agreeing with everything, I couldn't help thinking he knew he was about to lose his son to the dark side – gone forever, never to return. Never again would he see his boy run out in the colours of Wales and Bridgend. There seemed to be a finality about it as there wasn't any indication at that time that union would cave in and allow the legal payment of players a few years later, which was to prompt a return of players from league.'

A couple more hours of talks followed before both parties agreed in principle that Devereux would become the latest union international to make the switch to league, and that Laughton would return a week later with a contract to be signed to secure the deal.

'I went home and had a long chat with Alison, and my mam and dad', recalled Devereux. 'Mam said that type of money would be hard to earn in Wales. At the time I was working for Wimpey Homes as a land negotiator while Alison was working in the Special Care Baby Unit at the Princess of Wales Hospital, Bridgend. Between us we were earning just over £20,000 a year, so the opportunity and the financial rewards that went with it were too good to turn down. I had only recently turned down a once-in-a-lifetime trip to South Africa, and £35,000, but this latest offer was even better. We agreed I should accept, and Dougie duly turned up with a big smile on his face at successfully landing another catch

'It was just 48 hours before our wedding when I signed on the dotted line with Widnes. There was a moment when I was putting pen to paper when the enormity of what I was doing struck me and I had a "What am I doing?" moment, but there wasn't any turning back. I had signed for Widnes and I was desperate to be a success. In fact, I'd go further and say I felt I had to be a success.'

Devereux and Alison didn't want the news to reach the public domain before their wedding so Widnes agreed to stay silent: 'Dougie must have found that hard because he was a showman. I was walking around with a big smile on my face. People asked me why I was so happy but I'd palm off the question by pointing to our rapidly approaching wedding. It was a perfect reason to fend off more questions.'

Laughton was adamant it was money well spent, stressing: 'I can't remember ever having a cross word with John. When you change codes it takes a fair few games to adapt. It only took him about six.'

After a pause for thought, Laughton emphasised: 'I was fortunate to play with Billy Boston at Wigan and with Clive Sullivan for Great Britain, who were two other great Welsh players, but John was up there with them. I don't remember opposition wings beating him on the outside to score in the corner. He was great to work with, a coach's dream because he would take on board what he was told and just do it. There's no doubt about it, he was a top player.

'Not many players were capable of scoring some of the tries he did, when he knocked two or three guys out of the way to get over. The only other player I have seen who could do that was Billy Boston, and Billy was the best player I have seen.'

Devereux knew he was joining one of Britain's best league clubs, saying: 'What a team Widnes had! I had watched Jonathan's first game against Salford. He came on for the injured Tony Myler, straight to the wing opposite Adrian Hadley who had switched codes to Salford the previous year. Widnes smashed Salford and it was an easy baptism for Jiffy. Adrian Hadley looked like he was running through sand when Offiah went past him. Offiah was lightening. He was about 10m up on Hadley when he offered the ball to him, as if to say, "Come on, come and get it". I would have gone nuts if he'd done that to me and would have wanted to launch Offiah into the stand but Adolf couldn't get near him.'

With his transfer signed and sealed, Devereux could relax and enjoy his wedding. His best man was his Wales pal and one-time captain Bleddyn Bowen: 'We had become big mates after my Wales debut. He did a great job as best man, and he and his wife Denise even came on our honeymoon to Tenerife. Wow, what a holiday that was! We met a couple, Roy and Ellie, from Sidcup in Kent, who had got married on the same day as us and palled up. We had so much fun, mainly at night in the bars because we were all too hungover to do much in the day!

'We returned from our honeymoon to the home we had bought in the Garw Valley, a three-bedroom, mid-terrace house. We had only lived there for a few weeks. We'd bought it for £20,000 then sold it for £40,000. We got home on Monday and the following day Dougie was on the telephone, saying: "Welcome back kid, you're playing in the A team on Friday night at Naughton Park against Hull Kingston Rovers".

'I responded: "I'm not sure I'm up for that yet Dougie, I haven't done any training since I came back from the Lions' tour of Australia and my ankle was still a bit sore," but he wasn't having any of it, saying: "Don't worry kid, you will only have to do half a game just to show the spectators what we have bought".

'That was it then, I had been summoned and was on my way. Widnes wanted an immediate return on their investment. They knew me playing for their reserves would bump up the size of the crowd, and the ticket sales. I travelled to Widnes by train on my own and was met at Runcorn station by Eddie McDonald, chief scout at Widnes and Dougie's sidekick. Eddie drove me to the Hillcrest Hotel, at the northern end of Widnes, which was to be my home for the next eight weeks. I was nervous but excited. My foray into league was about to get under way.'

11

Making Waves with Widnes

'When Devs was fit and firing he was one of league's best wingers.'

Jonathan Davies

John Devereux's 13-a-side entrance came against Hull Kingston Rovers and he quickly discovered that Widnes had a strong A team. He also knew he was being thrown in at the deep end. His debut came before he had even trained with the club, introduce himself to his new teammates or had a chance to learn the game. Being a big-name signing meant he had to generate gate receipts for Widnes from day one. It also meant he had a huge target on his back and, sure enough, he copped it.

'Some big hairy-arsed second-row dropped his knees down hard on my chest and I popped two rib cartilages. I also took a knock to a knee on the hard ground and struggled to get out of bed the following morning. Hull's welcoming committee had done its job and I had been crocked in my very first game.'

Devereux discovered they didn't take prisoners in league, so to speak, with clubs operating in cut-throat environments. Players were viewed as commodities who were rarely treated compassionately. It was a case of getting up and getting on with it.

'From day one I was owned by Widnes and there wasn't any pussying around. The 'namby pamby' stuff you sometimes got in union didn't carry any weight with the guys in league. You all pulled your weight. It was straight-forward and brutal. Muzzy picked me up in his car for the journey to training where I had some physio and quickly learnt they loved needles. They gave you a jab of something or other to treat injuries in order to speed up recovery, or just to deaden the pain and get you back on the training paddock as quickly as possible.'

Devereux was shown the sacred den that was the first team changing room at Widnes, and those players fortunate enough to be regulars each had a locker with their name written on it: 'It was nothing fancy. The kitman Paul Hansbury, who everyone called Big Lad for obvious reasons, had written a name on the plywood door of each of the lockers in black felt pen. It was in felt pen because it was easy to remove and replace with the name of someone else. I hoped my name would soon be on a locker but knew it would be at the expense of someone else. It was dog-eat-dog but it was being in the first team that brought bigger bonuses, prestige and potential glory.

'I was greeted by some of the players, and couldn't get over how short they were. Muzzy towered above everyone. The next tallest were the two first team centres, Andy Currier and Darren Wright, who were both about 6ft 2in. "Where are the forwards?" I whispered to Paul, who just laughed and said, "They're here!" All of them were short but, fair play, they were all very powerful too.

'Kurt Sorenson was the captain, a Kiwi legend who had been at Widnes for many years. No-one knew his real age and no-one dared to ask because he was built like a brick shithouse and nobody wanted to get on the wrong side of him. Emosi Koloto, who had been signed from union, was, like me, about 6ft 1in, but rippled with muscle and was some player.'

Although Devereux's ribs were still painful, he was down to play again for the A team the following Friday, this time against Halifax and, again, at home. It was a steep learning curve but Laughton was doing everything in his power to get his new signing ready to make a play for the first team.'

While Devereux was a *bona-fide* Widnes player, there was a more secretive side to the A team, with union players often turning up for trials. Among them was one of the biggest names in Welsh rugby, a player who was to kick the British and Irish Lions to glory against the odds in South Africa with his metronome accuracy and who nowadays is an integral part of the Wales union team's management.

'There were lots of local boys in the A team set-up and sometimes, like a lot of other rugby league clubs, we had a number of AN Others in the team. Their names were never published or made known. The whole of rugby league was in on it and the media up north never blew the cover of any union player who was giving league a go because it would have finished their career in the amateur game,' explained Devereux.

'I remember going, I think it was around 1990, to a Warrington A team game and being greeted by several familiar faces from Wales who were having a trial as AN Other. Jiffy, Muzzy and Taity watched Neil Jenkins – yes, the Ginger Monster – play alongside Glenn Webbe, Huw Bevan, my old friend from school and college, and Pontypool centre Keith Orrell. I thought Neil had a great game but he decided that league wasn't for him after playing 80 minutes. He went home and became a household name for his exploits as a marksman. He was arguably one of the finest goal-kickers of a rugby ball in history and not switching to league didn't seem to stop him earning a good living from the side benefits of being a union international of some repute.

'Glenn also played very well but never signed for anyone. It was a shame because I think he was made for league and would have been amazing at it. Looking back, it's quite funny how so many players just want to have a go at league to see if they would like it or in the hope of being offered a lucrative contract.

'We met up with them in the Warrington clubhouse after the game and claimed to have photos of them playing that night before attempting to bribe them to keep it a secret, but it was just banter and we had a good laugh.'

Warrington were keen on signing Welsh players and, within a year, had made a triple signing, hoovering up Allan Bateman, Rowland Phillips and Kevin Ellis. They were to become club legends at Wilderspool but the loss of three more quality players was another huge blow to Welsh rugby union because it weakened the pool of players available to the national coach.

Devereux must have done something right in the A team victory over Halifax because he was named on the substitutes' bench for the first team's Lancashire Cup clash at Warrington. He recalled: 'Watching from the sidelines, I could see it was a tough derby match. Both teams hated each other and so did the fans. Halfway through the second half, our stand-off Barry Dowd broke an ankle. After waiting for him to be carted from the pitch, I was on for my first team debut, on to the wing, and what a baptism of fire it was. I was marking a quality winger called Des Drummond. He was a seasoned Great Britain international and he kept growling at me. All we seemed to be doing was standing under our own sticks after they had scored. We lost, but I had made the first team.

'My next game was going to be my home bow for the first team. Dougie picked me on the bench for our match against New Zealand, who were on tour. Naughton Park was packed to the rafters and midway through the first half Dougie nudged me in the ribs and said: "Go on kid, show us what you can do".

'Taking his words quite literally, I ran on, took up station on the right wing and immediately it kicked off. Well, the action between me and the Kiwi full-back Darrel Williams did. He ran in my channel and I flattened him with a tackle. I was still a tad green and I didn't really know how long I was supposed to hold on to him for. He wasn't amused and, as we stood up, he punched me in the face right in front of the referee and the main stand.

'The crowd was going nuts. I looked at the ref, thinking "What are you going to do about that?" Nothing happened and Williams punched me a second time. "Fuck that,' I thought, "you're having one back." It was absolute bedlam. The crowd roared as we went toe-to-toe before ending up scrapping on the turf and having to be pulled apart.'

Fight over, the ref produced the yellow card from his pocket and the pair were banished to the sin-bin for 10 minutes.

'I had been on the pitch all of 30 seconds! Dougie loved it. He knew from that moment that I wasn't going to be bullied and packed a punch of my own. Nobody was going to fuck around with me. Dougie had a huge grin on his face when I sat back on the bench, and repeated one of his favourite sayings: "Welcome to our game kid, you'll be alright".'

Jonathan Davies added: 'Devs certainly made an impact that day. It's not easy to make the transition from union to league but he managed it. When Devs was fit and firing he was one of league's best wingers. He was prepared to learn, was a diligent trainer and hated losing. He became a firm favourite at Widnes.'

Alison soon joined her new husband and Mr and Mrs Devereux spent eight weeks living in a hotel while a new house they had purchased was being completed. 'It was great having all your food cooked for you, beds made and the washing done free of charge,' he said.

The couple hadn't been told the address of their house because the new estate was still being built but they had a shock when they found out! It seemed the builder had submitted a request to the local council with the aim of making them feel at home.

'We'd bought plot number 33, but the developers hadn't put the street sign up when we moved in so we were in the dark over what it would be called. When the name was eventually revealed we couldn't believe it: they'd named it Porthcawl Close. It was as if they had done it just for us. We had a newly-built four-bedroom house and we couldn't have been happier as we started our married life,' said Devereux.

'The two of us loved our 10 years there and got on brilliantly with our next door neighbours, Ken and Barbara George. They were a little older than us and had three daughters but treated us as though we were members of their family. It was especially nice for Alison. It could be a lonely place for her when I was out, which was most days and nights, as I was also holding down a full-time job as well as having my training commitments.

'Alison was also fortunate to have Muzzy's wife, Suzanne, and Jiffy's wife, Karen, close by. Paul and Suzanne lived just a stone's throw from our house so were always in each other's homes and regularly went out together. As Alison got to know the wives of our teammates better – Caroline Tait, Susan Nicholls (later to be Koloto), Gaynor Currier, Denise Hulme – the circle of friends just grew and grew. The wives' friendship grew even deeper when the children started arriving with a baby boom in the Widnes camp.

'I loved training during my early years at the club, especially Saturday mornings as that was a short and sharp session. After training we were all given a free Chinese take-away of our choice, paid for by the club. It was so bizarre and certainly wouldn't happen today with such an emphasis on diet and nutrition. The perk continued for a number of seasons during the Laughton era. It was eventually stopped, not for nutrition reasons but because some players started taking the piss and ordering extra meals for their wives or girlfriends. The club said they wouldn't pay for them any more so that particular takeaway lost a lot of business as most of the players weren't prepared to stump up the cash themselves.'

During his first season at Widnes, Devereux tasted another of Dougie Laughton's favourite pick-me-ups – Ginseng: 'Dougie had heard that Ginseng was good for athletes as it increased energy levels, reduced inflammation from injuries and boosted the immune system. As a result, we were all given boxes of liquid Ginseng in small glass vials and told to take it every day. It may have tasted disgusting but the Ginseng certainly gave us a boost, though not in the way Dougie had intended. Within months, many of our wives were pregnant! Alan Tait was so taken by the additional energy boost that he also gave Ginseng to his racing greyhound.'

When Laughton returned to Widnes in 1995 following a stint with Leeds, he hatched a novel plan to put Chinese meals back on the menu, and save the club money, as Devereux explained: 'He got himself a Chinese cookery book, commandeered the kitchen at Naughton Park, turned chef and presided over the cooking of them. We were served them in the boardroom and tucked in. They were very nice and it was impossible for the players to abuse the system and bag extra meals to take home for partners.'

Devereux described Laughton as a character but wasn't too smitten on his coaching ability or style of management: 'I felt he treated me harshly during my formative time at Widnes, choosing to drop me for some big end-of-season games, like the Premiership final and the Lancashire Cup final, in favour of Jiffy, even though I thought I had cemented my place in the team. When it came to those games, he picked Jiffy on the wing over me even though Jiff seemed to have established himself in the team as a centre or stand-off.

'When everyone was fit, I became his easy choice to get the bullet. I remember Taity urging me to charge into Dougie's office and tell him he was wrong. He said Dougie would keep on doing it unless I took a stand. Taity reckoned he just wanted an easy life and didn't want any player giving him hassle, but Dougie knew I wasn't one to complain so carried on doing it.

'The ironic thing is that when Dougie came back for his second spell, he actually used to say: "Get the ball to Devs as much as possible." In mitigation, though, we had lost many of our star players by then.'

Devereux rated Phil Larder as the best coach he worked with at Widnes. A journeyman player before moving into coaching, Larder had played union for Sale before switching to league with Oldham, and later Whitehaven. He had been appointed director of coaching by the Rugby Football League and was instrumental in overhauling the structure of the code in Great Britain in an effort to catch up with Australia, who were undoubtedly the world leaders of the game. He then moved into club coaching at Widnes before taking the reins at Keighley and later Sheffield Eagles.

Yet, it was a move back to rugby union where Larder really found fame in the rugby world. He was appointed England defence coach by Clive Woodward while also working at Leicester Tigers. He stiffened the defence of the star-studded East Midlands club and they won four consecutive English Premiership titles as well as lifting Europe's Heineken Cup in 2001 and 2002, but his crowning moment came when England won the 2003 World Cup by beating Australia in the final in Sydney. Larder was also British and Irish Lions defence coach in 2001 and 2005.

'Phil knew his stuff and taught me so much. He also got the team more organised. He was more of a tactician and focused on the technical side of the game whereas Dougie's rugby philosophy was pretty simple; assemble a team full of players with lots of ability and bags of pace in every position and let them get on with it. Our training with Dougie was all sprinting, shuttles and games of "tick and pass", touch rugby to those in union. We would have a small number of basic moves from a ruck or a set play to get over the gain-line to put the opposition on the back foot. Lots of those moves came from the hooker and we had a few great hookers at Widnes.

'Australian Phil MacKenzie was brilliant at the base of the ruck, sniping and throwing dummies left, right and centre. He was a slick distributor as well. If McKenzie didn't play, either of the Hulme brothers, Paul and David, could deputise. They were local boys, had plenty of energy, were tough as hell, determined and, like us union imports, hated losing. The pair of them were so versatile. I couldn't believe how many positions both of them covered in the team – hooker, loose-forward, second-row, and both half-back positions. They were pushing it a bit going out any wider than that, though, because Dougie wanted pace from his centres and wingers. We had that in abundance with Martin 'Chariots' Offiah, who was the fastest player I had ever seen playing the game up to that point.

'Taity, the Scottish sprinter, was at full-back, Jiffy could play wing, centre, full-back or stand-off, and we know how fast he was over 10m and 100m. My centre partner, Andy Currier, was no slouch and I could shift a bit in my time. I honestly believe Dougie signed me on the back of the praise I had received from Jiffy, Muz and Taity about my ability and speed. Dougie had seen Jiffy playing before signing him and had jumped on an aeroplane to New Zealand to watch and sign Emosi Koloto. Emosi was a great player and gave up a lot to come to Widnes as he was pushing Buck Shelford hard for an All Black jersey at the time. I was gobsmacked when he signed and he was to prove to be awesome for us. Koloto, Sorenson, Esene Faimalo – known as 'Flymo' – and Joe Grima were rampaging forwards who were able to bust through the strongest defences.'

Widnes were a joy to watch as that quartet tore into teams and then off-loaded to the pretty boys in the backs to stroll over out wide or under the sticks. The early 1990s were special, but a bombshell was around the corner, and the timing couldn't have been much worse: 'We were playing Hull FC in the Premiership final at Manchester United's Old Trafford ground when Dougie announced he was leaving us for Leeds. We were in daze as he had come out with it before the game. We were united in thinking: "Why would you announce that now?" Our heads were in the shed and it wasn't a surprise that we went on to lose the final, our first defeat after three consecutive Premiership final victories.'

Apart from Offiah, Moriarty and Tait, the rest of the squad had day jobs. Tait's was club groundsman and had plenty of stick as all he seemed to do was drive a lawnmower.

'Some of us were lucky to be given company cars by our employers,' commented Devereux, 'and there were also the bonuses – £250 for a win and £50 for a loss – paid into your account, minus tax, each month. Some months we could make a few quid if we had four or five victories.

'We won far more than we lost but, unfortunately, in my time under Dougie, we were far too inconsistent. We would beat the top sides but slip up against some of the not so strong sides.'

12

Wales RL

*'That Wales RL team was packed with quality players, yet
Devs stood out.'*

Mark Jones

Wales played their first rugby league international match when they beat New Zealand 9-8 at Aberdare in 1908 in front of 20,000 spectators. England and France were the regular opponents for the Wales 13-a-side team, and encounters against Australia and New Zealand were relished if the Kangaroos or Kiwis were on tour.

The fortunes of the Wales RL team ebbed and flowed over the following 100 years as a direct result of the numbers of Welsh players who had left amateur rugby in southern Wales for professional rugby in northern England, and fixtures had come to a halt in 1984, primarily due to a lack of Welsh qualified players and Wales RL's struggle to field a competitive team. That lull continued for a few years, until a glut of union stars, led by Jonathan Davies, crossed codes following the bitter fall-out, finger pointing and sackings which had followed the humiliating 1988 tour of New Zealand.

Suddenly, a whole host of big names who had powered Wales to third position at the 1987 World Cup, and who were bursting with ambition and ability, were playing and starring in the 13-a-side code after signing for its biggest and best clubs. Among the stars that went north were John Devereux, Paul Moriarty, Dai Young, Rowland Phillips, Adrian Hadley, David Bishop, Mark Jones, Allan Bateman, Kevin Ellis and Jonathan Griffiths.

In 1991 Wales RL re-emerged from hibernation, with Devereux recalling: 'Clive Griffiths, who was to become our coach, and former player 'Big' Jim Mills, who would be team manager, started the ball rolling by meeting Rugby Football League chief executive and fixer Maurice Lindsay.'

Griffiths, who went on to be Wales' rugby union defence coach when they won a first Grand Slam in 27 years and lifted the 2005 Six Nations title, takes up the story, saying: 'Jim and I went to see Maurice in his office at RFL headquarters in Leeds with the idea of bringing back the Welsh team. We only had about 20 players to call on at the time but there was an on-going exodus out of Wales and the number soon grew. We got Maurice on board after we used his telephone to ring Jonathan Davies, who at the time was playing for Canterbury, in Australia. We asked Jonathan if he would be our captain and he jumped at the opportunity. So, Maurice said "Yes" and we were up and running.'

Phillips, Moriarty, Ellis, Jonathan Griffiths and Devereux were asked to attend a press conference at Naughton Park, the home of Widnes, for the big announcement. They were interviewed by reporters from TV, radio and newspapers and did a photo shoot.

'It was a day I haven't forgotten,' said Devereux.' We were asked what we thought about playing for Wales again and we all said the same thing, that we thought we'd never play for Wales again after going north, and that playing for Wales in front of our own fans was the one of the biggest things we all desperately missed. Nobody, and I mean nobody, ever turned down the chance to play for Wales. We were all passionate Welshmen so the opportunity of returning to the international stage, and being able to pull on that red shirt again, was music to our ears.

'We knew support for rugby league was there because Jiffy, Muzzy and I had been in the Widnes team that had beaten Wigan 24-8 in the Charity Shield at the Vetch Field, Swansea, 12 months earlier, in a match used to gauge the public appetite for holding more fixtures in Wales.'

Coach Clive Griffiths was full of passion and was fanatical about Wales starting with a bang when they lined up against Papua New Guinea at the Vetch on 27 October 1991. The team managers had some funding from league headquarters, although it was a lot less than England received, with Mills booking the Welsh squad into budget hotels, doing deals with companies and finding modestly-priced facilities where they would be allowed to train.

There was also a bitter-sweet irony in that one of their main sponsors was British Coal, which had been closing mines across the south Wales coalfield, and making tens of thousands of Welsh miners redundant, under the direction of Margaret Thatcher's Tory government.

Griffiths had assembled a strong squad, predominantly of ex-rugby union players who had gone to league, but it was laced with a few English-born players who qualified for Wales through their family heritage. They included the St. Helens winger Anthony Sullivan, the son of league legend Clive Sullivan, who had starred when Great Britian had won the World Cup, and the Carlisle hooker, Barry William.

Wales had a few training sessions up north, then travelled to Swansea and stayed at the Dragon Hotel on the Kingsway in the city centre.

'It was a little bit too central for Clive and Jim's liking but perfect for the characters we had in the squad. Phil Ford and Dai Bishop were the senior players and loved a pint or two, and it was Paul Moriarty's home town so we knew where all the best 'watering holes' were. But no-one took full advantage because we knew how important this first game was to us and our families. Training went well all week, apart from 'Bish' who suffered a minor groin injury.

'Clive was full of fresh ideas and was the first coach I worked with who analysed every player in the opposition squad. He would spend hours and hours watching videos and produce printed player stats. They were known as crib sheets and listed the strengths and weaknesses of the opposition squad.

'He would also compile a play book containing our moves and tactics and circulated a copy to every player. When Clive had his game head on, which was all week, he was so intense and never seemed to let up. Only after the games would you see a different side of him. I firmly believe that his preparation and coaching successfully released every ounce of performance out of the whole squad.'

The match took place on a Sunday night at the Vetch, the then home of Swansea City. It was a small stadium with a great atmosphere, especially with 11,422 fans crammed in. It was a cold October evening as the players and crowd proudly sang *Hen Wlad fy Nhadau*.

Devereux said: 'The PNG players were like rabbits caught in the headlights, even though league was their national sport back home in the Pacific. They were ranked in the top four teams in the world but a cold evening in Wales' second city under the floodlights was a million miles from the sweltering heat and stifling humidity they were used to.

'They didn't know what hit them. We played the perfect game Clive had prepared us for and he was beaming when we took a 46-0 half-time lead. Every player put in 100% and the tries flowed. Phil Ford bagged a hat-trick and was named Man of the Match ahead of Jonathan Davies who had bagged two tries and scored 24 points. The ball never seemed to come to my side of the field and my basket was empty after a 68-0 win, but it didn't matter because we had racked up a record victory. We had a great night out in Swansea after the game and there were a few sore heads the following morning when we said our farewells.'

Reminiscing about the team's performance, Clive Griffiths said: 'It couldn't have gone any better as we were well up at half-time. Papua New Guinea had played a series against Great Britain the previous year and won a game, so for us to beat them by such a big score was just brilliant. It was the start of something truly special.'

Devereux beamed: 'It was to become one of Wales RL's most successful decades in its history. We later played France at the Vetch in front of another bumper crowd of over 10,000 and were subjected to the same standard of preparation from Clive. This time the boys lifted the bar even higher, knowing the opposition had star players Dumas and Entat at half-back and were one of the top three international sides at the time. We won the game well, 35-6, and I scored a try.'

Teammate Mark Jones added: 'That Wales RL team was packed with quality players, yet Devs stood out.'

Unfortunately, Wales team manager Mills resigned following a row with Lindsay over Wales not being included in the World Cup tournament that climaxed in 1992. Griffiths was upset and going to follow suit but had a rethink and decided to stay. Rugby League HQ offered Welsh league legend Trevor Forster the role but he turned it down.

Devereux said: 'That's how Mike Nicholas came in as team manager. Mike had been an abrasive forward who played the game during the 1970s, for Aberavon at union before heading to league with Warrington. Mike had a bit of a reputation as an enforcer on the field, but in his new role he was more like Arthur Daley in the television series *Minder* – wheeling and dealing so we could stay in certain places and get our kit sorted for our next games.

'Our early successes had earned us a prime fixture against England in November 1992 at the Vetch, which was establishing a reputation as the new home of the Wales RL team. Preparation for the clash went into overdrive but we were going to have to play without our captain and talisman Jiffy, who was on the injured list.'

Devereux partnered Bateman at centre and was taking kicks at goal in Jiffy's absence. A crowd of 10,243 roared on Wales as they took a 12-11 lead. The home team were taking the game to England but weren't converting pressure into points.

'As half-time approached, all we had to show for our efforts were two tries, a conversion and a drop-goal, and our inability to keep the scoreboard ticking over came back to haunt us when we spilled the ball and Lee Crooks scored for England. It was a huge blow, and as the second half progressed the England pack was becoming more and more dominant. Their key players – Ellery Hanley, Crooks and Garry Schofield – used their experience to take the game away from us.'

The 36-11 defeat was the new-look Wales' first loss, but it provided numerous lessons, some of which came in handy a little later down the line, and provided further incentive for future battles with England.

'We had noticed the English were always kitted out better than us, stayed in better hotels and travelled like premier footballers,' said Devereux. 'We were all funded by rugby league headquarters in Leeds but we could see it was not a level playing field. The excuse that kept coming back for the unfairness of it was that England were crowdfunded and had more cash and more of everything as a result.'

Wales faced France the following month in Perpignan. It was the team's first away game, and trip abroad, since being reformed. The French had a strong side and were very comfortable playing in familiar surroundings. It was an exciting and entertaining match which made the very small crowd of 3,700 a great disappointment. Starting for the first time was Gary Pearce, the ex-Wales, Bridgend and Llanelli outside-half, from Hull, Dai Bishop from Hull KR and Rob Ackerman, the player whose place Devereux had taken in the Wales union team six years earlier, from Carlisle.

Speaking fondly of the trip to the Catalan stronghold in France, Devereux said: 'We had prepped well and old heads in our team helped make the difference. We raced into a lead in the first half and should have made easy work of the game but France seized on an opportunity, charging down a kick from Phil Ford at full-back and scoring a try. However, we rallied and scored tries through Allan Bateman, myself and Ackerman, with a drop-goal from Gary ensuring we edged it 19-18.'

Wales' next game took place, against the touring New Zealanders, who were one of the world's top teams, in a massive fixture at the Vetch. It was a daunting fixture, for the players and their coach, as Devereux recalled: 'Clive was so hyper before it. He did his usual prep and we trained well all week, using Swansea University as our base.'

A disappointing crowd of just over 6,000 saw a hard-fought game. Wales got some points on the scoreboard through a brace of penalties from Jonathan Davies, and it got even better when Gerald Cordle scored a great try after chasing a kick-over-the-top. New Zealand had a great kicker themselves, the ex-union player Daryl Harrigan who played club rugby in Australia for Canterbury. He kept the Kiwis in touch with some penalties and then Jason Mackie scored a try just before half-time to inch them ahead.

Davies repeated his magic of the first half with another kick-over-the-top for former Cardiff winger Cordle to grab a second try to regain the lead for Wales. But a mistake from Devereux following the restart was seized upon by the Kiwis with Sean Hoppe scoring to make it 22-17 to New Zealand. Penalties were exchanged and the score was finely poised at 24-19.

Wales then thought they had snatched it when Devereux attempted to atone for his costly error: 'With a few minutes of the game remaining, Jiffy hoisted a bomb right on the Kiwis' goal posts and, as it came down, I jumped above everyone, claimed the ball and landed over the try-line to score. My celebrations were short-lived, however, as Adrian Hadley was alleged to have pushed a Kiwi in the act of me scoring and the try was disallowed. Our final chance had gone and we lost the game. We were gutted. What made it worse was that we knew we should have won but had blown it. The main positive we did take from the encounter was that our performance sent out a clear message that the Welsh side was heading in the right direction and was targeting the 1995 World Cup.'

Wales were improving as a team and strengthening as a squad with a steady stream of new recruits arriving. More players joined league ranks from union, while Griffiths and Nicholas had also identified more Welsh qualified players from the existing professional ranks.

'From union, Peter Williams, the ex-England and Orrell outside-half, whose pass I had intercepted at the 1987 union World Cup to score in the quarter-finals was welcomed into the Welsh squad, while former Swansea, Wales, and British and Irish Lions flanker Richard Webster was now with Salford. Our England-born contingent was also boosted with the introduction of Ian Marlow from Beverley, Mark Moran from Leigh, Mark Perrett from Halifax, and Daio Powell from Bradford.'

Devereux unfortunately missed a scrappy 13-12 victory over France at Ninian Park, the then home of Cardiff City, because of a recurring back injury, saying: 'I was disappointed to be a spectator. It was a disc problem in my lower back that I'd picked while playing for Great Britain in the Kiwi Test series the previous October and I was to miss most of the second half of the season. It required some intense treatment and time on the side-lines. My physician was the brilliant Dr. Yousef Yousef, an Egyptian consultant neurologist at the private Alexandra Hospital in Cheadle, Manchester, who performed three procedures on my lower back.

'Over the course of several months he would insert a large needle into my spine, an epidural, for a procedure called an epidurogram, which involved a cocktail of steroid and other anti-inflammatory drugs. They'd sedate me and I had to curl up on my side on the table in the operating theatre. The sedative did its job and my head felt as woozy as if I'd drunk 10 pints of beer but, at the end of a six-month treatment programme, the procedures were a success and had cured my lower back problem. I could finally put my shoes and socks on unaided.'

13

RL World Cup Final Ends in Tears

'Devs was the consummate professional during the time that I knew him as his coach. He had all the physical and mental attributes necessary to succeed.'

Clive Griffiths

It's a quiz question which many may struggle to answer but here goes: Who was the last Welsh rugby union international to play in a Rugby League World Cup final? The answer is John Devereux, although an emotional clash with Australia in front of a then 13-a-side Test record crowd of 73,631 at Wembley on 24 October 1992 is one that he's more likely to want to forget, and which earned him the unwanted nickname Steve 'Ranoff'.

The Wales team had been reformed too late to take part in a convoluted tournament, so how the heck did Devereux end up playing in the final? The story is almost as long and convoluted as that World Cup. It was played over three years and was contested by just five countries – Australia, Great Britain, New Zealand, France and Papua New Guinea – on a round-robin, home and away, basis with each team having eight fixtures and the top two facing each other in the final.

Australia went through the group stage unbeaten, with Great Britain and New Zealand each winning five and losing three to finish level on 10 points, but due to a superior points difference – 136 to 83 – GB went through to meet short-priced favourites Australia at Wembley.

Devereux had only switched codes a few months before the tournament had kicked off, when GB had beaten New Zealand at Wigan's Central Park in November 1989, so it was too much to expect him to be involved at such an early stage of his league career.

It didn't take him long to force his way into the GB frame, though, and he was called up for the following summer's tour of Papua New Guinea and New Zealand after fellow Wales international Anthony Sullivan had damaged a hamstring during the first training session of the trip.

'Alison and I were at home, looking at travel brochures for a nice relaxing summer holiday after my first campaign with Widnes when our phone rang,' explained Devereux. 'It was David Oxley from Rugby League headquarters in Leeds, with the news that Anthony was out. I couldn't believe it. I had been playing league for less than a year and I had been called up for the GB tour.'

Holiday plans were put on hold as Devereux was kitted out with team attire for the tour and flew out of London Heathrow on 24 May 1990. Some 30 hours and three flights later he was arriving in Goroka to witness Britain beating Papua New Guinea in their opening Test. His decision to buy a Sony Walkman, complete with rechargeable batteries, had proved wise as it allowed him to listen to music on the journey and ease the boredom. Devereux arrived in the country a couple of hours before the opening Test and was taken directly to the ground in what turned out to be a hair-raising experience.

'I was the only passenger in a small van with side windows,' he said. 'It was more than 100 degrees Fahrenheit and we were slowly inching our way through the crowds. It was like being in a furnace and there was no escape. At this point the local supporters realised I was a GB player, rather than a British journalist, fan or RL administrator, and it started to turn ugly. They began banging on the windows and rocking the van from side to side. I honestly thought they were going to turn it over. I knew that cannibalism had existed there right up to 1978 and there have been claims in more recent years of it still being practised by at least one tribe, so all sorts of thoughts were racing through my head. I had never experienced anything like the reception I got that day but, thanks to the skill of the driver, we got to the ground in one piece.

'If the atmosphere was raucous outside the ground, it was nothing compared to what I experienced inside. It was total mayhem and the match had to be stopped a couple of times because of the crowd locked outside the ground going berserk. We lost the game, 20-18, but that was the least of our concerns as the police made no attempt to calm the supporters and only had one plan, Plan A, which was to fire tear gas at the spectators and rubber bullets in the air, then wield their weapons and get stuck in. People began dropping out of trees they'd climbed in order to watch the match as a tear gas cloud blew toward them, and the players had to run for safety and put wet towels over their faces to lessen the effect of the gas. I was sat by the side of the pitch and couldn't believe what I was witnessing. We soon realised this was the norm, however, as similar scenes happened at all our matches in PNG.'

Devereux's GB debut came a few days later. He crossed for two tries but it didn't persuade coach Mal Reilly to make a change for the second Test, which GB won 40-8. There were huge sighs of relief as the tourists travelled to New Zealand via a few days in Cairns, the Australian holiday destination for visitors to the Great Barrier Reef.

'I'd had an upset stomach and was feeling rough for a couple of days but I was determined not to miss the white-water rafting. I had done it with the Lions the year before and it was a great laugh,' said Devereux.

As Dai Young had found out with the Lions, rafting could be dangerous. Reilly though wasn't concerned by the hazards lurking under the surface of the water on the fast-flowing river.

'Mal was a headcase and decided to tackle the rapids on a body board,' recalled Devereux. 'They were dangerous enough to tackle in a boat, and the guides and safety instructors thought he was mad. It was impossible to disagree but Mal didn't care. Holding on to a plastic board with handles, Mal somehow made it to the end. He was completely knackered as he did it without flippers, because none were big enough to fit his feet.'

The down time continued the next day when the squad boarded a catamaran, paid for by sponsors British Coal, and set sail at 7am for the Great Barrier Reef. When it arrived two hours later, Devereux dived overboard and lay on a small mound of sand sticking out of the sea, in the middle of the Pacific Ocean.

'It was heaven. The chap running the trip asked who wanted to snorkel or scuba dive, but strongly advised against it for anyone who had consumed alcohol in the previous 12 hours. Dai Bishop, the former Pontypool favourite, quickly hid his can of beer behind his back and I reckon that all the players and team management on the boat had been on the booze the previous night, and a few like Bish had enjoyed a can or two already that day, and it was only 9am.'

The warning did not perturb Devereux: 'I hadn't taken the opportunity to scuba dive when with the Lions, and really regretted it, so had vowed to take any future offer when it came, and here was my chance. We had a quick lesson on what to do in an emergency and were given sign language calls to communicate underwater.'

It was a once in a lifetime experience for most of the players, but the adventure could, as Devereux explained, have easily ended in tragedy: 'We were in a group who were swimming deeper and deeper when Denis Betts swam past me doing breast stroke, which we had been told not to do. One of his arms accidentally caught the mouthpiece of my breathing apparatus and ripped it out of my mouth.

'During the safety drill they had shown us how to put it back in your mouth and expel all the water from it by breathing out, but I panicked and went straight up to the surface. Luckily, I was only 10 feet below the water line and was able to surface before running out of breath. Regaining my composure I had another go and was so glad I did. It was such an amazing experience being at the bottom of the ocean surrounded by fabulous coral of all colours and an array of exotic fish.'

The party soon departed for Auckland where Devereux, somewhat ironically, was roomed with Betts at the Park Royal Hotel in the city centre. Training sessions were mostly held in the mornings which freed up the afternoons for golf, shopping or tanning. Devereux had some catching up to do as he had arrived in PNG with milk bottle white skin.

The catching up extended to a nice surprise: 'Maurice Lindsay, the tour manager, called me to his hotel room after a training session. I didn't know what he wanted. I knocked and entered as one of the other players was leaving. "Sit down at the desk, John," Maurice said, as I noticed the wad of cash on the table. He explained that each player got a daily allowance of about 12 New Zealand dollars for phone calls and other incidentals and handed me my allocation, back-dated to my first day on tour. I left the room clutching a few hundred dollars so I was well happy. I didn't even know about the payments so it came as a nice bonus. Most of it went on phoning home, beer and presents.'

Devereux wasn't selected for the opening Test with New Zealand and had a couple of days off training after feeling unwell from the upset stomach he'd picked up in Papua New Guinea, and his golf was all to pot as well, adding to his frustration. The squad watched newly-crowned Five Nations champions Scotland push the All Blacks in their union international, after which Devereux and Alan Tait, who had starred for Scotland before switching to league with Widnes, joined the Scots for a booze-up afterwards.

Tait had picked up an injury and was scheduled to leave for home so didn't have to train the following morning while Devereux missed it with a self-induced hangover. Thankfully, the management thought his suffering was a recurrence of the stomach bug so there were no repercussions.

Devereux was a spectator as Great Britain produced an against-the-odds 11-10 Test victory over New Zealand, which was disappointingly followed by a midweek defeat in Wellington, but they bounced back with Devereux playing well in a physical victory over the Māori, and they backed it up in terrible conditions against Taranaki in New Plymouth

Devereux then watched Great Britain win the second Test 16-14 in Auckland from a seat in the stand alongside All Blacks ace John Kirwan, who had terrorised Wales at the 1987 union World Cup and the following year during the so-called tour of death.

'We had a free bar at the hotel that night so there were a few of us very worse for wear the following morning, including me. Next stop was Christchurch. My roomie on this leg was Martin Offiah but that arrangement didn't last long. Chariots wasn't a big drinker but he'd definitely had a few that night. How did I know? Well, he found his way back to the room after I'd already hit the sack – I had to be up for early training while he had a day off – then picked up the phone and tried to order room service which woke me up. I wasn't best pleased. We had some strong words and I told him he was out of order, then he was back and forth to the toilet being sick through the rest of the night. I went to see Maurice the next day to ask for a room change and ended up getting a room to myself.

'The boys lost the third and final Test match 21-18, partly due to Martin dropping the ball over the try-line as he attempted to put it down one-handed. It was a bit embarrassing and the team were fuming as they had lost their win bonus.'

Looking back on that tour, Devereux said: 'League was the top sport in PNG and the people were mad for it. They were strong and so passionate about the game and it was an experience I will never forget. I always thought Tonga was one of the poorest rugby nations I had visited until I went to PNG. Hardly anyone wore shoes, so it must have been strange to wear rugby boots. Rugby is a path to escape poverty so the incentive was there for them to showcase their talent against Great Britain and get snapped up by overseas clubs.'

He also said that he found touring harder with Britain compared to Wales and the Lions in union: 'There was something lacking and I didn't enjoy the training. I found league tours a bit too stiff and I didn't really take to the coaching methods and negativity of Reilly and assistant coach Phil Larder in pointing out your weaknesses before kick-off and telling you not to make the same mistakes.

'I probably drank a little too much with the boys after games and struggled a little the next day in training, unlike others like Jiffy and Gary Connolly who were two of the best pound-for-pound drinkers I know.

'There were lots of characters on the tour, like Bish and his gang, but that also led to a split in the camp, especially when Bish smashed Keith 'Beefy' England after coming back from a mid-week night out. The tour doctor had to be woken at 3am to stitch Beefy's head. Mal was so angry he wanted to offer Bish out for a fight – it would have been a good scrap if it had happened!

'Then there was Bobbie Goulding's infamous night out in Auckland when two Kiwis started taking the piss out of him, and the GB team as a whole. Bobbie picked his moment and followed them into the toilets, where he battered them both. He was arrested and appeared in court a few hours later. Jiffy had to go to court and give a character witness statement. Bobbie was young and naive and could consider himself fortunate not to have spent longer being locked up.'

Twelve months later, Devereux returned to Papua New Guinea with the Great Britain squad as part of their 1992 tour to Australia. He'd had a good season at Widnes, scoring 35 tries, and made the shortlist for two prestigious awards: Player of The Year and Man of Steel.

'I thought I was in with a shout,' he said, 'but Castleford's Graham Steadman was named Player of The Year, and Wigan captain Dean Bell was a worthy winner of the Man of Steel. I was definitely improving and looked forward to another major tour to the southern hemisphere.'

Devereux made a miserable start to his bid to make Reilly's Test team, being twice tackled into touch when in possession and dropping two scoring passes during a 25-15 success over Highland in front of 8,000 spectators in hot and steamy conditions.

'I had blown my chance of playing in the opening Test against Australia because I knew the way Mal worked. He pulled me to one side and said I hadn't made the Test side because I hadn't taken my chances in the opening game of the trip.'

After missing out, Dev's head was 'in the shed' during his next outing, against Queensland Residents in Townsville, going off with a knee injury during a narrow 14-10 win. Devereux was happier with his performance during an 11-10 win at Illawarra but failed to make Reilly's team for the second Test, a 22-6 defeat.

The Scotland rugby union team were also in Australia and staying at the same hotel, the Manly Pacific, so Devereux caught up with his pals from the Lions tour of Australia in 1989, coach Ian McGeechan, Craig Chalmers and brothers Gavin and Scott Hastings. Their match with Australia took place 24 hours after the RL Test so Devereux and some of the 13-a-side colleagues formed a cunning plan to watch it.

'We had hired a pink Cadillac and a gang of us, with our team doctor at the steering wheel, followed the Scottish team bus across the Sydney Harbour Bridge and into the Sydney Football Stadium. The police escort didn't mind us hugging the back of the bus and we didn't even stop for any red lights or to pay our toll on the bridge. It was such a laugh and was a great night despite Scotland being beaten.'

Great Britain squared their series with Australia but went down in the decider before heading for New Zealand, where a visit to a go kart track provided more entertainment.

'Mal was a nutter behind the wheel. He quickly crashed his kart, turning it over, then manhandled it upright, jumped back in and set off in pursuit of the field. Ian Lucas was the unlucky driver when Mal rejoined the pack and, in his desperation to get past, barged Ian's kart off the track. It went flying through the air and over the safety tyre wall. Billy McGinty took the chequered flag with Mal second. It was hilarious but Mal and Ian could easily have been injured in the mayhem.'

Devereux's morale rose when he was picked as a substitute for the opening rubber with New Zealand but he didn't get on during the 15-14 defeat. He drowned his sorrows by getting drunk and couldn't remember the antics which had occurred back at the team hotel. That all changed when he saw the lack of hair on the head of winger Alan Hunte the following morning: 'Suddenly, it all came back to me. Alan had been pissed and made the mistake of leaving his room unlocked.

The others who had been on the lash then sneaked in because it was too good an opportunity to miss. Alan lay in a drunken stupor so Kelvin Skerrett thought it would be a good idea to shave 'Hunty's' hair.

'Kelvin got his electric hair clippers and set upon Alan. We were in stitches watching. I was thinking I would love to see Hunty's face when he woke up and looked in the mirror because it wasn't a pretty sight. When he walked into breakfast a few hours later it was obvious he had noticed the unexpected overnight trim. He'd shaved everything off to restore some dignity and make good of the mess Kelvin had made. Hunty turned to us and warned: "I will find out who the culprits are, and I will get you back".'

Devereux finally got to make a Test appearance on the tour when he came on as a blood replacement for Martin Offiah in the 19-16 victory that secured the series for Great Britain. The tour was over and it was time for home but, at the back of his mind, he'd heard the whispers that Hunt was planning to extract revenge on the barber shop gang on the flight home.

'We heard he had bought a few tubes of hair removing cream, so Andy Platt and Kelvin raided his suitcase at the airport. They found some and we thought it was job done, emergency averted.'

On the flight home, Devereux had been given the role of official invigilator for Lee Crooks' attempt at Australia cricketer David Boon's unofficial world record for the number of cans of beer drank on a flight from Sydney to London: 'Apparently, the record was 55 and 'Crooksey' got off to a fast start by downing three of the cans we had taken on board before the wheels of the 747 had left the tarmac. He was up to about 22 a few hours later when he hit the wall and fell asleep.'

That was the cue for Hunt to begin his revenge mission. Devereux had dozed off but woke up and immediately sensed something was amiss because he had two sisters and knew what hair removal cream smelt like.

'I went to the toilets, removed my hat and looked in the mirror. There was a dollop of hair removal cream on my head and it was starting to melt some of my hair. I quickly washed it off, put my hat back on, returned to my seat and dropped off again. I don't how much time passed before the cabin lights were switched on, but I woke to one of the funniest things I have ever seen.

'Dean Sampson, the Castleford prop, had blond spiky hair cut in a flat top. He usually looked like a fatter version of Johnny Bravo but, when he got up out of his seat, did a big stretch in the aisle and took his baseball cap off, he had a bald patch on top of his head and looked like a monk. Dean's reaction was priceless after he realised what had happened. He went berserk and wanted to kill Hunty. The irony was that the real culprits, Kelvin and 'Platty', had escaped scot-free.'

Devereux must have made a positive impact on that tour which, coupled with a rousing start to the following club season with Widnes, resulted in him being picked on the replacements' bench for the 1992 World Cup final against Australia at Wembley.

'I was playing with lots of confidence so felt selection was a just reward. We stayed in a posh hotel in St. Albans, the place used by the England football team and clubs preparing for games at Wembley. Training was good and the whole squad had a real buzz about it. We fancied our chances against Australia, especially at home.

'It was my first time playing at Wembley and it was a truly special place, steeped in history. The playing surface was like a snooker table, flat, green and firm. Travelling to any stadium on a team bus and with a police escort was always special. It took a good 45 minutes to reach the ground, and the buzz of being driven along Wembley Way surrounded by our fans was incredible.'

Devereux overheard a player say: "Imagine being the person who fucks up today?" It was a statement which will haunt him for the rest of his life.

The game was tight with both teams trading penalties and GB took a 6-4 lead into half-time. Phil Clarke had a dead leg and he was getting treatment while Gary Connolly had also been injured, leading to Reilly putting Devereux in the centre.

'There was nothing between the sides. Our half-back Deryck Fox bombed their full-back Tim Brasher with an up-and-under near the Australian sticks and Alan Tait rose like a salmon leaping out of a Scottish river and caught the ball. All he had to do was fall over the line and ground the ball, but he got tipped slightly in mid-air and landed on his back. As he tried to ground the ball for a try, the Aussie defence pounced on him and snuffed any chance of a try out by getting under the ball. I couldn't believe it, I felt it was our chance to put the game to bed.

'Minutes later, the Aussies were attacking my right side of defence. I was mindful that Phil, my second-row defensive partner, was carrying his leg so I was standing closer to him in defence. Steve Waters, as he picked the ball up from a ruck in the middle of the park just outside our 20m line, saw that I was tight to Clarke so held the ball and ran diagonally which caught me ball watching as he sent a sublime pass out to Steve Renouf, my opposite number.

'Renouf was a lightning centre and had got on the outside of my right shoulder. I tried to adjust and put a cover tackle in but he was too quick – the quality of the pass from Walters had done me. Renouf was gone, and scored a try in the corner to put them 10-6 ahead. We tried our best to snatch the lead back but ran out of steam as the best team in the world closed the door on us.'

Devereux was distraught: 'The game ended and I was beside myself. I had never cried on a rugby pitch but, after the final whistle, I sank to the floor and the tears started flooding. I was utterly devastated, for my teammates, the fans, and my family and friends watching. Ellery Hanley came over and picked me up off the turf but I was still so upset.

'He said: "Come on John, it's not all your fault. We had chances in that game and we didn't take them. I've made similar mistakes in my career, you just have to dust yourself down and go again, be stronger and better next time".

'Our changing room was like a morgue. Most people were silent, apart from a few who were talking quietly in corners to other players. They were probably saying how shit that attempt of a tackle was on Renouf. To make matters worse, I was selected for a drugs test and it took me several hours hanging around in the stadium with the doping control officer before I was rehydrated sufficiently to produce the required amount of urine.

'After dinner back at the hotel, I drowned my sorrows. The torment didn't end there because some of the players' wives travelled home with us on the bus. They weren't happy their husbands had missed out on a £5,000-a-player win bonus. I could hear comments like: "There goes my new conservatory, there goes my new kitchen, there goes my new car." A bonus of 5k would have bought any of those back in 1992.'

Some years later, Devereux was chatting to Clarke about that game at a rugby event: 'Phil said, without prompting: "JD, it wasn't your fault, you were covering me as I was struggling with a painful dead leg. Walters saw that and exploited it with a great pass timed to perfection to Renouf. Don't beat yourself up about it, mate".'

Devereux may have wanted to forget the nightmare but, each time the Wales squad gathered, he was teased by his teammates and members of the management. Clive Griffiths, who was the Wales coach, said: 'After the final the Welsh boys started calling him Steve 'Ranoff'. Our boys used to shout at him: "Steve's ran off." The banter was ruthless and relentless with Devs copping it big time but it was in jest because we knew he was some player.'

'Devs was the consummate professional during the time that I knew him as his coach. He had all the physical and mental attributes necessary to succeed. He was tough, aggressive and skilful. He played hard and also partied hard after a win.

'He had a combination of strength and speed, and was a real powerhouse of a player. Not only that but he had a big engine and this showed in his high work ethic, in whatever position he played. John understood the game, playing with great skill and his versatility was a bonus.

'I'll never forget his horrendous jaw break injury against Australia and his sheer determination to get back in the red famous shirt, which he did and helped Wales win the European Championship for the first time in 57 years. He had amazing powers of recovery, and was real passionate man and team player.'

14

Implosion at Widnes

'Whenever he returns to Widnes, he is given a very warm welcome because this is a rugby town and he fitted right in. John was, without a doubt, one of the finest players to ever wear the Widnes jersey.'

Jim Mills

Frank Myler, a legendary rugby league figure and a stalwart of the Chemics, had taken over from the Leeds-bound Dougie Laughton ahead of the 1991-92 season. Myler had helped Great Britain lift the World Cup in 1960 and was the last captain of a GB side to have won a Test series against Australia on antipodean soil, coming from behind to take it 2-1 in 1970.

He clearly came with a healthy pedigree, a huge amount of respect and a big reputation. 'Frank was a great player. He had been out of coaching for quite a while but fancied another crack at the league title,' said Devereux. 'We started off the season with a surprise defeat at Workington in the Lancashire Cup but then went on a great run. Apart from defeats to Wigan and Halifax, we won 11 of our next 13 games.'

Widnes seemed to be on the up, but the wheels came off in the league as they slumped to a fifth-place finish, with eventual champions Wigan beating them 42-16. 'The only competition we were doing well in was the Regal Trophy; beating Workington, Carlisle, Featherstone Rovers and then St. Helens in our semi-final to set up a showdown at Central Park, Wigan against Dougie's Leeds in the final. We smashed them 24-0 and Dougie's face was a picture at the end of the game,' grinned Devereux. 'He had spent big money assembling a new Leeds team and we battered them.'

More change was afoot at Widnes, however: 'Phil Larder came on to me during the 1992 Great Britain tour to Papua New Guinea, New Zealand and Australia. He told me he was taking over from Frank and would bring more structure to our play but his tenure started badly and without a ball being kicked as we lost one of our best players in Martin Offiah. He had signed for Wigan for a world record fee of £440,000.'

There was a second hammer-blow when the accomplished Alan Tait left for Leeds in another big-money deal. 'Offiah and Tait were irreplaceable really,' said Devereux. 'Alan was a great player in his own right while Martin was uncatchable if you put him away. Nevertheless, we still started the league campaign brightly, winning our first three games, However, the new powerhouses in the league, Bradford, St. Helens and Wigan proved too strong for us.'

Offiah and Tait had been sold to raise desperately needed funds with Widnes' very future under threat from mounting debts, as Devereux recalled: 'The shit hit the fan just after Christmas. The whole squad, management and backroom staff were summoned to the club for an emergency meeting, and we assembled in the weights room under the stand. An old, dilapidated, dirty, dusty and very small place, it was a strange venue to hold such an important meeting. Our chairman, Big Jim Mills, walked into the room accompanied by two well-dressed gentlemen wearing pin-stripe suits. The contrast between our surroundings and these two city slickers was startling and illustrated the difference between old school rugby league and modern day finance.

'We had no idea what we were about to hear from Jim, but were quickly told that the taxman had issued a winding up order on Widnes and we were about to go into financial administration. It was a massive shock to us all. We knew money was tight at most clubs, but Widnes were regarded as a top-three team in the league and had been known as the cup kings, having regularly got to the twin towers of Wembley in the Challenge Cup and to Premiership finals held at Manchester United's Old Trafford.

'However, partly due to bad business management and a number of players having clauses in their contracts concerning how their income tax was deducted, the club was crippled financially. As players, we had been unaware of the magnitude of the problem until that meeting and sat there in disbelief at what was happening to us and our club. We had thought selling Offiah would sort out any money problems the club had, but we were so wrong because the problem ran much deeper. It transpired that the money from selling Martin had gone straight to pay off debt to the Inland Revenue but it wanted more, and it was money the club simply didn't have.'

Widnes were different to clubs like St. Helens, Wigan, Leeds and Warrington. Those clubs each had a board of wealthy directors stumping up their own money to pay for players and contracts, but Widnes had a committee of smaller, local businessmen, ranging from an insurance salesman, a nightclub owner, a retired director of ICI, a pub landlord, a solicitor and a director of a local demolition and scrap metal company. They were as equally committed and passionate but only a few of those were able to put money into the club, so the job of balancing the books was much harder.

Laughton had gambled on getting more success at Widnes. They were regular winners of the Premiership Grand Final, the Lancashire Cup and the Regal Trophy. In Devereux's first year at the club, they faced top Australian outfit Canberra Raiders at Old Trafford for the World Club Championship.

Not getting to the Challenge Cup final at Wembley, though, was financially crippling for a club that had big debts to pay. Laughton had promised the committee the big money they were spending would be recouped by the cash generated from Wembley finals, and that they would relive the heady days when Widnes made annual pilgrimages to north London.

'You could probably sum up rugby league back then as being played by professionals but run by forward-thinking amateurs,' said Devereux. 'The priority for the club now, of course, was staying afloat. The administrator explained there would be no player contract payments made until all the creditors had been fully paid and the majority of that money was heading to the taxman.'

The only way we players could get any decent money each week was by winning. Each member of the match-day squad was paid a bonus of £250 a game per win but only got £50 each if they lost. The effect was profound.

'Some players had mortgages and other had loans to pay, but we all had everyday living costs. Muzzy was on the long-term injured list and, after hearing what the administrator had to say, broke down. The emotion of the moment poured out of him. He asked how he was going to pay his mortgage and other bills from win bonuses if he couldn't even play. The only income he could get would be statutory sick pay from the government. Tears were rolling down his face. It was a desperate situation and, in the end, Muzzy was forced to cash in some of the investments he had made and which were intended for later life, in order to put food on the table and pay his bills.'

The incentive to win couldn't be greater, with Devereux pausing before saying: 'I won't forget in a hurry what happened, or the date – 13 January 1993 – but it certainly motivated us. Our survival instinct kicked-in and we went on a 14-match unbeaten run which also took us to the Challenge Cup final for the first time since 1984. Going to Wembley was the Holy Grail for us.

'We beat Dougie's Leeds superstars in the semi-final at Wigan's Central Park, hammering them 39-4. Believe it or not, we had negotiated a special win bonus package to beat Leeds in that semi and a smaller win bonus for the final. Some may think that was strange but it was more financially lucrative for the club to actually get to Wembley than to win the final. We had gone to the board and said: "Wouldn't it be better to pay us £4,000 each for winning the semi-final and getting us to Wembley because that's how the club will earn the big money?" The board agreed, which is why David Myers ran up to a television camera after scoring a try in the semi and counted one, two, three and four with his fingers, in celebration at the bonus money coming our way.'

The town and the club were buzzing again. Laughton had promised the club he would take it there when he had assembled his team of 'Harlem Globetrotters', but they had failed three times under him, including losing in a semi-final in 1989 at Liverpool's Anfield ground to St. Helens. Rick Thackeray was in the clear and seemingly set to score a try which could have won it, but he fell over as if a sniper had shot him from the stand.

Discussing Widnes' cup performances of that period, Devereux described how: 'During my first season we lost at home in the first round to Oldham, a Second Division side. It was a shocking result. We had another first round defeat the following year, losing to St. Helens at Naughton Park. Having home advantage hadn't done anything for us.

'However, after reaching the 1993 final under Phil Larder, we were on a high. We had three good wins on the trot but, bang, the wheels came off and we lost four of our next five league games. We also went out in the first round of the end-of-season Premiership competition, to Leeds, the week before the Challenge Cup final. I guess the main reason we hit a slump in form was that players didn't want to get injured before the final, with intensity levels and commitment dropping off as a consequence.'

Devereux hurt his back quite badly in that last game before Wembley when trying to make a try-saving tackle on Leeds centre

Simon Irvine: 'I was trying to emulate the famous JPR Williams shoulder-charge tackle for Wales against France at Cardiff Arms Park in 1976 that sealed a Grand Slam victory, but my attempt was no way as good or effective as JPR's. I twisted my lower spine in contact and it felt like I'd broken my back. We went to Lilleshall to prepare for the final, staying there for three days, where I had intense physiotherapy for the first two days. It was touch and go whether I would be fit for the final with Wigan.'

It was a final to forget for Devereux and for Widnes, who lost 20-14: 'We were only on something like a grand each for the final. We played our hearts out and should have won it but Wigan beat us. I probably had the worst game of my career. Offiah, who was the fastest thing I've seen on a rugby pitch, was part of the reason. I lost my focus and became distracted – every time I had the ball I just wanted to run through him. The first time I tried, I was caught by an elbow to the side of my head and lost the ball, coming around to see Dean Bell scoring under the sticks for Wigan, but I was stubborn and kept trying to do the same thing, with the same outcome each time. If there's any advice I could give to a youngster, it's don't lose focus by getting engulfed by the emotion of the occasion or becoming fixated on your opponent. Just play your own game.

'I wasn't the only one to lose my head. Richie Eyres used to wear an arm guard because he'd previously broken a forearm, but Richie being Richie, went a step too far and used to slot a piece of metal into the guard to stiffen it up and help protect his arm. He also used it to inflict some pain on whoever he smashed with his forearm. He stupidly tried to take Offiah's head off but missed. Although he didn't catch Martin, it was a wild challenge and he was sent off. Richie and Martin were mates as well, so it was mad!

'Even though I was very strong and had good muscle definition in my shoulders and arms, I still chose to wear shoulder pads to protect myself. I also wore an arm guard to protect my forearm, which was susceptible to damage if it caught a player's head in a collision. As Paul Moriarty discovered to his cost just before the Challenge Cup final against Wigan at Wembley in 1993, a solid hit without an arm guard could result in a broken arm. Allan Bateman broke his arm in a similar manner when tackling an opponent who'd ducked his head at the last second.

'Jonathan Davies claimed I tried to take his head off after he left Widnes for Warrington during the 1993-94 season, but I would never do that to any player, let alone my good friend Jiffy. He still brings it up today and I always tell him I was joking.'

A promising footballer in his youth who represented Wales at the Boys' Clubs level, Devereux loved the game and, with so many top class sides on his doorstep, was frequently spotted in the crowd at soccer matches with his pals.

'Paul Moriarty was an Evertonian Blue, I was a Liverpool Red, while Jiffy never really made his mind up – he generally supported the side that was playing the best football and winning everything at the time!

'We got to know some footballers very well, like fellow Welshmen Mark 'Sparky' Hughes and Clayton Blackmore at United and England centre-half Dave Watson at Everton. Dave was a big fan of league. We would get tickets to football matches from them and it was great, rubbing shoulders with those boys.

'Me and Muzzy played a lot of golf with Sparky and Clayton, and we participated in both Sparky's and Bryan 'Robbo' Robson's testimonial golf days. Robbo's was great and finished with a dinner back at Old Trafford, with special guest, Franz Klammer, the famous Austrian downhill skier who came with his entourage. Another special guest was Liverpool comedian Stan Boardman who provided the entertainment.

'Stan loved to tell stories about the Germans in the Second World War and how he didn't like them because he claimed that they'd bombed all the chip shops in Liverpool. It's safe to say Stan went for it big time and kept referring to Franz as if he was German and not Austrian, saying he was in more bunkers on the golf course than Hitler was in during the whole of the war. Klammer's manager went absolutely mad and stormed out of the dinner. I could only conclude that a Scouser cracking jokes at a Manchester United player dinner was never going to go down well!'

Widnes may have imploded, but Devereux had made an indelible impression on the club and the town, as Jim Mills warmly recalled: 'John was one of several tremendous Welsh players who came to the club and he soon became a favourite of the fans who admired his powerful running, strong hand-off and total commitment to the team. Even now, whenever he returns to Widnes, he is given a very warm welcome because this is a rugby town and he fitted right in. John was, without a doubt, one of the finest players to ever wear the Widnes jersey.'

15

Meninga and Manly

*'I rushed downstairs to the medical room and Devs was lying there
with blood coming out of his mouth. It was a horrific injury and you
could see his jaw was broken.'*

Clive Griffiths

Perhaps he can still feel the pain, but John Devereux remembers it as
if it was yesterday, the sickening incident which saw his jaw shattered
with pieces of bone protruding into his tongue.

It was a Wales versus Australia encounter at Cardiff City's former
home, Ninian Park, and Devereux was marking Mal Meninga, the
tourists' pile-driving 19st centre and captain. It was a clash of giants,
in more ways than one, as there was previous history between the
pair, emanating from a clash Down Under when Devereux had a stint
with Manly Sea Eagles in the National Rugby League.

He had eased his way back to fitness for the start of the 1994-
95 season after missing nearly all of the second half of the previous
campaign with a back problem. Devereux had only managed to play
a few games when he was selected to play for Wales in the centre,
against the mighty Kangaroos at Ninian Park. They were touring
Great Britain and it was the first game of the tour. It was also the
Wales debuts of Iestyn Harris and Scott Gibbs.

'I will remember that day for the rest of my life,' he explained. 'It
was eight minutes past three on the 30 October 1994 when I went
to tackle a man mountain named Mal Meninga. It was pouring with
rain and I got everything wrong.

'The collision was sickening with a bone-shattering impact on
my lower jaw, after it had made contact with big Mal's shoulder. It
happened at high speed with two large immovable objects colliding
head on. He was bigger than me, though, and I went in too high and

exposed my face. The pain was excruciating, the worst injury I had ever experienced. My jaw bone was smashed into four pieces and one piece of jaw bone had gone straight through my tongue. The blood was everywhere.

'I was conscious throughout and I immediately knew I would be out of action for a long time. As I headed off the pitch I remember Rory, our physio, handing me a white towel. I cupped it around my jaw and it was claret red before I had reached the touchline.

'I thought he had done me with an elbow because it was such a pinpoint and forceful hit but, when I looked at the video, I had caught the best dipped shoulder in the game. Maybe there was a little bit of extra grunt in his charge because of what had happened when I was playing for Manly against Canberra in Australia the previous year when Mal had lifted me off the floor with a forearm to the chin in a tackle. Mal was cited for that one and had been punished with a two-game ban. As a result, he missed a match against New Zealand because of it. I don't know if he held that against me that day at Ninian Park but I certainly came off second best.'

Wales coach Clive Griffiths chipped in: 'I rushed downstairs to the medical room and Devs was lying there with blood coming out of his mouth. It was a horrific injury and you could see his jaw was broken. Jonathan Davies, who was injured and had missed the game, was also there. I looked at him and he gave me a shake of the head. It was clear Devs wouldn't be returning to the field of play. Our doctor confirmed as much

'I've always felt Devs went high, a bit like you see in rugby union, and caught the shoulder of Meninga. Mal didn't have the shoulders of a normal man, they were enormous. He was a giant of a man, with legs like tree trunks, but he was quick and had the skills of a stand-off.

'Devs went for the ball with an all-in tackle but, unfortunately, collided with the granite shoulder of Meninga. I don't think there was any malice and no action was taken by the authorities. Sometimes, league can be lenient in dealing with incidents but I don't think it was on that occasion. It was just Meninga had shoulders which were like concrete blocks.

'Mal used to drop his shoulder and would-be tacklers bounced off him. Devs was a giant in his own right, was fully committed and was determined to smash Mal. It was a rugby collision, pure and simple, and Devs came off worst. Even now, I can visualise it and hear the crunch!'

Devereux had been joined in the treatment room by Wales captain Dai Young, who had been pummelled during an almighty fight: 'Dai came in with a large cut above one eye and a huge egg of a swelling above the other like a scene in a *Rocky* movie. I remember Dai saying: "Strap it up, I'm going back out there," but as they were putting elastoplast on his head, the blood was seeping through it. That match was absolute carnage, on and off the pitch. Kevin Ellis got hammered by David Furner who hit Kev about 50 times and the swelling closed both his eyes – he looked like Chi Chi the panda.'

Devereux's match was over but Young did go back into the fray. It was a physical game with a lot of niggle, fighting and off-the-ball cheap shots. Wales lost the fighting, the collisions and, ultimately, the match, 46-4.

Griffiths added: 'I had to make a quick assessment of the situation with Devs and Dai because two of our best players were off the field. Dai was sat next to Devs, nursing cuts above both his eyes, and with his face covered in blood. Dai said he was going back on, so I said: "You had better get stitched up then." I put Dai back on for his pride but he was unable to last it out because the cuts reopened.'

Six weeks earlier, Devereux and his wife Alison had been in hospital for the birth of their second daughter Ellen. This time, they travelled by ambulance to Cardiff Royal Infirmary, and waited in the Accident and Emergency Department until he was summoned for an X-Ray, still clad in his Wales kit: 'The damage was clear to see and I was operated on that night. I would be sidelined for 13 weeks.'

Alison had rushed to the Wales dressing room but was met at its door by Allan Bateman, who had been ruled out of playing in the match by injury. 'Allan advised me not to go in,' said Alison, 'as it wasn't a pretty scene, but I told him I was going in to see John. It was like walking into a war zone because there was blood everywhere. Seeing Dai Young being stitched up and John with his jaw smashed it wasn't a pleasant experience and we were soon on our way back to the Cardiff Royal Infirmary, this time for an unwanted reason.'

Devereux had crossed swords with Meninga after being loaned to Manly by Widnes for the 1993 Australian domestic season. He had left for Sydney, accompanied by Alison and three-year-old daughter Jessica, a day after being in the Widnes team which had been beaten

20-14 by Wigan at Wembley in the 1993 Challenge Cup final in front of a crowd of 78,348.

'Six months earlier,' Devereux explained about his Australian adventure. 'I had received a telephone call from Eddie McDonald, who had been chief scout at Widnes and Dougie Laughton's right-hand man, asking me whether I fancied a spell with Manly Sea Eagles playing in the National Rugby League as soon as our season at Widnes was over.

'Eddie had moved on from Widnes and was doing some wheeling and dealing when he sounded me out. He seemed to have contacts everywhere, having been involved in the sport for so many years, and, true to form, had fingers in pies in Australia.

'He was big mates with Eagles coach Graham Lowe and told me Graham had made an inquiry into the possibility of me playing over there during the British off-season. I was gobsmacked, as offers like that didn't come very often, and not many Brits had been to play in Oz. The only players I knew who had been out there were the very best of British: Ellery Hanley, Jonathan Davies, Martin Offiah, Andy Gregory and Joe Lydon. My good friend and teammate at Widnes, Andy Currier, had also played for Balmain Tigers the year I signed for Widnes.

'To receive an offer was an honour and I couldn't wait to get over there. It wasn't for megabucks, to be honest, but I would have gone for nothing just to have the experience. I was offered 1,000 Aussie dollars a game plus a living allowance of $500 a week, a car, a rent-free apartment, and a free return flight for the mother-in-law. All I had to do was play virtually a full season back home, stay fit and fly out there at the end of it.

'Everyone playing rugby league in the UK was so envious of Australian RL, which was flying high with Tina Turner contracted to promote the game with her hit song *The Best*, and we would watch the highlights of the games back home on *The Footy Show* with Fatty Vautin, Blocker Roach and Peter Sterling. The State of Origin series between New South Wales and Queensland – with players playing for the state in which they were born – was awesome. Those matches were brutal and no prisoners were taken as clubmates came up against each other for state bragging rights.'

New Zealander Graham Lowe, later a Sir and the only non-Australian to coach a State of Origin team, had been coach of Wigan. He had turned the Lancashire club around, guiding them to their first Rugby League Championship in 27 years in 1986-87 and later that year, he steered Wigan to glory over Manly in the World Club Challenge. It was a first for Wigan and a huge boost for British rugby league. Lowe then went on to mastermind triumphs for Wigan in the 1988 and 1989 Challenge Cup finals.

Lowe had headed to the Sydney suburb of Manly in 1990 to coach the Sea Eagles and used his Midas touch on them to reach cup finals in each of the next two years. It saw him appointed Queensland boss for the State of Origin battles, with his Maroons winning a gripping series against New South Wales 2-1.

Former Widnes man McDonald had bought an apartment overlooking the magnificent Sydney Harbour and got talking to Lowe. Manley wanted a player who could figure at wing or centre and Devereux soon discovered that he fitted the bill: 'Graham didn't take too much convincing because he knew all about me, following his stint with Wigan. The deal was done and I managed to get a flight ticket for my mother-in-law thrown in to keep Alison happy while we were settling into life in Australia.'

Devereux had some important business to take care of before heading Down Under, with Widnes having reached the final of the Challenge Cup against, of all teams, Lowe's former club, Wigan. The cash-strapped Widnes may have lost, but he came through it unscathed and arrived at London's Heathrow Airport the following day to board the flight for Australia. However, potential trouble was looming.

'Graham had been forced to stand down from his position at Manly due to health problems. A blood clot had threatened to not only end his coaching career but had put his life in danger. Bob Fulton, a straight-talking and notorious Australia coach, had now taken over at the club and we were *en route* to Sydney, unsure whether he wanted an import signed by his predecessor.

'I'd never met Fulton but his reputation went ahead of him. He didn't mince his words and was ruthless. I told Alison that, even though I had an agreement with Manly, to be prepared for the worst and to be told by Fulton he didn't want me. I feared our stay in Australia may be short and we would soon be heading in the opposition direction back to Britain. I had a game-by-game contract so there wasn't any guarantee, especially if Fulton wasn't smitten on me.'

The anxiety of the Devereux family was eased when Frank Stanton, the chief executive of Manly, met them at Sydney Airport after they emerged from customs control following a long and tiring journey.

'He was a lovely guy and had brought a bouquet of flowers for Alison and a cuddly toy for Jessica. Frank drove us to the Manly Pacific Hotel, where I had stayed with the 1989 British and Irish Lions, and checked us in. We had a lovely room overlooking the sandy beach and the Pacific Ocean. We woke up about three o'clock in the morning because our bodies hadn't adjusted to the time difference and ordered burger and chips from room service. It seemed like bliss but I still hadn't met Fulton and didn't know whether he would give me the big heave-ho or allow me a chance to show what I could do.

'The following morning Frank turned up at about 10am to show us the lovely apartment where we would be staying for the duration of our stay in Manly. Then he took me to training, which was led by the other coaches with Fulton watching from the touchline. Once I recognised who he was I kept an eye on him.

'It seemed like an eternity before a guy called over to me and said: "Devereux, Bob Fulton wants to speak to you." I trotted over to him and he said: "Alright mate, look here, I didn't bring you to the club. If you don't shape up, we will put you on the next ship home." He was certainly old school and blunt but I got the message. It concentrated my mind and I made an impact on my debut on the wing and won him over. Soon, he was picking me at centre and even had me kicking goals. Not many remember it, but I'd been a goal-kicker early in my union career.

'There was a host of big names at the club, including Ian Roberts. It's been widely reported Gareth 'Alfie' Thomas, the former Wales union captain and ex-league player, was the first openly gay professional rugby player, but it's not true as Ian had come out years earlier, in 1995 actually. Ian was a huge man and one of the Australia national team's best forwards.

'Just before I arrived at Manly, Ian had tackled Garry Jack during a match against Balmain Tigers afterwhich Jack allegedly made an unsavoury remark and Ian hit him with a flurry of punches, shutting both of Jack's eyes. The conflict didn't end there because Jack took Ian to court years later in an effort to receive damages, claiming he was taking a stand because other Manly players had allegedly taken part in the beating and had left him with scarring and traumatic injuries to his face. The dispute was eventually settled out of court with Roberts paying Jack a sum of money.'

Devereux was to make 15 appearances for Manly and was keen to stay on, but Widnes wouldn't have any of it and insisted he honour his contract with them and return to Naughton Park. Nevertheless, he had made a favourable impact in the NRL, with his former teammate Des Hasler, the Australia international, saying: 'Devs had a good season out here. Bob and everyone else were happy with the way he played and wanted to keep him, but Widnes put a block on it. JD was a victim of his own success. It was a real shame he couldn't stay and probably a sliding door moment for him because Manly went on a top run in 1995 and got to the NRL final.

'John played some good footie and was hard to mark. He ran smart lines and had good footwork. He was tough and also was very good defensively. Cliffy Lyons put him through a hole on his debut and JD ran half the length of the field, then stepped the full-back for a try. It was certainly some entrance to Manly, and the rest is history for he never looked back. Cliffy was a great player and a master at putting players like John into space. It would have been interesting if John had stayed on. I believe he would have forged a hugely successful career in the NRL.

'There was a lot of pressure on JD when he came to Australia but our fans loved him and viewed him as a really honest player. When you go overseas to play there is a certain expectation on you to perform and he achieved it by making a difference and a positive impact. The Australian game is a bit more competitive than in Britain and he had a determination to prove himself. The opposition fans were ready to pile into him but he soon silenced them. JD was all-in and his teammates and the fans respected him for that.'

Devereux even got a form of revenge against Brisbane Broncos star Steve Renouf, the helmeted player who had out-witted him to win the 1992 World Cup final with a game deciding try for Australia.

'Brookvale Oval, Manly's home ground, was the scene for the big rematch after what he did to me at Wembley, but this time I got the better of him. I learned a lot out there because they were big on analysis of opponents and the skills training was miles ahead of that in the Britian at the time. A few other players and I were full-time professionals so I'd gone from training a couple days a week in the late 1980s, to full-time training with Manley. My best mates at the club were Kiwis Tony Iro and Daryl Williams.'

Although Devereux twice tangled with Meninga and was sent off three times during his career, he never considered himself a dirty player. His first dismissal came early in his league career following a brawl with Keith England.

'The second time I got my marching orders was a lot cleaner. We were playing Huddersfield and they had a young second-row who ran at me. He stepped inside me, catching me off-guard and flat-footed. I left my right arm out there and coat-hangered the lad with my forearm. He crashed to the ground and I started walking before the referee had time to pull the red card out of his pocket.

'My final sending off came just after I had turned 40 and was playing for Maesteg in a Glamorgan County Silver Ball final with Banwen, on neutral territory at Caerphilly's Virginia Park. The day started off miserably and ended badly. Ninety per cent of the team had only got back from Benidorm on the morning of the match. Allan Bateman, Kevin Ellis and I were the only players who hadn't gone to Spain.

'I walked into the changing room and it was like a scene out of a zombie film. The lads had been on the pop for a week and we were expecting them to win a game in which we were odds-on favourites, but being on the piss for a week had taken a toll and it showed when the game commenced.

'The Benidorm returnees were sweaty, some were being sick, and many were green in complexion. We were going to get beaten, and that's how it went, mainly due to their openside flanker getting away with murder at the rucks. Midway through the second half, I'd had enough of the referee not penalising him for infringing and decided to take the law into my hands. There was a ruck on the halfway line and I saw the flanker killing our ball illegally yet again, so I ran from my position in the centre, which was about 15m from the ruck, and did some tap-dancing on him as the ball was nearby.

'That was the catalyst for a mass brawl to erupt. I was at the bottom of a pile of bodies chuckling to myself. When it broke up and order was restored, I was regaining my feet when the referee produced a red card and sent me off. I was gutted. I did the walk of shame off the pitch, but decided against going straight to the changing room. Instead I joined the Maesteg boys in the dugout, where I got pelters off some women who were supporting Banwen. I spent the remainder of the game winding them up, but they had the last laugh as they picked up the trophy.'

16

Wales and Samoa Go to War

'It was a war and everyone was willing to die for the cause in one of the most brutal and physical rugby league games ever.'

Willie Poching

Wales had been a shambles at the 1995 rugby union World Cup in South Africa, with a change of coaches before the tournament and in-fighting between players from the Cardiff and Swansea clubs during it.

Coach Alan Davies, his assistant Gareth Jenkins and team manager Robert Norster had quit following a whitewash in that year's Five Nations Championship and after failing to secure a vote of confidence from the all-powerful general committee of the Welsh Rugby Union.

Drafted in for the World Cup by the WRU, and on a caretaker basis only, were Cardiff's Aussie coach, Alex Evans, Swansea's Mike Ruddock, who was to later guide Wales to a first Grand Slam in 28 years, and Pontypridd's Dennis John. Of the three, Evans was put in charge and it's fair to say it wasn't a happy camp.

That disharmony was obvious for all to see by performances on the pitch. Wales were comprehensively beaten by a Jonah Lomu-inspired New Zealand before crashing out of the tournament at the pool stage with a toothless display against Ireland in one of the most boring internationals of all-time when both teams opted to repeatedly kick the ball long in what resembled aerial ping-pong.

The shambolic mess wasn't a surprise to anyone who knew rugby because most of Wales' best players were now being paid to play league and were off-limits with union not yet having gone 'officially' professional. It meant Evans, Ruddock and John were, like Davies,

Jenkins and Norster before them, shuffling half a deck of cards, so to speak.

The cards the coaches really needed were in the north of England and that became apparent when the RL World Cup was held in Great Britain later the same year. Of course, the basic requirement for any team is to have harmony, a settled squad and management, and results that had instilled confidence. Wales certainly had all those facets as they prepared to face France and Samoa at the group stage. How the rugby union coaches would have relished the prospect of picking from such a stellar cast list that wore the red jersey of Wales RL: Jonathan Davies, John Devereux, Paul Moriarty, Adrian Hadley, David Young, Rowland Phillips, Scott Gibbs, Scott Quinnell, Allan Bateman, Iestyn Harris, Mark Jones, Kevin Ellis and Anthony Sullivan.

While it was painful for union fanatics, it was the best of times for Welsh sports followers as they savoured the growing momentum and confidence of the league team, and waited with anticipation at the prospect of Wales attempting to avenge the shock 1991 union World Cup exit at the hands of the then Western Samoa, with both teams packed with former 15-a-side stars. First up though was the not-so-small matter of accounting for France at Cardiff's Ninian Park.

'We had faced the French so many times we knew each other's style and plays very well,' recalled Devereux. 'We knew we couldn't be complacent and would have to be near or at our best against them as they were very dangerous opponents. Anyone who has been up against French sides would tell you, once the French lads get their tails up, they are almost impossible to stop.'

Wales had prepared for the tournament with a training camp at an outdoor pursuits centre in Pelena, near Pontrhydyfen in the beautiful Afan Valley north of Port Talbot. Nowadays, tourists have called the area 'Little Switzerland' for its outstanding natural beauty and its extensive, world renowned mountain bike trails. All that was lacking was a training pitch!

'We didn't have permission to use a rugby union ground as a training venue, so we travelled around the valley in the team bus with our coach Clive Griffiths and team manager Mike Nicholas looking for a suitable ground to train on, and found a pitch next to the main road running through Pontrhydyfen. We also had a few opportunities to do some team bonding, which involved going into Swansea or Bridgend for a few beers, I can't quite work out how the hell we ended up back at my home town of Bridgend, because it wasn't the best for nightlife.'

Preparations complete, the Wales squad moved to Cardiff for their game against France, staying at the old Crest Hotel, now the Holiday Inn, at the castle end of Westgate Street, next to the Arms Park and only a minute from the Horse and Groom on Womanby Street. It brought back fond memories for Devereux of that day when he discovered he had been selected for his Wales union debut.

Griffiths turned up with an Irish guy named Kieron in tow. None of the squad knew Kieron but he was to give the players a talk, quickly winning them over.

'It turned out he was good at motivating people and worked on the psychology of sport,' said Devereux. 'He introduced himself and then he had us all lying on the floor doing visualisation exercises, using mental anchors to get us to a good place and explaining how powerful a 1% increase in team performance could be when it was multiplied by 13 players. I, and probably most of us, had never experienced anything like it and he had a great reaction from the squad.'

Any nerves or anxiety of letting down the country were eased with a comprehensive 28-6 victory over France, in front of a crowd of more than 10,000. Paul Moriarty starred in the pack with Anthony Sullivan on the wing scoring a hat-trick of tries. It was a solid start to Wales' bid for glory but there was a bigger challenge to come if they were to advance to the knock-out stage.

France didn't have much time to recover from the fixture with Wales and three days later were beaten 56-10 by Samoa. The Samoans sent out a message with their winning margin and the Welsh stars knew they would have a big challenge on their hands when they played them a week later at their favourite Vetch Field ground, which had been the scene of so many memorable league experiences.

Wales checked in at the Dragon Hotel, on Swansea's Kingsway, knowing this would be a much sterner test, with Devereux saying: 'We were switched on and there was a big game feel. We prepared well and felt ready for the win-or-bust match that evening with a big crowd expected. You wouldn't believe how special it was and how Kieron had us bouncing off the walls.'

There was electricity and tension in the air, and the kick-off had to be delayed by 20 minutes to get the capacity crowd into the ground for a real hairs-on-the-back-of-the-neck night. It was the return of the stars of the Wales team that had finished third at the 1987 World Cup and had pocketed a Triple Crown the following year, but who had headed north after being lured by the money of league. Wales boasted an exceptional line-up and Welsh fans were desperate to see them get stuck into the big-hitting Samoans.

'It was a lovely crisp October evening and the fans were piling into the stadium, hoping to see the Welsh boys do the business on Samoa and reach the semi-final, versus England at Old Trafford,' continued Devereux.

'What we didn't know, as we were getting ready in the changing rooms at the Vetch, was that Clive had decided to invite Kieron back to give us a pre-match psych-up. He had us lying on the floor of the changing room doing meditation and visualisation exercises. He talked about family and friends, and made us all feel 10 feet tall and utterly invincible. Mark Jones, his face and neck smothered in Vaseline, was pacing up and down and snorting like a raging bull. 'Scooby', as we all knew him, was so pumped up he started head-butting walls and punching doors – and he was only on the bench!

'Suddenly, the changing room door opened and a police inspector walked in to tell us that the kick-off was being delayed because there were so many fans still trying to get into the stadium. With Scooby, Kelvin Skerrett and Neil Cowie prowling around like caged lions I didn't think there would be anything left of the changing room if we had to stay a minute longer.

'After waiting for what seemed an eternity, the order finally came to head out for battle. Jiffy led us out, with his son Scott – the Welsh team mascot for the game – walking alongside him. Scott was beaming, the stadium was packed and the atmosphere was electric, as we sang *Hen Wlad fy Nhadau* with real passion.

'We lined up our side of the halfway line for Samoa to do their *Manu Siva Tau* – the Samoan version of the Polynesian *Haka* ritual. Beforehand, the boys had decided that we would stand on the halfway line and face them full-on with our arms locked together. I was in the middle of the line, on the centre spot, with Martin Hall, the Wigan and Great Britain hooker. The Samoans completed their performance then, in a show of defiance and intent, started to walk towards us in slow deliberate steps with their arms raised as if they had spears in their hands.

'Martin grunted "stuff it", or something like that, and started pacing towards them, dragging me with him. The Welsh straight line quickly changed to an arrowhead, with me and him at the tip of it. By the time the Samoans finished I was nose to nose with Inga Tuigamala, a beast of a rugby player who I was marking that night. Then there was a little bit of an in-your-face stand-off with no-one prepared to back down.

'It was about to kick off, in more ways than one and, when the whistle blew, all hell broke loose. I can't remember who took the ball to them first but he got absolutely smashed. Samoa had some huge players in their team and I think almost everyone would say it was the hardest game of rugby they had ever played. The crowd could hear and feel the hits as both sides took no prisoners. It was just brutal.'

At one point, Hall lurched like a punch-drunk boxer when his legs turned to jelly after he was the recipient of a ferocious hit, yet he managed to stagger back into the defensive line and make a vital tackle seconds later.

There were some comical moments, however, as Devereuex recalled: 'Muzzy took a knock to the head and was off the field having some treatment. Rory, our physio, said that Muzzy "didn't know who he was" so Clive, quick as a flash, replied: "Tell him he's Ellery Hanley and get him back on there!" It was mental.'

Samoa star Willie Poching, who later shone for Australia said: 'It sounded like the whole country was singing the Welsh national anthem. It was a war and everyone was willing to die for the cause in one of the most brutal and physical rugby league games ever. I still bear the scars! We went at it hammer and tongs; battering the hell out of each other. Players were going down left, right and centre and then getting back up for more. I was fortunate because I was at dummy half most of the time, so I was passing the ball to the other guys who'd get smashed. For both teams it was do or die. It was an absolute classic and an honour to be part of a game that's still revered.'

Jiffy Davies added: 'The crowd came with expectations and the game didn't let anyone down. I knew, looking at the side that we had, we could play any type of rugby and if they wanted to mix it, our boys were not going to take a step backwards. I had a feeling it was going to be absolutely brutal, one hell of a match, and it was.'

A young Iestyn Harris crossed for the game's opening try, then Samoa replied with Brian Laumatia carving open the Wales defence. A smart kick by Davies enabled Sullivan to bag Wales' second try, with Ellis going over late-on to seal a 22-10 win to set up a semi-final against England. Scott Quinnell, who relished the high-octane physical encounter with Samoa, was named Man of the Match.

Each Welsh player gave his all that night and it was a truly magnificent performance against a formidable opposition with a number of that Samoa team playing top level rugby league in Australia.

'Not only that,' said Devereux, 'but we had avenged the defeat our union team had suffered against them in 1991.The crowd at the Vetch knew they were watching players who would have starred for Wales at union if they hadn't gone to league. I honestly believe, if there hadn't been an exodus and we'd had the right coaches in place, Wales would have been real challengers for the 1991 and 1995 union World Cups, and in the Five Nations.

'It was brilliant for us to hear the crowd singing *Bread of Heaven* and other Welsh hymns as we thought those days had gone when we went to league. The singing gave us that extra little bit we needed to put Samoa to bed. They kept coming at us, but our defence held firm and, although Jiffy's goal-kicking was off on the night, he and Iestyn landed the drop-goals for us to close out the game. It was fantastic to be able to celebrate with the fans, and we did a lap of honour to thank them for their support. The atmosphere was just incredible.'

Devereux had sliced a knee open during the game and had to go to hospital to have the wound stitched. 'John Fairclough, who was a consultant orthopaedic specialist, was our team doctor and he took me to hospital in his Toyota Landcruiser. It was a beast of a car! He actually drove from Swansea to Cardiff's University Hospital of Wales and opened one of the theatres himself to operate on me. I had to have a number of stitches on the inside and on the outside of a nasty cut near the patella tendon of my left knee. I was panicking whether I would be fit for the semi-finals but, thanks to John, I made it.'

Celebrations were still in full flow when Devereux and Fairclough arrived back at the team hotel in Swansea, but would the party come back to haunt them? 'A lot of the boys were drinking but, in hindsight, I think we should have thought better of it as we had the biggest game in our history against England just six days later and they had a few extra days to prepare. There were a lot of bruised bodies in our camp the day after beating Samoa and going on the piss certainly hadn't helped our recovery. Don't get me wrong, our preparation for England was decent but every recovery day was vital.'

Whichever way it was viewed, nobody could hide from the fact that Wales were physically drained by the intensity of the seismic clash with Samoa. Old Trafford, scene of so many golden sporting memories, was half full with 30,000 English and Welsh spectators sitting side by side in the stands on a sunny Saturday afternoon.

'A lot of people had said the game with Samoa was our final but we were determined to prove them wrong. The match began at a ferocious tempo. We exchanged a few penalties but then failed to slow down their momentum. England got a roll on and we also dropped off a few tackles. I still believe we were suffering a bit of a hangover from the match with Samoa.

'Paul Newlove scored in the corner for England and we went in at half-time 7-4 down. We knew we had some work to do in the second half to contain and get the better of an England team that was laced with match winners. Andy Farrell popped a ball to Tony Smith, who sent Denis Betts in for a try, while Bobbie Goulding was orchestrating his forwards and creating space for his runners.

'Muzzy was sin-binned and being a man down against England was a body blow. They worked their man advantage well and it was Bobbie who kicked to my corner and behind me for Martin Offiah to score unopposed. I would have loved there to have been a television match official back then to check if he was onside.

'His second try came from another lovely kick behind me. I scrambled to cover my line and, as Offiah caught the ball, I pushed him as hard as I could in an attempt to force him over the dead ball line. The referee gave the try, which was at best very dubious. Judging by the look on the face of Offiah, he didn't seem convinced he had scored.

'The damage had been done. A great try from Rowland Phillips gave us a ray of hope but more brilliance from Goulding put Phil Clarke into space for a try to put an end to our World Cup dreams. We didn't have enough power and fuel in the tank to match England for the 80 minutes and they were worthy winners on the day, but I do wonder if the outcome might have been different had we had the same preparation time as them.

'We were gutted, as we believed it was our time. We had put together the strongest squad since being reformed a few years earlier and the camaraderie was the best I have ever experienced between a group of players, in union or league. Clive would always say we under-performed and didn't fulfil our destiny but I felt we gave it everything we had.'

Welsh rugby league was on a high despite the semi-final disappointment but it didn't last long. The impact of union going open and offering hefty wages prompted a return to the 15-a-side code. Davies, who had been at the forefront of the exodus north, was one of the first to move, joining Cardiff. Young joined him, while Scott Quinnell signed for Richmond, and Gibbs for Swansea.

Eventually, almost all the players in the squad who had gone to league returned to union and the team that beat Samoa and pushed England to the limit would never play another game together. Sadly, Welsh league's golden era was over.

17

The Toughest Fight of My Life

*'I was caught up in a nightmare situation and didn't know what was
going to happen next'*

John Devereux

It should have been a night to remember, a celebration of the best of British sport but it turned into a nightmare which still haunts John Devereux.

He didn't expect it to turn out that way when he accepted an invitation to join his pal Jonathan Davies at the BBC Sports Personality of The Year awards at the Queen Elizabeth II Centre in central London. It was December 1994 when the pair travelled south from Widnes to England's capital for the awards evening hosted, for the first time, by former tennis player Sue Barker.

They weren't the only rugby league stars in attendance as the all-conquering Wigan squad had been nominated for the best team award. The Wigan team, including Shaun Edwards, Andy Farrell, Jason Robinson, Martin Offiah, Denis Betts, Frano Botica, Gary Connolly and the late, great Inga Tuigamala had been in action earlier in the day and had turned up *en bloc*.

'We had a great night at the awards. It was a pleasure and privilege to be there, sitting in the audience with the *crème de la crème* of British sport,' said Devereux.

Damon Hill was voted Sports Personality of The Year by the public even though he had failed in his quest to be crowned Formula One world champion. Hill had been beaten to the title by a point in controversial circumstances after being taken out in the final Grand Prix of the season, in Australia, in a collision with Michael Schumacher. Neither of them finished the race, meaning the German won the world title. Hill even shared a Christian name with the Welsh rugby star for his full name was Damon Graham Devereux Hill.

'I love cars,' said Devereux. 'I'm a huge fan of F1 and have been to some Grand Prix races. Trevor Lloyd, whose father David originally came from Bedlinog, near Merthyr, and who had been a footballer with Wolverhampton Wanderers, had a garage, Lloyd Motors, in Ellesmere Port, had become a good friend while I was playing at Widnes.

'He came to our matches and was the sponsor of Paul Moriarty. Trevor used to invite me and Jonathan to the British F1 Grand Prix and other events. We had access to the paddock at some races and David Coulthard was among the drivers I met. I also had a ride in a touring car, as a passenger, on a test day and have never been so scared as the driver threw the car into the corners with minimal braking.

'So, it's fair to say I was delighted when Damon picked up the prestigious Sports Personality award. It was even better when I found out we shared the same name, Devereux. Who would have thought that? I was quite proud!'

When the formalities were over, Devereux, Davies, members of the Wigan squad, who had won the Team of the Year award, and other sporting stars headed for the post-event party.

The festive fun was, however, to turn sour later, a downcast Devereux explained: 'What happened next was embarrassing and humiliating, although I feel, to this day, I was the one singled-out and made an example of.

'Towards the end of the after-show party I was with some of the Wigan boys as they headed to the cloakroom to collect their kit bags. They'd played that afternoon in Hull then travelled straight to London after the match, dropping off their bags in the cloakroom on their way in.

'To this day I have no idea how it started, or who it was, and it definitely wasn't me, but a charity box that was located in the cloakroom was picked up from the counter and passed around like a rugby ball. An improvised game of rugby began and the kit bags were used as crash mats when diving to score a 'try'. It was just a bit of innocent, if boisterous, fun, and as far as I was aware the charity box had then been returned to the cloakroom counter before we left.'

After the impromptu game ended, its participants piled into taxi cabs and headed back to their hotel for more drinks. The following morning Devereux and Davies, who had not been involved with the high-spirited game of rugby in the cloakroom, caught a train back to Widnes. The pair had enjoyed a great time and that was the end of the Sports Personality of The Year experience as far as Devereux was concerned.

Unfortunately it wasn't, as a startled Devereux was to find out a couple of weeks later when he was collared by Wales and Widnes rugby league colossus Jim Mills, who was a big shot at the Lancashire club: 'I was injured at the time and was attending the Boxing Day derby clash away to Warrington at Wilderspool when Jim approached me and said: "Can I have a word?"'

'Jim asked me if I had got into any trouble at the event in London. I looked at him, bemused, because I didn't know what he was talking about. I had completely forgotten about the game of rugby in the cloakroom, but my heart rate shot up when he said he had been contacted by the Metropolitan Police and that they wanted to speak to me about something that happened that night.

'I agreed to meet the police, even though I had no idea what they wanted to speak to me about, and two officers from London came to my house in Widnes. They were very friendly and asked me a number of questions because, according to the building's CCTV, I had been identified as the last of the group of players to leave the cloakroom. I answered their questions as best as I could and confirmed I was present at the event and the names of other people who were present with me. Apparently my great friend Denis Betts had also been spoken to, but no one else. The police then hit me with a bombshell. They said there had been a complaint from the QEII Centre, alleging a charity box had been damaged and its contents were missing.

'They went on their way and I thought that was the end of the matter, but, to my surprise, a week or so later, I received a phone call from the Metropolitan Police saying I had to go to London to give a formal statement and be questioned under oath. They advised me that I should take legal advice and appoint a solicitor to represent me. I was gobsmacked. I couldn't believe it, thinking: "What the hell is going on?"

'I spoke to Jim Mills again and he gave me the name of a solicitor he knew well from Liverpool, Brian Kavannagh, and I made an appointment to see him. We met in his office and I explained what had happened in the cloakroom. Brian agreed to act for me in the case and explained what would happen next.

'I was summoned to attend Bow Street Police Station at a specific date and time, and Brian and I travelled to London by train. The police wanted to take a formal statement from me and it soon became clear during questioning that the Met were taking this extremely seriously as the alleged incident had taken place at a high-profile event and it seemed that the authorities at the QEII were eager for someone to be seen to be punished.

'I wanted to assist them and answered each question honestly, explaining and clarifying everything I knew, just like when the police had visited me at my home. Brian and I were then shown some closed-circuit TV footage of me and a few other people who had been identified as being present in the cloakroom playing a game of rugby. It also showed us leaving.

'Interview over, we left for the railway station and held a debrief on the train *en route* to Liverpool. Brian said that, in his opinion, the evidence was inconclusive and he didn't think the Crown Prosecution Service would pursue the matter any further. I was mightily relieved but, a few days later, Brian called me to give me the bad news that the CPS had decided to pursue the case and I would have to go back to London to be formally charged, which happened on 31 December.

'Because I had been charged, I could not talk about the case and could not put my side of the story. That would have to wait until I went to court. It wasn't the best way to end the year and totally destroyed our family Christmas. I had been used to seeing my name on the back pages of the tabloids but what happened over that period certainly opened my eyes to how the gutter press operates.

'They descended on our home in Widnes and I was shocked at how despicably many of them behaved: one so-called journalist pressed a finger on the doorbell and kept it ringing for ages in an attempt to get me to come to the door, and on another occasion, I lay in the boot of the car and was driven out of the garage and away from the house. It was awful for me but it was far worse for my wife who went through hell during that period. Also, all these years later, I can only but apologise again to my neighbours for the distress this caused them too, having the road filled by camera vans and the pavement packed with journalists and film crews.

'A court appearance in London was looming in the New Year and I was fraught with worry. It felt like my whole world was imploding and that my rugby career, my professional reputation and my personal integrity were all in jeopardy. It was a nightmare situation because I knew I hadn't stolen anything, yet I didn't know what was going to happen next.

'Attending court wasn't straightforward. On one occasion, there was an adjournment and we went home from London to Liverpool having got nowhere. All those days spent with Brian were at a massive cost to me but I was adamant I needed and wanted to clear my name.

'The date for the court hearing was finally set and I met a barrister who would represent me. It was a world I wasn't used to. It was a horrific and stressful time for everyone in my family.

'I will maintain to my dying day I did nothing wrong other than get caught up in some tomfoolery. I am an honest person and have never stolen anything in my life. I would never take money from anywhere, let alone from a charity box. Throughout my life I've given so much time helping to raise money for charities. I am an ambassador for Prostate Cymru and have regularly supported fund-raising activities for Velindre Cancer Centre in Cardiff. I'm also a trustee of the Welsh Rugby Players Benevolent Fund, raising money to help former Welsh rugby players who have fallen on hard times. I give to charities – I don't take from them.

'A dark cloud was hanging over me until I could prove my innocence. I was anxious and nervous when I entered Bow Street Magistrates Court for the hearing. My barrister and the prosecution did their stuff and it didn't take long before the charge of theft was dismissed – I wasn't guilty. That was what I most wanted.'

However, it wasn't the end of the proceedings for Devereux as a lesser charge remained, of criminal damage to the charity box: 'I just wanted the nightmare to end, and because I had definitely taken part in the idiotic 'game' that night, I thought I should do the right thing and take responsibility. A charity box had been damaged during a foolish escapade and I had been involved. That was fair enough, but what happened next was a hell of a shock.

'Concluding the case of criminal damage, the chair of the magistrates called me a "rugby hooligan" – something I will remember until my last breath – and fined me £5,000 which had to paid immediately. I was in such a state, and so relieved that the charge of theft had been dropped, that I wrote a cheque at the back of the court and handed it to the clerk without thinking. Looking back however, that appeared to be such an excessive amount for an item that would cost just a few pounds to replace. It was clear to me that I was being made an example of. All told, including my legal costs, the ordeal cost me about £15,000, but it wasn't about money, it was about preserving my reputation as being an honest person. I wasn't a thief and the court acknowledged that.'

The story was on TV, radio and headlines were splashed across newspapers, yet although the case had ended and a verdict had been reached, its repercussions continued: 'I felt the affair tarnished my opportunities of working outside the game, as a media pundit or after-dinner guest speaker, for a number of years. I had appeared on *A Question of Sport* and had a reasonably high profile but the invites dried up on the back of the court case and it took years for them to reappear.'

The effect on Devereux was painful and his normal cheery persona disappeared as he struggled to come to terms with the ordeal, with dark thoughts going through his mind.

'I was so low and felt so desperate that it was the one and only time in my life where I could have put an end to it all. Although I had been exonerated of theft, it didn't stop some supposed fans of other clubs chanting about it on the terraces and calling me a thief. Even now, on social media, anonymous keyboard warriors have brought it up and had a pop at me. People like that, who like to smear and demean but hide their real identity, are despicable human beings, but it says more about them than it does about me.'

Devereux and his wife had survived a hellish few months and wanted nothing more than to put the incident behind them. With two young daughters growing up, the couple were determined to look forward to happier times: 'I can't thank Alison enough, and it needs placing on the record how grateful I am of her support. Without Alison I don't think I could have handled that nightmare. We've been together since our schooldays and I knew that she was the one for me, but I couldn't have foreseen back then how important her strength and determination would be during our married life. That was a dark and traumatic period which had a huge and deep impact on Alison. It also taught me a lesson that thoughtless actions can have serious consequences and hurt the ones you care for most. My admiration and love for her know no bounds – *diolch cariad*.'

18

Back to Rugby Union

*'Come on, we're going. Widnes are in breach of contract and
John Devereux is leaving, goodbye.'*

Simon Cohen

John Devereux had stayed loyal to Widnes despite the club's money
troubles and the loss of some of their best players to rival teams,
but found himself in an unusual position as the new Super League
loomed on the horizon.

He was the only player at the Chemics, their then nickname which
later became the Vikings, who had been offered and signed a contract
with media tycoon Rupert Murdoch's News Corporation. Murdoch's
empire included *Sky*, *The Sun*, *The News of the World*, *The Times* and
a number of other publishing and television outlets throughout the
world.

Rugby league was embroiled in a civil war, with the Australian
Rugby League making serious financial offers to big names in an
effort to stave off the threat posed by Murdoch, who wanted to
broadcast matches on his satellite television channels.

Jonathan Davies, Devereux's teammate at Widnes before joining
Warrington, was one of the stars who had been targeted by the ARL,
which was supported by Kerry Packer and Optus Vision, Murdoch's
bitter broadcasting rival, for television rights and supremacy in the
sport.

Super League Australia ran parallel to the ARL for one season
before a peace deal was reached with the competitions uniting to
form the National Rugby League. If you were on the wanted list of
either organisation in the league civil war that took place before the
coming together you were literally quids in, as Devereux and Davies
were to find out as the cash was splashed around.

Davies went to Wigan to meet the ARL officials who had come to Britain to try and sign players in the battle for control of the sport with Murdoch, and there was a lucrative spin-off off another Welsh star.

'It was quite funny,' revealed Devereux, 'because Kevin Ellis, a teammate of Jiffy at Warrington and with Wales, had tagged along with him for the ride. Kevin got lucky because, at the meeting, the ARL chiefs turned to him and asked if he would be interested in playing in Australia too.

'Kevin couldn't believe his luck. He'd gone with Jiffy as company and was now being offered pots of money. It didn't take him long to agree to a deal and he quickly put pen to paper as the money on offer was too good to turn down. The ARL and Murdoch's mob had millions of pounds in their war chests and were prepared to use it in an attempt to get their way. Jiffy also signed for the ARL and would be heading Down Under to play for the Townsville Cowboys in northern Queensland.'

Devereux's deal with News Corporation meant he was committed to remaining with Widnes, but could the club afford to pay his lucrative Super League contract while competing in the division below it?

Widnes had finished a disappointing 14th in 1995, which was the lowest during his time at the club. The following season was going to see the launch of the new Super League format in the UK, with summer rugby being among its innovations. The Chemics thought they had a place in the inaugural Super League season based on their performances over the previous 10 years, but there was a late and unexpected twist.

'We were cut from the 11-team Super League because its bosses had pulled a flanker,' said Devereux. 'Out of the blue they announced they had picked London Broncos rather than us because they wanted a club in England's capital city. We were the odd one out. It was unbelievable. We were in a state of shock because we thought our history and what we had brought to the league as Wigan's main rivals in the 1980s and early 1990s would ensure us a place.'

The repercussions were enormous for Widnes because it meant lower crowds and a lower income. It was the first time Widnes had dropped out of the top flight and it was a bitter pill to swallow. Their axing from Super League resulted in the club's well-documented financial problems descending into a full-blown crisis.

It was another nail in the Chemics' coffin, and Devereux started the new season seeing his pals and some of his former teammates who had moved on and were basking in the razzmatazz as Sky spent millions of pounds promoting its new Super League summer tournament, bringing in bigger crowds and more money.

'Prepping for the new season was a bit odd because I was the only player at Widnes to have signed a Super League contract, which had been tagged on to a new deal I had committed to at Widnes. Our collapse into financial administration meant that a lot of familiar faces had left the club the previous season despite us reaching the 1993 Challenge Cup final. I had gone to play in Australia for Manly over the summer and, at the end of that loan period, I was offered a long-term deal by the Sea Eagles, but Widnes didn't want to sell me and I had to return to Naughton Park.'

Fast forward three years and Devereux's agent at the time, Alan McColm, was calling him to say he had links with Sky's News Corporation and could get me a Super League contract. I didn't hang around signing the deal because it was a lot of money. It would keep me at Widnes and, I thought, playing Super League in the UK.

Rugby was going through a period of major change and it wasn't just in league. Union had gone open, allowing the payment of players, in a move in which the repercussions are still being felt today in Wales and England because neither country has found a way of making the 15-a-side code economically viable. The International Rugby Board – now World Rugby – chairman, Vernon Pugh, made the announcement in August 1995, but it wasn't until the following year that professionalism really came in with a galaxy of league stars switching codes on short-term deals or returning home permanently, as some Welsh lads did.

Devereux was a prime target for union clubs and with Widnes languishing outside of Super League the possibility of him being lured away increased. It wasn't long before he received a telephone call. It was former Wales outside-half Paul Turner, then the coach of Cheshire club Sale, who made the first move.

'We were into the new league season when I got a call saying Paul wanted to speak to me about the possibility of playing on loan in union with Sale at the end of the season with Widnes. I never expected to be able to play union again because we had become ineligible after breaking our amateur status and playing league. Anybody getting paid to play league had been deemed *persona non grata* by union authorities ever since clubs in northern England broke away from the Rugby Football Union in 1895 and began paying players.'

It had taken union a century to follow suit, and the boot was now on the other foot, so to speak, with union clubs in England, Wales and France soon paying bigger wages than league clubs in Britain. Overnight, professionalism essentially ended the movement of top Welsh union stars to league. The gloves were off and the moves were being made the other way.

'It was music to my ears,' said Devereux, 'and I jumped at the chance to play union again. What also made it attractive was the chance to link up with Paul, as Sale's training ground was only about 30 minutes away along the M56 from my home in Widnes.

'The deal was done quickly, suiting all parties, with Widnes receiving money from Sale for agreeing to the arrangement, and I signed a contract to play union, and get paid – what a novelty! It also meant, I would be playing rugby all-year round, league in the spring and summer, and union in the autumn and winter.'

It wasn't just the rugby union clubs that were looking to recruit former union stars, as Devereux recalls: 'In early 1996, a number of former Welsh internationals now plying their trade in RL were contacted by the WRU about the possibility of returning to play in Wales. We agreed to meet and a secret rendezvous was arranged at the old Celtic Manor Hotel. I remember travelling down with Paul Moriarty and Dai Young after training with our clubs, and other players were present, including Jiffy. Representing the WRU was Glanmor Griffiths and Vernon Pugh QC, with a few other committee members. They asked if we were interested in returning and what would it take to get us back, not just at international level but also for Welsh clubs, then began to indicate which clubs they'd offer us to. Apparently, I would be going to Llanelli or Pontypridd, Paul to Swansea, Dai to Cardiff and Jiffy to Llanelli. After the meeting the WRU sent us all contracts and I remember Paul faxing his contract back to Cardiff from the newsagent close to where we both lived in Widnes. Disappointingly, there must have been a change of heart at the WRU's end because their central contracts plan never materialised and I never heard from them again. Jiffy and Dai did return to Welsh club rugby via a different route and Paul went back to Swansea that October. After hearing nothing from the WRU, and knowing Paul Turner at nearby Sale wanted me, I opted to play for the Sharks for the 1996-97 season.

Devereux's dream of working with Turner failed to materialise though as the mercurial, former Newbridge, Newport, London

'1989 was a very memorable year. I was happy to continue playing rugby union but when Dougie Laughton offered me a life-changing fee to join Widnes, and team up again with Jonathan Davies, my career path took a northern twist.'

'Within a year of going north I was back in Wales with Widnes, for the 1990-91 season-opener, the Charity Shield, when we beat Wigan 24-8 at The Vetch in Swansea. The game was held in Wales to test the potential support for a reconstituted Wales RL team.'

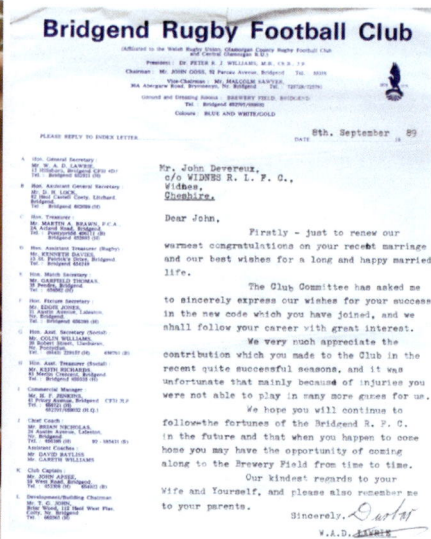

'1989 was also a special year as it was when I married Alison. We'd been together since our schooldays, and moved to Widnes just weeks after our wedding.'

'Contrary to the public perception, many rugby clubs were very kind and supportive when their players switched to rugby league, as this letter from Bridgend illustrates. They understood the situation and wanted me to succeed. I'll be forever grateful for the way they handled the situation.'

'My higher public profile led to several new experiences, including an appearance on A Question of Sport alongside former cricketer Ian Botham and boxer Herbie Hide.'

'As a big money signing I knew I needed to show the Widnes fans that I would repay their faith in me, and I think I managed that. I didn't take a step backwards when challenged by those wanting a piece of me, and took plenty of steps forward to score 125 tries in 225 appearances.'

'Cup finals and trophy triumphs came thick and fast during my early years at Widnes. In 1993 (below) we celebrated after beating Leeds in the Challenge Cup semi-final at Central Park. Rugby genius Phil Larder was the architect of much of our success and went on to change the face of rugby union. Paul Moriarty, in the sunglasses, didn't let his need for crutches to get in the way of a changing room party.'

'On the charge against Leigh at Naughton Park during my first season with Widnes (above).'

'One of my 125 tries for Widnes (below left). Despite my expression I was always happy to score!'

'After victories against Workington, Carlisle, Featherstone Rovers and St. Helens, we faced Leeds in the 1992 Regal Trophy final (below right).'

'Andy Farrell didn't take any prisoners as a player, even as an 18-year-old, as I quickly discovered. He took the same attitude into coaching as his outstanding results with Ireland have demonstrated.'

'The Widnes team that faced Leeds at Central Park in the 1992 Regal Trophy Final which we won 24-0 after a rugby masterclass from Jonathan Davies who scored a try, three goals and a drop goal.'

'Widnes missed out on the first year of the new multi-million pound Super league and I spent my final years in rugby league's second division, playing teams like Phil Larder's Keithley Cougars (left) and Featherstone Rovers (below).'

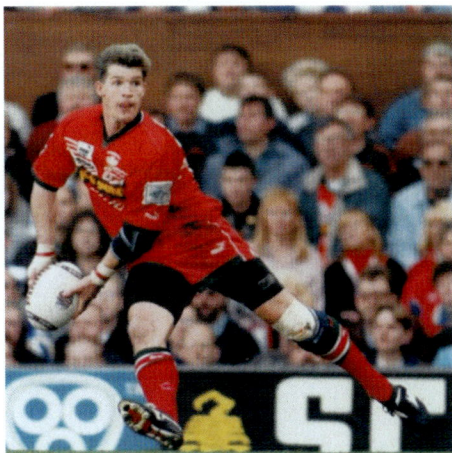

'Pulling on that red shirt was such an emotional experience on every one of the 12 occasions I played for Wales RL.'

'The union exiles and the Welsh heritage players from northern England combined brilliantly, and we had an outstanding team, winning the European Championship in 1995, and reaching the World Cup semi-finals in 1995 and 2000.'

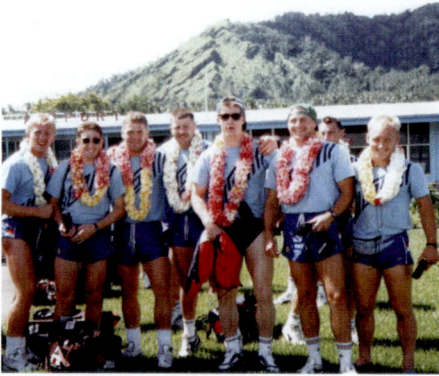

'On tour with Great Britain to Papua New Guinea and New Zealand in 1990.' (left)

'Three Welsh recruits to league went on the tour (left lower). I played five matches, including the mud bath in Taranaki (below) and scored two tries, while Dai Bishop played in six games and scored one try, but neither of us made the cut for the five Tests. Jiffy scored 6 tries, 34 goals and played in every Test. We drew the series with Papua New Guinea 1-1 and beat New Zealand 2-1.'

'The 1992 World Cup Final (below) against Australia has bittersweet memories for me. It was one of the pinnacles of my career, and I was the last Welshman to play in rugby league's showcase event, but we lost the match 10-6 and the man I was marking evaded me to score the winning try: "It wasn't your fault" I was told years later, but it still hurts that we were that close to being World Champions.'

'We found success in 1993 when the Great Britain team whitewashed New Zealand in a three-Test series. There were actually four Tests against New Zealand that autumn as Wales were first up to face the Kiwis, but we narrowly lost 24-19.'

'It was a good Test series for me as I scored a try in the opening match, which we won 17-0. I then scored two tries in the 29-12 second Test victory, but didn't trouble the scorer in our final 29-10 win.'

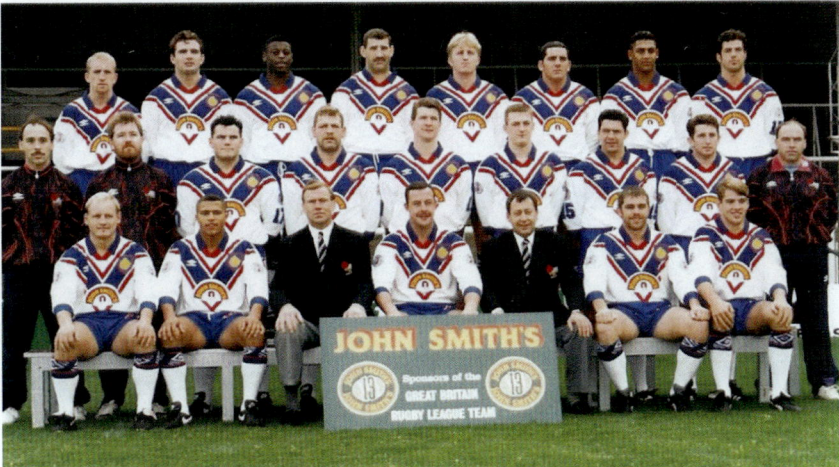

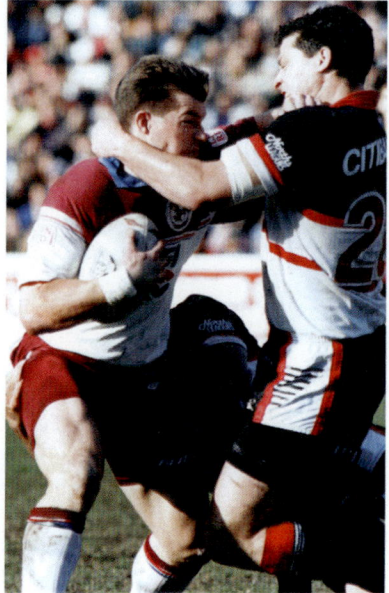

'I enjoyed a fantastic, but far too short, spell playing in Australia's ultra competitive National Rugby League for Manly Sea Eagles. I scored two tries in 15 games and would have happily stayed there for much longer, but Widnes demanded I return to Lancashire.'

'Rugby union becoming a professional sport coincided with financial difficulties at Widnes, so when Sale came calling in 1996 I jumped at the chance. Another move, to Worcester on loan, followed from January to May 1999, before I headed home to Wales and an emotional return to Bridgend for the 1999-2000 season. Scoring tries again at the Brewery Field meant a lot to me.'

'My return to Bridgend lasted for three seasons, from 1999 to 2002, during which I made over 60 appearances and scored eight tries, including this one (above) against Dunvant at the Brewery Field. We had some fun at the end of my last game for the Ravens (below left) before I left for a season with Pontypool RFC.'

'My last three seasons in rugby union, 2003-06, were spent with Maesteg RFC (below right), a lovely old club a few miles away from Pontycymer, and it was with them that I played my final game, against Ebbw Vale.'

'I finished my playing career with the Bridgend Blue Bulls (above), and still enjoyed causing havoc in opposition defences. I ended on a high with two British Championships in the Amateur RL Conference in 2003 and 2005.'

'After retirement as a player I followed in the footsteps of Welsh greats Jim Mills and Mike Nicholas, spending six years as team manager of the Wales RL team (below). It was a great honour and I was pleased to be able to give something back to the game that had given me so much.'

'My Groggs - amongst my favourite rugby mementos of an eventful career.'

'As well as being a proud ambassador for Prostrate Cymru, I'm a passionate fundraiser for the Velindre Cancer Centre in Cardiff (below left) and a trustee of the Welsh Rugby Players Benevolent Fund. Whether speaking at events or sponsored bike rides, I'm committed to doing what I can for these excellent causes.'

'Lyndon Thomas (below right) has been such a good friend and mentor for over 40 years. His guidance helped me secure a job with a house builder after I left college, and he pointed me in the direction of the pharmaceutical industry when I returned to Wales.'

'From my lovely mum and dad, Valerie and Peter, to my wonderful wife Alison and our two gorgeous daughters, Jessica and Ellen, and the newest member of the Devereux clan, my grandson Beaudie, I've been truly blessed with an incredible family and I cannot adequately express how much they all mean to me.'

'Being capped by Wales in rugby union and rugby league was very special, and to have played for Great Britain RL and for the British & Irish Lions was the icing on the cake. I've had a career I can be proud of. Only a few Welsh players can show these caps at the end of their careers, as a double dragon and double lion, and I consider myself fortunate to be one of them.'

'During 2023, as this book was being written, I was inducted into the Welsh Sport Hall of Fame at its annual ceremony in Cardiff. My dear friend Jim Mills presented the award, which meant a lot, as did the presence of a large number of friends from Cyncoed who'd kept the secret from me. It was a lovely night and one I'll always cherish.

Welsh, Sale and Wales play-maker, along with Sale chief executive Brian Wilkinson, were then released by the club.

'By the time I started my new adventure, Sale was under a bit of a cloud and didn't have a coach. I'd hardly got my foot through the door when it transpired John Mitchell had been promoted to head coach. 'Mitch' had played for New Zealand on tour but had never been capped by the All Blacks. He'd also been a housemate of Warren Gatland in New Zealand and knew his stuff.'

Mitchell and Gatland had been teammates at provincial side Waikato – they had given Devereux and Wales a stuffing during the humiliating 'tour of death' in 1988, and Mitchell had been a player-coach in Ireland before becoming Turner's assistant coach at Sale while continuing to perform as a player.

The hard-nosed Kiwi quickly made an impression on Devereux, who wasn't in the least surprised Mitchell went on to become head coach of the All Blacks at the 2003 World Cup in Australia and have two stints as an assistant with England, as well as occupying prime positions with South Africa's professional rugby franchises.

'He was brilliant. Mitch was a fine player and was equally impressive as a coach. He had so many modern ideas and they were great to see and hear. It was refreshing and we started the campaign well. I loved being back in union. What struck me in my first game back was how easy it was, physically, compared to the rough, tough and high-octane world of league. I made a number of breaks and, at times, I was going through like a proverbial knife through butter.

'We had some exciting backs at Sale but we struggled in the scrum against the big teams. At that time, everyone was on the hunt for world class tight head props and second rows. We did well enough to finish fifth in the English Premiership, just missing out on fourth and a place in Europe's new and growing Heineken Cup the following season. If we had beaten Leicester at home in our final match of the season, we would have taken fourth from them. The match ended in a 20-20 draw but will always be remembered for an horrific injury to our second row Charlie Vivian. Martin Johnson, who captained the British and Irish Lions to glory in South Africa in 1997, and England to the World Cup in 2003, cleaned him out of a ruck and Charlie suffered a badly broken leg.

'There was a bad atmosphere after that game, over that controversial incident and the whispers and veiled threats concerning Mitchell's eligibility to play for Sale. He had played a number of games for the club during the early part of the season and made a big difference to the performance of the team, but it had emerged he may not have had the correct registration criteria to play in the Premiership. Word had got around that if Leicester hadn't qualified for the Heineken Cup, they would have sued the rugby authorities for allowing him to play for Sale. As soon as Mitch knew there was a potential problem with his registration, he stopped playing and concentrated on his coaching.'

Sale had a chance to avenge that defeat in the final of the Pilkington Cup at Twickenham after beating Richmond, Orrell, Northampton Saints, and then Harlequins in the semis. By the time of the final, the new rugby league season had started and Devereux was back at Widnes, unable to play for Sale in the showpiece event. He did manage to go and watch the game at Twickers, however, but was disappointed when Leicester won 9-3 in a dour encounter.

'I had really enjoyed that first season back in union, it was a breath of fresh air for me after so long in league. Being back at Widnes and playing in the Second Division was tough. We played in Cumbria against Workington, Whitehaven and Barrow, and against Yorkshire sides like Dewsbury, Batley and Hunslet. I won't make any bones about it, that was tough.

'Before I left to go back to Widnes, Sale had made advances to me about signing full-time for them. Mitch was attempting to build a side to compete with the best in England and Europe and I was chuffed he wanted me as part of his plan to rebuild the squad.'

The Sale side was going to look a lot different the following season but there was a major stumbling block, Widnes would not let Devereux go. Dougie Laughton had returned to Widnes as coach. He had left Widnes in 1991 to go to Leeds and had built a brilliant side there that competed with Wigan, but he still couldn't topple them off the top spot. In the end, Dougie parted company with Leeds and returned to Lancashire.

'We had so many new faces at Widnes, including lots of kids, and there were only a few players left from the great times of a few years earlier, like the Hulme brothers, David and Paul, who were still putting in a shift week in, week out. They were not big physically but were tough and could play in virtually any position in the team, and quite rightly regarded as club legends. Steve McCurrie, who signed for Widnes as a promising 16-year-old, was another still there and we had a few local lads who had returned from rival clubs.'

But, just before the end of the 1996-97 season, the club's money troubles returned and Devereux became a victim of a growing crisis.

'I suppose it didn't help Widnes that they were paying me a contract that, although subsidised by News Corporation, was still at Super League level. I could see a potential problem coming. Sure enough, Widnes missed paying my monthly wages on a few occasions so Simon Cohen, who had become my agent, decided to see what offer Sale were prepared to make me to go and play for them full-time.

'Their offer was a lot more than what I was on at Widnes, so we called a meeting with Chemics' chairman Tom Fleet and club president Tony Chambers to discuss options. It was apparent Widnes were struggling to pay my contract and other player contracts so Simon offered them a way out, they could release me – I was owed over £12,000 by Widnes by that stage – and I would walk away from my league contract and sign for Sale. However, there was also another spanner in the works as I had been working for club director Sam Evans' demolition company for five years as a contracts manager.

'He wasn't happy with the prospect of me leaving the club, or his company. It was an awful meeting during a terrible time for me and my family. At the end of the meeting, during which the directors claimed to have done nothing wrong and obviously believed that my contract with them was watertight, Fleet basically said I'd only leave Widnes over his dead body. With that, Simon got up and said: "Come on, we're going, Widnes are in breach of contract and John is leaving, goodbye."

'I felt so bad I was leaving Widnes on such terms but loyalty works both ways. I had been ultra loyal to Widnes. I could have asked for a move at any time during my years with them but hadn't. I've subsequently found out that Wigan came in for me a few years earlier and I was never told, but, hey, that's life!

'Widnes were the club I had served for eight years of my rugby career and I had given my all, 100% in every game. I had and still have a strong bond with the fans, having stuck with Widnes through the good and the bad times. They were the only professional league club I played for in Britain.

'I love Widnes to this day, the fans living in the town and the friends we made as a family, but the reality of professional sport is it is a business and players have a short career to maximise their earnings.'

It was Sale who provided that opportunity with Widnes' failure to pay Devereux's salary on time and his worries over their future pushing him through the exit door.

19

Sharks, Warriors and Ravens

'Would you be interested in coming back to play for Bridgend?'

Leighton Samuel

The ink had barely dried on the three-year contract John Devereux had signed with Sale Sharks, which cemented his full-time return to rugby union, before he hot-footed it to a boot camp with the British Army to link up with the players who were halfway through their pre-season team building and bonding exercises at the Army's Catterick Garrison near Richmond in north Yorkshire.

Devereux wasn't given the time to view the facilities at the camp, which houses the Army's largest garrison, or to discover it once housed one of Yorkshire's largest cinemas, the Ritz, which had more than a thousand seats. Opened on 21 December 1940, the Ritz had closed in July 1977 following declining usage with its site being transformed into a health and beauty salon.

The Sale squad stayed at the Vimy Barracks, which were named after a famous First World War battle when British, French and Canadian soldiers joined forces to attack the German front line. The battle, for a strategic ridge near Arras in France, claimed thousands of lives on all sides and four members of the Canadian Corps received the Victoria Cross, the highest military award of the British and Commonwealth honours system, for their actions and bravery during the battle.

'I was unaware of the importance of the base or its history when I was let in by security at one of its entrance gates and pointed in the direction of our accommodation,' said Devereux. 'The only thing I knew at that time about Catterick, was its dentists tended to be busy on Mondays fixing the teeth of soldiers who had broken or chipped them while prizing opening the tops of beer and lager bottles with their gnashers during weekend drinking sessions.'

There was hardly any time for Devereux to put his bags down before he was ordered into a team meeting, and be greeted by some new faces. Sale's two new signings from New Zealand, Shane Howarth and Simon Mannix, were there along with Ireland back-row forward Dion O'Cuinneagain.

Howarth was later to make major headlines for the wrong reasons with Wales after being unveiled as a key player in the eligibility scandal which rocked Welsh rugby in 2000 following an investigation by a Sunday newspaper that revealed he was ineligible for his adopted country because his claim of having a Welsh grandparent was found to be untrue. Flanker Brett Sinkinson was another Kiwi who got caught up in it for the same reason. He'd also got a number of caps under Wales coach, Graham Henry.

'I hadn't met Shane previously but knew he had been capped by New Zealand. The All Blacks don't give caps away – to this day they haven't, unlike nations such as Wales who have handed them out like confetti – so clearly he was class. As far as the other Sale players, though, I knew most of the lads from my stint at Sale the previous campaign.

'We stayed in the same dorms as the soldiers, the majority of whom were on summer leave. They were mostly Gurkhas and Fijians who couldn't go home because it was too expensive. The physical training at the base was brutal, and coach John Mitchell beasted us to such a degree some of us were physically sick. There were lots of cross country runs but they were made harder by us having to carry heavy objects, like a telegraph pole and tank tracks welded into the shape of a large stretcher. We finished off the last day doing the assault course. Mitch then put together a file for each player containing our goals for the season and the team charter and regulations. He was very thorough and used a lot of sports psychology in his coaching.'

Despite the success of the training camp, the start of Sale's 1997-98 campaign didn't go to plan with defeats to Saracens, Newcastle Falcons, Harlequins, Leicester and Bath. The losing streak was broken by a draw with Gloucester but it was followed with another defeat against Northampton Saints.

'The team then travelled to London to play Saracens at Vicarage Road, the home of Elton John's Watford Football Club. 'Sarries' were a formidable team that included the great Michael Lynagh, Australia's 1991 World Cup winning play-maker and one heck of a player at outside-half, flanker Francois Pienaar, who captained South

Africa to glory in the 1995 tournament, and the great French centre Philippe Sella, who was one of the best and most difficult opponents I faced during my career, whether it was at international or club level.'

Sale lost a terrific encounter and were heading back to Manchester on the team bus when Howarth took a call on his mobile phone from Wales' first Kiwi coach, Graham Henry. Quickly nicknamed 'The Great Redeemer', Henry had taken the helm following the humiliating tour of South Africa, and the record 96-13 defeat against the Springboks in Pretoria in June 1998.

According to Devereux: 'Henry had been at Vicarage Road and told Shane that he and I had played well. Then he apparently asked Shane if, assuming he could prove his eligibility, he'd be interested in playing for Wales. That phone call certainly made for some interesting conversations on the long journey north. Shane did find an alleged Welsh grandparent and was capped 19 times by Wales, but a newspaper investigation revealed the grandparent was in fact English.'

A World Rugby hearing hauled the Welsh Rugby Union – who didn't offer any defence – over the coals and Howarth's second international career with Wales was over. He'd been a major figure in Wales' record-equalling winning streak under Henry and had picked up in excess of £130,000 in appearance money and win bonuses from the WRU.

'It left a sour taste in the mouth with many people,' said Devereux, 'as that money and those caps could have gone to a qualified player. I can't understand why players born and brought up in one country would want to appear for another country. I certainly wouldn't because I'm Welsh and proud of it. I suspect money may come into it because the financial rewards of switching countries to play for some countries are considerable.

'Nathan Hughes, the Fijian who played for England, was a rarity in being honest why he made the switch, saying it was for the money. Others come up with different reasons but being highly paid has to be a huge attraction. I hate to say it but there's an argument Test rugby is becoming like club rugby with players 'transferring' from nation to nation, which is plain wrong.'

As part of his three-year contract, Devereux also took up a role in Sale's marketing department. He was given the job of putting together the match day programme for home fixtures, which was something he enjoyed: 'I really got into it and tried to make it interesting and informative for the spectators. I added sections like news from the physio's bench featuring the injured players trying to get back to fitness.

'Including the coach's view from Mitch and the chairman's notes was also important and I was also keen on publishing a fairly accurate team line-up as I felt we owed that to our loyal supporters, but it proved to be extremely difficult as Mitch never liked publicising who was playing until just before a game. I suppose the only consolation for our fans was the team at the time more or less picked itself as we didn't have a large squad.'

Sale, with its location in rugby league's heartland, was in an ideal place to sign big names from the 13-a-side code and Devereux was joined at the club by Widnes pair Darren Wright and Adrian Hadley, Bridgend old boy Kevin Ellis from Warrington and Barrie-Jon Mather from Wigan.

One of the attractions of first-class rugby union are the European club competitions, and a trip to Clermont Ferrand to face Montferrand, who subsequently were rebranded as Clermont Auvergne, and to Montpellier in Europe's second-tier Challenge Cup stuck in the mind of Devereux: 'We were due to play them on consecutive weekends so Mitch thought it would be a good idea if we stayed in France and used the time to train and prepare for the Montpellier game. He also calculated it would save both the money and time spent travelling. We stayed in an outdoor pursuits centre called Club Correze which was then owned by Ged Byrne from Wigan RL.'

Sale played Montferrand in round one of the cup on 7 September 1997 at the Stade Marcel-Michelin in Clermont. They were some side and had fantastic support. The city, which is situated almost slap bang in the centre of France, lay in the shadow of a huge Michelin tyre factory, with the stadium named in honour of the company founder's son who fought with the French Resistance during the Second World War and was murdered by the Nazis at their Buchenwald death camp in January 1945. The company employed thousands of locals and were the main backers of the club. It wasn't a great start to the tournament for Sale as they were beaten 25-16.

Devereux had a funny feeling it was going to be a long week in France: 'The bad start to the trip continued when we got to the pursuits centre. It was a beautiful location in the mountains but that wasn't good enough for some. We had barely checked into the dorms when one of our props, Paul Smith, lost his rag as he wasn't happy with the centre's low star accommodation rating. He threw his ruck sack on to a bed in anger then saw it bounce straight through a window.

'Once we'd settled in, we discovered it was actually a very nice place and Ged and his wife couldn't do enough for us. We did a lot of fitness training, and had time to practise and perfect our set moves. Mitch also thought it would be a great idea if we did a team-based mini-triathlon, in and around the reservoir. Firstly swimming across it, before cycling and running around it. Adolf Hadley and I were not the best swimmers so we donned life jackets. Adolf actually put two on and everyone took the piss out of him. We swam breast stroke while fast swimmers, like Mitch and Matthew Tetlow, put their heads down in the water and did front crawl all the way.

'I was with Steve Diamond, who went on to coach Sale and Worcester Warriors, and we looked for the shortest route to swim. We quickly spotted a short cut that avoided the need of swimming the whole width of the reservoir. By swimming to the wall of the dam on our left and then running across the wall itself we could reach the bike station with minimal swimming required. When we got to the bikes, Adolf was still swimming across the reservoir, ensuring his team were going to be last out of the water. Unknown to us, though, someone had thought it would be funny to sabotage the bikes by undoing the wheel nuts. When we grabbed the bikes, the wheels fell off. It was hilarious!'

After the loss to Montferrand, Sale's players were determined to give a better account of themselves following a 200-mile plus, four-hour bus ride to Montpellier, a beautiful city on the Mediterranean coast, but were well-beaten 30-12.

Devereux remained with Sale but, come January 1999, his 10-year spell 'up north' in league and union was coming to an end. Sale had decided he was surplus to requirements and put him on the transfer list. They planned to use any fee they received for him in a bid to sign South African tighthead prop Dawie Theron.

'I had been recovering from a broken ankle and Sale, in fairness, had been 100% behind me and had never put me under pressure to return to action, until that point. So it was somewhat ironic that when I finally received the green light to return to action they had a change of heart. Adrian Hadley, who by then had become team manager, had called me into his office for a chat with him and Mitch, saying nothing was wrong when I asked him why the meeting had been arranged. There clearly was though. Mitch said Sale needed a world-class tighthead prop and I was the key to the deal for Theron going ahead.

'To say I was extremely angry and disappointed was an understatement. I knew I had so much more to offer Sale as a player and fumed they wanted me to leave. The ankle injury had also, temporarily, put paid to my Wales team aspirations but I believed I was still good enough to play international rugby. I may have been 33 but, as far as I was concerned, I was still at the top of my game and fired up physically and mentally for when I returned to action.

'The meeting ended with me putting Mitch straight. I told him he may be putting me on the transfer list but it didn't automatically mean another club would come in for me and pay the sort of transfer fee he needed in order to sign Theron. I also pointed out it would be a gamble for a club to sign me after a year out with a dodgy ankle. I asked Mitch if I could fight for a place, prove my worth and maybe force him to look at another option rather than sell me, but he didn't have any intention of doing that so the only option I had was to look elsewhere.

'I knew it was, at the end of the day, a business decision and Mitch had to do the best he could, but it was still annoying to be treated in such a way. We were also good friends off the field. When he arrived at the club his wife didn't know anyone and felt a bit lonely, so Alison made a big effort to help her and their two children, Daryl – who is now an international cricketer – and his sister Keira, settle in. They were regular visitors to our house in Widnes.'

Devereux's agent, Simon Cohen, suggested there may be an opening at Worcester Warriors. Although they were competing in the Second Division of English rugby, they were flying high. Cohen knew Les Cusworth, the former Leicester and England outside-half who Hadley had unceremoniously swatted aside while scoring a try during a famous Wales win at Twickenham in the 1988 Five Nations. Cusworth was director of rugby at the club and Cohen suggested it would provide a great platform to get Devereux back in the shop window, so he agreed to join Worcester on loan.

'Little did I know how good that loan move, which started in January 1999, would turn out to be. I really enjoyed my time there and the players and coaches were great. The only drag was that it was a 200-mile round trip from my home in Widnes every time we trained and played. Warriors were a semi-pro club at the time, training three nights a week in addition to playing games, so I was clocking up the miles.'

Worcester had been a struggling team until multi-millionaire Cecil Duckworth began his association with the club two years earlier. Duckworth's Worcester Engineering Company had pioneered the introduction of combination boilers before being bought out by Bosch in 1992, a deal which earned him a reputed £30 million. Duckworth then became executive chairman of Worcester RFC and bank-rolled the rise of the club, transforming Sixways into a state-of-the-art venue – it was one of the first to have an indoor training barn – and the fortunes of the team as it climbed through six divisions to reach the English rugby's pinnacle, the Premiership.

'I only met Cecil once. He was a likeable eccentric, like the scientist in *Back to the Future*. Sometimes Mr Duckworth would sit in his Range Rover at the edge of the training paddock and watch go through our paces. Other times, he'd be in his distinctive pink Bentley, but he certainly had put his money where his mouth was and was building a lovely sports complex at Sixways when I was with the club. He had just started building new hospitality boxes and a stand at one end of the ground and had also overseen the construction of a new clubhouse.'

While Devereux was full of praise for the financial commitment and efforts of Duckworth to put Worcester on the rugby map, he was not enamoured by the clobber the club's benefactor made the players wear following matches: 'We had to wear what I can only describe as ice-cream seller blazers. Mine cost me £90 and I wore it about six times. It was horrible and I hated it, but I had to weigh that minor irritation against the state-of-the-art indoor training barn he'd built, that was so useful when we had bad weather.'

Devereux's debut came in a 51-3 win over Blackheath in London, and the victories continued. There was a load of great characters at Worcester with try-scoring machine Nick Baxter, and Tim Smith, a former Gloucester full-back of some repute, as well as several up-and-coming local lads who were great fun.

As the race for promotion heated up, Worcester had a big game, in more ways than one for Devereux, at home against one of their rivals for promotion, London Welsh. The Exiles were coached by his Wales rugby league coach and good friend Clive Griffiths.

'Clive, as I would expect because he's a class act, was doing a great job at London Welsh and they also had my old Widnes mate Andy 'Adge' Currier playing in the centre.'

It was a tight game heading into the final minutes, with London Welsh just edging the contest when Currier caught Devereux with a high tackle. Worcester were awarded a penalty right in front of the sticks, which was slotted over for a 14-12 victory. Griffiths was gutted as the defeat had almost certainly put his famous old club out of the race for top spot and automatic promotion to the Premiership.

Worcester's penultimate game of the season, against Rotherham, and the final game against Bristol would decide which team would get automatically promoted. The squad of players who had got Worcester within touching distance of the top flight were hopeful they would be kept on and get the opportunity to play in the Premiership the following season, but, as the end of the season approached, Devereux was picking up vibes in the changing room that not every player had been offered a new contract: 'It became apparent the club were being very selective, offering some long-term contracts and some other players only getting extensions until the end of the season. Problems started to arise and the contract negotiations caused plenty of unrest in the camp. A number of players were involved, which meant the turmoil was bound to have a negative impact on the performance of the whole team.'

It was clear that Worcester liked Devereux because, halfway through the loan spell, club coaches Duncan Hall – who had come to England with Bob Dwyer when Australia's 1991 World Cup winning mastermind was boss of Leicester Tigers – and Phil Maynard, along with Les Cusworth, approached him to ask whether he would be interested in playing full-time for the Warriors?

'I said I would think about it,' revealed Devereux. 'I hadn't said "Yes" immediately because Simon was negotiating a severance package from Sale but nothing had been agreed. He had advised me to accept Sale's offer, as the money may not be there at the end of the season amid rumours of money issues. Kevin Ellis had already decided to take the offer Sale had made him and departed the club.'

It was at that point when Devereux was unexpectedly called by an old friend, Peter Burnett, who used to be the landlord of the Royal Hotel in Pontycymer. It was a boozer where Devereux had spent a lot of time before going north and when he visited friends and family.

Peter or 'Bush' as everyone knew him, told Devereux he was sitting next to a chap named Leighton Samuel, a Welsh businessman who had just bought Bridgend RFC from the administrators. It transpired the Ravens had been just 20 minutes from going out of business when Samuel came to the rescue.

'I only realised we were on speakerphone, and Samuel was on the call, when the club's new owner chipped in and asked: "Would you be interested in coming back to play for Bridgend?"

'Leighton had purchased the debt on the club and his next job was to rebuild the team, bringing in some marquee signings to generate some interest in Bridgend and attract other big names. Leighton was listening-in as I told Bush I was interested and I suggested the three of us meet to see what sort of money Leighton had in the pot for contracts.'

Samuel, however, was unaware there was another carrot dangling in front of Devereux, because Bush had previously told the centre that two investors from Cheltenham, who had allegedly made millions in energy, were looking to invest some of their money into a sports hospitality and security business, Coliseum Promotions, and Devereux had received a job offer to join the Cardiff-based business. Bush's ambition was to attract well known sports stars, and investment from well-connected businessmen, to make Coliseum the biggest hospitality business in Wales and had already recruited some big names such as Jonathan Davies, Robert Jones, Wayne Hall (the ex-Bridgend and Wales hooker) Bob Harris (the ex-Ebbw Vale and Blue Dragons rugby league forward), former boxing champion Floyd Harvard and businessman Matt Southall senior.

'When I heard that news from Bush, I became a bit more interested and thought maybe there was a possibility of getting back home to Wales. It wasn't a case of Alison and I being desperate to come home because we had a lovely home and friends in Widnes, but the thought of playing semi-pro rugby with Bridgend and then building a career for life after rugby with Coliseum was becoming increasingly attractive. The sister company of Coliseum was Olympus Security, which was fronted by Pat Strutt and Peter Guchii, who was once a bodyguard to Madonna and other stars. Olympus went on to be the security firm made famous by its work on the television show *Big Brother*.'

Those few months at Worcester offered Devereux an opportunity to weigh up what he would like to do as a next career move and where he would like to go.

'What I did have, was the chance to cut all ties with Sale despite having 18 months left on my contract and, after mulling over it for weeks, I decided to go with the offer from Bridgend combined with starting a new career with Coliseum.

'While I was considering my future, the unrest in the changing room at Worcester had spread. A few players had, it appeared, decided to down tools and we started losing games. The rot started in the match against Leeds and continued at Coventry. It was obvious that the players who were unhappy with how the contracts were being offered were now putting automatic promotion under threat.'

The day before Worcester played Rotherham in the crunch, penultimate game, Devereux had travelled to Wales from Widnes and signed for Bridgend. Former Lions flanker Richard Webster also signed the same day, joining from Bath. The pair were Samuel's opening signings.

'With that done I jumped in the car and drove the 100-miles to Worcester with a grin on my face. The grin soon disappeared after the battle with Rotherham at Sixways kicked off. The match was tight but I could see certain players didn't seem to care and were not playing at their normal standard.

'That's what happens when you mess-up your man management. To make matters worse, with about 15 minutes left on the clock, I jumped to catch a bouncing ball and, as I collected it, I landed on one leg and hyper-extended my right knee. I felt a sharp pain and had to go off. It was to be my last game for the Warriors and, to make matters worse, we were defeated 35-27.

Worcester's bid for promotion had gone and they would have to wait until 2004 before eventually reaching the Premiership. Duckworth passed away in 2020 and the money dried up. The club went through various owners before sadly entering financial administration in September 2022 which resulted in the club being wound up.

'Cecil would be turning in his grave at how the powers that be at Worcester had allowed the club to get into that mess after the vast investment he had made in the stadium, the company, the squad and the rest of the management. It was a scandalous end to a great club.'

20

The Green Green Grass of Home

*'I felt most, if not all the Welsh clubs, had failed to grasp the
professional era as well as their English counterparts.'*

John Devereux

John and Alison Devereux had spent 10 years living outside Wales,
with their daughters Jessica and Ellen being born while the family
were domiciled in Widnes. While they had been happy in the north of
England, when the decision to return to Bridgend was taken, Alison
went into over-drive.

'My wife didn't waste any time after I signed for the Ravens. The
ink was still wet on the contract with Bridgend when our house
in Widnes was listed and sold very quickly. Then Alison set about
scouring the town for a new family home and found and secured a
house on a lovely new development in Pen-y-fai, on the outskirts of
the town, and the purchase was quickly completed. It was a perfect
location, being only five minutes from the Brewery Field, the home of
Bridgend RFC.'

Many Welshmen who went north in the 1960s and '70s never
came home. The great Lewis Jones, Jim Mills, Clive Griffiths, Mike
Nicholas, Bobby Wanbon, Roy Mathias, Glyn Shaw and others settled
in Lancashire or Yorkshire.

'I could see why because there was so much to do and we were so
close to Liverpool, Manchester, Leeds and the Lake District. Alison
always says the shops were better up north and she and the girls were
so happy there, with lots of lovely memories.

'It was a terribly sad day when we said goodbye to our friends
in Widnes. Our neighbours Barbara and Ken George had been like
surrogate parents to us and were like grandparents to our girls, who
adored them, and their three teenage girls.

'The only thing me and Ken ever argued about was football, because he was an Everton blue and I was a diehard Liverpool red. We left the town wondering where the 10 years had gone because it seemed to have passed in a flash. It was a good time to be going home but it was tough to leave. It was a very emotional farewell for us all when our neighbours stood on their doorsteps to wave us off. Alison burst into tears and cried all the way to Knutsford.'

The Devereux family arrived back in Wales on one of the most important dates in the history of Welsh rugby. It wasn't the return of John Devereux that was being shouted from the roof tops on 26 June 1999 but Graham Henry's Wales beating South Africa for the first time, in the opening fixture at the still-under-construction Millennium Stadium. Devereux tried the patience of Alison by getting into a car to head for the centre of Cardiff to watch the Test match, while the family were still moving in.

'The removal vans were coming along the street as my lift arrived. I wasn't popular with the wife and family but I had to go because it was a dry run for Coliseum Promotions, who were the newest hospitality business in town. Peter Burnett and I were travelling to the capital to meet up with the other team members of Coliseum. The sun was out when we left Bridgend, but the storm clouds were brewing and it was pouring down in Cardiff as a summer shower pelted down on a hot and humid afternoon.'

Building contractors were working 24/7 to get the stadium finished in time for the start of the 1999 Rugby World Cup, with the first game scheduled for 1 October. It was going to be a fabulous stadium and it only cost circa £121 million, thanks to some tough negotiating skills from WRU chairman Glanmor Griffiths. The true cost of the stadium was revealed when John Laing, the construction company who built it, suffered a huge financial loss on the project and was bought by a rival firm for £1.

The stadium had to pass a few test events prior to the start of the World Cup, and only 27,000 fans were allowed in to watch the magnificent 29-19 triumph over the Springboks. The unfinished part of the stadium was literally a building site with huge lattice girders propping up the four corners of the ground. The rain was pouring off the roof like a waterfall on to the spectators below and people were getting soaked. As well as the rain it was also windy and a piece of scaffold blew off the roof and landed on a woman watching the game, breaking an arm. It could have been so much worse.

It was a great result for Wales but Devereux realised there was much to do before the World Cup to get Coliseum up and running. There were negotiations to ensure the company had the best venues for events before and after Wales' pool fixtures against Argentina, Japan and Samoa. The Cardiff office was in Charles Street – the head office located in Cheltenham – and on its first day it was packed with all the new recruits.

'It was heck of a team but I suppose, looking back, you could say that we were a bit late trying to book venues as most had been booked months earlier by other companies. Nevertheless, Bush had a knack of talking to people. Either that or was he just a pretty good bullshitter! He managed to secure the Angel Hotel for hospitality packages and a celebrity speaker for all of Wales' pool matches with options for the knockout stage, but the opening match clash with Argentina was a big reality check for us.

'The Dragon Suite at the Angel Hotel held around 250 people and we had 200 match tickets. The trouble was we were a new company and we didn't have an established company database to pull from. We were relying on advertising, which was costly, backed up with our extensive connections, yet still found ourselves with around 100 spare tickets which needed offloading.

'We had to pull in the services of dual-code international David Bishop to offload most of those spare tickets. They were a mad few hours, but we pulled it off. It was a major learning curve for us. We did smaller events for the Japan game and the crunch match for qualification to the quarter-finals, against Samoa.'

After defeating Argentina 23-18 in the tournament's opening game, and easily despatching Japan 64-15, Wales lost 38-31 to the Pat Lam-inspired Samoa but still topped the pool. The quarter-final against Australia was a massive game with most of the 74,000-crowd screaming their support for Wales, but that wasn't enough to prevent a 24-9 defeat against the eventual champions.

The World Cup was over for Wales but the Coliseum team was still in the tournament. It had a sell-out for the final when Australia beat France 35-12, and brought Billy Thompson, an ex-league referee from the 1970s, from the north of England as guest speaker. He was, at the time, among the best public speakers on the after-dinner circuit and it was a great occasion.

When the tournament ended, Devereux was able to concentrate on being back with Bridgend RFC, the team he had watched as a boy alongside his father when the Ravens twice lifted the Welsh Cup in the 1970s. His career had come full circle and he was living his dream of bringing the curtain down on it with the club where he had started his senior career.

Its new owner Leighton Samuel was very much hands-on. He had a family company called Decor Frame, which made picture frames and mirrors for all the main stores in the UK – like B&Q and Homebase – and two factories churning out his frames, one in Port Talbot and another in Bridgend. He had bought the club, which owed around £150,000 to creditors, but made sure he would not pay anywhere near the figure.

Samuel's aim was to assemble a side that could compete with the top teams in the UK and Europe, but he started to ruffle feathers when he wanted to rebrand the Bridgend badge. Samuel was a friend of Andrew Brownsword, the owner of Bath Rugby and boss of Hallmark Cards, and copied the design for the new Bridgend badge from Bath's. He was full of ideas and spent a lot of his time at the club as he started to upgrade its function rooms, angering some members when he did away with all the club memorabilia from the main function room upstairs and put them in a metal storage container.

The revamp generated another income stream by opening up the room – renamed from the Bernie Davies Suite to the President's Suite – which had big windows with great views of the pitch. Davies had been a major and loyal sponsor of the Ravens over many years with his builders merchants business, but the upgraded rooms were more modern and could be rented out for weddings and other social occasions not connected to rugby. Samuel also opened a restaurant downstairs, called Sadlers, that was open all week to the general public, along with the main supporters' sports bar.

The upheaval continued when a new stand, complete with executive boxes, was built opposite the main stand. It meant the symbolic Sony scoreboard was demolished after being there for as long as Devereux could remember.

'Leighton received a lot of criticism for demolishing it, which made his blood boil with anger. He always said: "What money did Sony give Bridgend for that advert? Absolutely nothing!" I could see he was waging war on the hangers-on and the gravy-trainers who had rocked up at games in the past and had been given free beer and food. Those days were well and truly over!

'Leighton and his wife Rhian even staffed the turnstiles. You should have seen the faces on some of these locals who rocked up to games expecting to get their normal free admission, and other perks, when they were confronted by Leighton – it was brilliant!

'What Leighton overdid, though, was to get too involved with these people in those situations. He should have had taken a step back and have someone else deal with the moaners. I witnessed an occasion when Leighton was having a ding-dong slagging match in the front of the rugby club with the granddaughter of a club stalwart who had played for Bridgend in the 1950s, and whose family had been given free tickets to games ever since. Leighton brought that to an end and they were upset with what he'd done.'

Selected by Bridgend's coach, Brian Powell, a former RAF officer and fitness instructor, Devereux's debut was a home friendly against Bath. It was the battle of the Adidas kits and the Bath badges. It was a beautiful warm August day and a large crowd turned up to watch Bridgend edge a close game. But there was controversy.

'Richard Webster was smacked full on the chops by Bath back rower Ben Sturnham. The noise of the punch was unreal. 'Webby's' nose exploded and he had to be dragged off the field by Bridgend officials to stop him attacking Sturnham. In the official squad photo for the season Webby was sporting a black eye.'

Webster only managed to play a handful of other games for Bridgend after that, as his knees had gone. Perhaps he was lucky to get a contract at Bridgend but Leighton was inexperienced in the area and should have had insisted that Webby – with his history of knee problems – had passed a medical before signing.

'I felt most, if not all the Welsh clubs, had failed to grasp the professional era as well as their English counterparts,' commented Devereux. 'It was far from a professional environment, with the attitude of some players still being amateur, while it's safe to say the administration of the game was definitely amateur.'

Samuel had a soft spot for Tongans and signed a number of them. The first to sign, in 1999, was a rugged back rower called Maama Molitika. As hard as nails yet still only 19, he was some player and would become a main man at Bridgend during his time there. 'Josh' Taumalolo – an electric full-back – then joined from Ebbw Vale and delighted the home crowd when he came into the line at full pelt.

'Leighton accommodated them in a big house he had bought on Bridgend's Park Street, which became well-known local landmark because of its residents, and the Tongan contingent would regularly receive mail addressed to the 'Tongan Embassy' in Bridgend.'

It wasn't the only Tongan outpost in Wales as, around that time, there was also a 'Tongan Embassy' in Ebbw Vale where the Faletau family lived. The back garden of the house in Park Street was dug up for a traditional Māori *Hāngī*, where its inhabitants would slow cook foil-wrapped food underground, covered with hot stones.

'Uiniati 'Winnie' Moa was the next Tongan to join. He was a prop forward who possessed the biggest calf muscles I had ever seen. His English wasn't great but it was better than another Tongan prop named Tevita Taumoepeau, who just growled at people. Maama should have been used as an interpreter in training and team meetings to help Tevita, but he didn't stay long with us and left for the Blues Super Rugby franchise in Auckland, where he became a world-class player.

'The last Tongan Leighton signed was Aisea 'Idris' Haveli. He was electric, the quickest winger I had seen since Martin Offiah. Idris' party trick was to chip the defensive line and use his speed to get to the ball first.'

When regional rugby was introduced in 2003, he was in the Samuel-backed Celtic Warriors set-up, but when the plug was pulled on the Warriors after one season, Haveli switched to the Scarlets.'

Bridgend were in the Welsh-Scottish League and trained three evenings a week. A trip to Aberdeen to face Glasgow Caledonian Reds, later to become the Glasgow Warriors, saw the Ravens win 17-10 on Rubislaw Playing Fields. Things got more hostile later with a massive fight erupting, as Devereux explained: 'After the game we went out in the granite city to celebrate our win and the boys were going for it. A bar was offering pints of Red Bull and Vodka for a few quid so the boys piled into it. It didn't take long for the alcohol to take effect on some of the Tongans as they were not the most accomplished drinkers.

'Trouble was brewing and it kicked off when one of the Tongans took a fancy to a young lady. There was a hitch because she wasn't single, and with her boyfriend. A punch was thrown and it erupted into a mass brawl. We stood out as targets in our club issue light blue shirts and fawn-coloured jackets. I was outside the pub when it started and went in to try and break it up, by which stage Winnie was piling into the locals. Richard Webster and I were trying to get our boys out of the bar and away from the trouble, but Winnie didn't move, and stayed there scrapping, so Webby punched him full-on in the face in an effort to get him to wise up.

'We managed to get Winnie out alive but there was a sting in the tail. Webby had cut his hand on Winnie's teeth when he walloped him and the pair of them were covered in blood. Webby's nightmare had just started because, on returning home, his hand become swollen and he ended up in A&E in Bridgend, admitted with suspected blood poisoning and spent a week on a drip!'

Bridgend's season had started with victory over Swansea and a draw with eventual league champions, Cardiff, but then they proceeded to lose 12 out of the next 15 games. Webster put paid to Powell's time at Bridgend by venting his ill-feeling about the coaching methods when Samuel called him and Devereux into his office to discuss the growing crisis. With Powell gone, Samuel brought in Dennis John, the former Pontypridd and ex-Wales caretaker coach, as head honcho.

'Webster became his assistant and video analyst after retiring from playing, a position he took very seriously. The squad we had at Bridgend had loads of potential. There was a good blend of experience and youth, plus we had some flair in the three-quarters and knew Samuel had the ambition to bring in new players when he could.

'Dennis was ok as a coach. He went back to basics at the start, with a squad you would like to assume already had a good grasp of the basics. I can best describe it as the goldfish syndrome. The fish learnt a trick but, by the time it did a full circle of its bowl, it had forgotten what it had just been taught.

'There were many training sessions where the coaches wasted so much time by going over the things they had covered in previous sessions. Give me a £5 note for every team meeting I've attended where the coach highlights something, calling out a player for his error and the next week the player makes the same error, and I'd be a rich man!'

Bridgend drew Gloucester, Spain and Biarritz in the European Challenge Cup. Biarritz were some side and had a back-rower playing for them that hardly anyone had heard of. His name was Serge Betsen and he had a stormer against the Ravens in both games.

'The trip to the popular surfers' resort of Biarritz on the French Basque coast was a brilliant experience. Biarritz boasted France great Serge Blanco as its president. He was a giant on the field but when I saw him that weekend I guessed he must have eaten his twin brother since the last time we'd clashed, in 1987, because he was huge.

'Our president, JPR Williams, came on the trip with us and the two of them soon got down to sharing a glass of wine and chatting all things rugby. It was an absolute privilege to be in the company of two of the greatest full-backs rugby has ever seen. It's what rugby is all about.

'We were hammered 29-6 but had a great night in Biarritz after the game. We drank bottles of cheap red wine like they were pints of beer. I was smashed and went for a Chinese meal with big Steve Ford, our captain and second-row, and a few others at the end of the night. I don't know why I did, as I was later told I fell asleep in the restaurant. Steve finished his meal, and mine, then picked me up and carried me back to our hotel.'

The next morning, with quite a few players suffering from bad hangovers, Dennis John took the Bridgend team to the beach for a run. Ford got into the spirit and stripped to his cycling shorts, but they were full of holes.

'It wasn't a pretty sight although the run was the best medicine we could have had. A Kangaroo Court was then held back at the hotel with a number of players and officials in the dock. The funniest one was when the judge, outside-half Paul Williams, and the jury voted to remove JPR of his legendary status as the world's best No.15.

'JPR was genuinely distraught. The judge's findings were that he believed Serge Blanco was a better player. It came off the back of JPR telling everybody the night before, how good he was as a player: "Do you know what? I am more of a legend in France than I am in Wales and I was so good I could have been an All Black." He had us in stitches.'

The return match wasn't much better and Bridgend were hammered 30-11, with Frano Botica having an exceptional game for Biarritz. He told Devereux that when he returned to New Zealand after spending some time with Llanelli, he'd bought a hotel but had run out of money renovating it. He needed cash and had signed a lucrative deal with the French outfit to help him finish the building work.

Devereux played in most matches that season and was satisfied with his performances but, while the rugby went well for him, it wasn't going to plan at Coliseum Promotions. Its success at the World Cup became a distant memory as the pressure to generate revenue to pay the overheads mounted on its full-time employees including Devereux.

'We had to bring in a lot of business to keep the big wheel turning as our combined salaries were high. We were all very well connected and could get in front of most chief executives or managing directors of top companies if we needed to, but it wasn't easy getting business. The lack of a database flummoxed us.'

Coliseum offered hospitality packages in different sports – tennis at Wimbledon, horse-racing, and F1 Grand Prix, among others – but it came to a critical point around April 2000 when Devereux was summoned with a couple of others to a crisis meeting at the company's head office in Cheltenham.

'Pat Strutt, the general manager of the group, was up front and said, unless we could pull in enough business to cover the overheads by June, they were shutting the operation down. Faced with that ultimatum we rallied and worked our socks off booking events, including the boxing great Marvellous Marvin Hagler in Swansea and Cardiff.'

Those events, and several more, were being organised but the writing was on the wall for Coliseum Promotions. The business was seriously floundering, and the high hopes generated at its launch quickly disintegrated as its lack of hard-nosed acumen and solid grounding in events management became increasingly obvious to all involved. It ceased trading in June 2000, just a year after being established.

Samuel, on hearing what had happened at Coliseum, called Devereux into his office and told him not to panic. He had a new venture called Global Sports Travel Management and offered Devereux a job and an immediate start. Everything was going well until Samuel asked him to organise some rugby hospitality events alongside the travel business.

'I madly agreed. It just added to the pressure levels. Hospitality in Wales was hard. It certainly wasn't London where budgets spent on hospitality were 10 times those of any company in Wales. The king of hospitality, Mike Burton, always used to say there was only one game where you could make money in hospitality in Wales and that was Wales against England. I found out the hard way he was correct.'

Dennis John, with Leighton Samuel's agreement, signed a raft of players for the 2000-01 season, including lock Paul Clapham, scrum-half Huw Harries from London club Harlequins who was also installed as captain, outside-half Craig Warlow, Cardiff flanker Jamie

Ringer and South Africa back-row forward Shawn van Rensburg from Neath. It was still a semi-pro environment, but pre-season training was anything but.

Huw Bevan, Devereux's school and college friend, had retired from playing and was coaching strength and conditioning at Bridgend. He was extremely professional and introduced scientific analysis to training and matches.

'We also used to do pre-season runs on a Saturday morning at the legendary Merthyr Mawr sand dunes, on the coast near Ogmore-by-Sea. It was brutal running up and down the 'Big Dipper', a huge dune over 100ft high where gold medal winning Olympic athletes such as Steve Ovett, Seb Coe and Darren Campbell had come for strength training.'

Dennis John frequently tinkered with the team that season and Bridgend had a mixed campaign, finishing fifth in the Welsh-Scottish League. Devereux had been in and out of the side and, off the field, was hit by a bombshell when it was discovered that the chap in charge of Samuel's sports travel firm, and who was supposed to ensure the business was licenced by ABTA, the trade association of UK-based travel agents, had overlooked that crucial detail, and was promptly sacked.

'We had effectively been trading illegally for months. It was sad as the venture seemed to have had so much potential. Leighton summoned me to tell me he had been forced to shut down the business. I was devastated.'

Devereux then turned to his close friend Lyndon 'Trooper' Thomas, who had advised him on so many aspects of his life and career from when he had played his first game for Bridgend as a 17-year-old and who had helped him find his first job after leaving college.

'We were weighing up some options when, out of the blue, he said: "Have you ever thought about being a medical rep?" Most of my college friends went on to be PE teachers but a few, such as David Bryant and Huw Davies, had tried their hand at pharmaceutical sales and were still working in that industry, so I thought it must be decent.'

Thomas said that he knew a friend who was a manager of a pharma company and he would ask her advice. That led to a meeting with Andrea Robertson who said Devereux would be an ideal candidate for a role, but her company didn't have any vacancies at the time. However, she knew someone who did and was looking to build a new sales team so he met with Jane Bridges, as Devereux explained: 'We got on well and she introduced me to one of her directors Mike Blackburn, just to make the agreement official, and I was offered a job. It was a part-time role, working mornings only, so that I could still do my rugby training in the afternoons or in the evenings.

'I loved the new role but, just when things were going well, Dennis decided to change the times of mid-week training to mornings *and* evenings, so we were training twice a day. It caused me so much stress in my new job. We would train at Pencoed RFC and Pencoed Comprehensive school at 9am and, after training, I would literally have to run to the changing room, get showered and then shoot off to see doctors in their surgeries.

'They were the days when the job was much different. I would take some doctors out for a meal at least once a month and discuss our products with them. It was more relaxed and sociable. Some 22 years later, I am still doing the same job, but it has changed beyond recognition from those early days.

'Now I cover a much bigger territory, the whole of Wales, and don't see GPs or practice nurses anymore, as the balance of power shifted from GPs being able to prescribe whatever they wanted, to today where I have to see the new decision-makers in the NHS. It's mostly pharmacists who sit at the top of the tree in procurement and they make decisions whether to use a new drug based on NICE [National Institute for Health & Care Excellence] recommendations, which are mainly cost-based versus clinical need.'

In preparation for the following season's new Celtic League, which included the Scottish clubs and Irish provinces, Samuel spent big in the transfer market, bringing future Wales and British and Irish Lions captain Gareth Thomas, and Dafydd James, who had made the Lions Test team in Australia a couple of months earlier, back to the Brewery Field.

Devereux, who was six months into his job with Innovex Pharmaceuticals, was finding it difficult to mix rugby and work, and didn't need any drama, like when the team stayed at a budget hotel in Paris after a defeat at Castres.

'During the night we were woken by a commotion. It transpired a pair of thieves had broken into Dennis' room while he was sleeping. He awoke to see them rifling through his stuff and started screaming and shouting at them. One jumped out of a first floor window and vanished into the night while the other tried to leg-it down the corridor but met Maama Molitika who coming up the stairs after a night out. Seeing the guy running towards him and hearing Dennis shouting "Stop him!" Maama decked the guy, knocking him out, and he was still coming around as the *gendarmes* arrived to arrest him.'

Bridgend suffered back-to-back defeats against a Munster team that included a host of promising young players, including Ronan O'Gara, Peter Stringer, Paul O'Connell, David Wallace and old heads in seasoned Ireland internationals like Peter 'The Claw' Clohessy, Mick Galway, and Anthony 'Axel' Foley, who sadly died suddenly in France years later while part of the province's coaching team. There was more drama after a night out in Cork to drown their sorrows.

'I had lost my hotel key but was staying on the ground floor so I tried to get into what I thought was my room via an open window at about 1am. I was squeezing my way through the window but had miscalculated. It wasn't my room but Leighton's. I had a shock when he woke up shouting, "Who is it?" I bailed out of the window and am, to this day, not sure if he knows that it was me! Sorry Leighton!'

Dennis John was axed following another loss to Castres and a defeat to Harlequins, with Wales backs coach Allan Lewis being appointed as his successor. Lewis made it clear he wanted Bridgend to go full-time the following season, but Devereux was unable to commit due to his employment as a pharmaceutical rep.

'I had a good relationship with Leighton and wanted him to tell Allan Lewis to keep me, not necessarily to play every game but to help bring on youngsters like David Bishop, who was joining from Treorchy. However, Allan was having none of it. He didn't want a 36-year-old part-time centre and, to my disappointment, Leighton didn't back me up. My final game for Bridgend was against Newport and I was very emotional after the final whistle. I had a wry smile at the club's end of season presentation evening, though, when I was named Players' Player of the Year, which wasn't bad for an old git and meant such a lot to me as it was chosen by my teammates.

'Despite my disappointment, I didn't cut my ties with Leighton and introduced him to the then Rugby Football League chief executive Nigel Wood. The formation of the Celtic Crusaders RL team was in the embryonic stage, financed by Leighton following the collapse of the Celtic Warriors union team in 2004. The Crusaders were awarded a

Super League franchise in 2009 but the team never got the support it deserved and moved to Wrexham, eventually withdrawing its bid to renew its licence.

Devereux wasn't done with league though, later serving as Wales team manager and playing for Bridgend Blue Bulls amateur team.

21

2000 RL World Cup

*'John had always been one of the first names on my team sheet and I
had no hesitation in bringing him back in from rugby union for the 2000
RL World Cup. True to form, John rolled back the years. It raised a few
eyebrows, until the games started! He was just a class act.'*

Clive Griffiths

Paul Moriarty and John Devereux were back in Wales playing for the
union clubs where they had made their name, Swansea and Bridgend
respectively, and had thought their days of playing rugby league on
the big stage were well and truly behind them.

When Devereux's telephone burst into life, he didn't have any
inkling who was on the other end. He wondered who it was, what
they wanted, and whether he should answer. When he did, it soon
became apparent it was a plea for help from a longtime pal. It was
Wales boss Clive Griffiths, who had been coach of Moriarty and
Devereux during their 13-a-side Wales international careers.

'We had an off-the-wall idea that coaches sometimes have, about
trying to get Paul and John into our squad for the World Cup,'
explained Griffiths. 'John had always been one of the first names on
my team sheet and I had no hesitation in bringing him back in from
rugby union for the 2000 Rugby League World Cup. True to form,
John rolled back the years. It raised a few eyebrows, until the games
started! He was just a class act.'

The 2000 Rugby League World Cup was under way and Griffiths
had a problem, namely a lack of fit bodies after his squad had suffered
a few injuries during physical clashes with South Africa and Lebanon.

As Devereux explained: 'Clive needed some reinforcements so he
tried me and Paul. He knew Paul and I were still playing rugby, albeit
union, and had a wealth of experience of league. Clive surmised

it wouldn't take too much time for us to be reintegrated back into league, even though we were both at the wrong end of our 30s.'

The pair agreed in principle to join the squad but had to get permission from their clubs to allow them to be available for the rest of the tournament. Wales' next game was on 5 November, against New Zealand at, of all places, the Millennium (now Principality) Stadium.

'Neither of us had played at what is, in my view and in the opinion of many, the best rugby stadium in the world, so there was a chance we might tick off another important box in our long careers. I put the proposal to Bridgend and was given the green light to join the squad, but Paul was initially refused permission by Swansea. However, it was always going to be a long shot to get me involved for the game with the Kiwis and, in the end, I spent it watching from the bench so never got to play at the stadium.'

New Zealand had uncovered a star in Lesley Vainikolo, a winger who was built like another Tonga-born giant, the legendary Jonah Lomu, and had been dubbed 'Volcano' by Australian great and television commentator Peter Sterling while starring for Canberra Raiders in the National Rugby League.

Vainikolo well and truly erupted against Wales with a hat-trick of tries as New Zealand won convincingly 58-18. He was an exceptional talent and went on to score 35 tries in 68 appearances for Canberra before bagging an incredible 149 in 152 outings for Bradford Bulls in the Super League. Gloucester then lured him to union with a big money offer.

Although he could have played for Tonga, Vainikolo qualified for England on residency and made his debut for the Red Rose against Wales at Twickenham in the 2008 Six Nations. It was Warren Gatland's opening match as Wales coach and what a match it was, as the men in red overturned a half-time deficit to beat England and go on to complete a Grand Slam.

'Volcano scored 36 tries for Gloucester in 87 appearances but just didn't click for England. He was ditched after just five caps. I guess, at times, he did look like a fish out of water in union, but he was a prolific scorer at club level, and in league, and it was a surprise England didn't persevere with him for longer and give him a chance to find his feet.

'He was such a handful for New Zealand against Wales at the Millennium Stadium that I expected more from him. Perhaps England were the wrong union country for him because they were averse to throwing the ball around and playing unstructured rugby.'

Devereux felt strange seeing the Wales league team playing at the citadel of Welsh rugby union. The attendance was about 17,000 so, if truth be told, large swathes of the stands were empty, and the atmosphere was pretty flat as home supporters didn't have much to shout about, such was the one-sided nature of the contest.

Even though Devereux had joined the Wales squad, he returned to his home in Bridgend that night to pack his bags. The plan was to travel to the team hotel in Runcorn, on Merseyside, the following day. Before he set out, he received a phone call: 'It was Muzzy, saying Swansea had, after all, decided to allow him to join me in the Wales squad. He was on his way and it was a mad rush to get ready before he came by to pick me up.

'We set off on the three-hour drive and had just passed Hilton Park Services on the M6 when Muzzy said he needed a pee. I said we should have stopped at Hilton Park, and suggested he stopped at the next services. Then he drove straight past them! He was getting increasingly desperate and I was metaphorically pissing myself with laughter. We reached Knutsford Services, Sandbach, but still didn't stop, saying he'd be ok until we got to Runcorn.

'Defying nature, Muzzy pressed on towards the Runcorn Premier Inn and, by the time we got off the M56, he was in a lot of discomfort. As we arrived Muzzy stopped the car by the hotel entrance, told me to park it and jumped out to head straight for the gents, but it was far too late. As he got out, steam was rising from his shorts and he faced the dreaded walk of shame past reception desperately trying to avoid further embarrassment.

'I was laughing hysterically as I parked the car, trying not to sit on the wet part of the driver's seat, wondering why he hadn't stopped at one of the services he'd zoomed past. As I headed into the hotel, where I was welcomed by members of the Welsh squad, Muzzy appeared from the gentlemen's toilet looking very relieved but wet!'

After a shower and change of clothes, Moriarty joined Devereux for a few pints with Clive, Mike Nicholas and the boys in the bar that night and paid the price the next day.

'Muzzy and I probably had one or two too many because we slept late the following morning and missed the bus taking the boys to training.'

'I don't know how many they had,' said Griffiths. 'In those days, players, even though they were professional, tended to drink a bit more. We had told the squad, management and support staff the bus taking us to our training ground was leaving at 10am. At 10.02 there wasn't any sign of Devs and Muzzy. Iestyn Harris asked if he should go and get them from their room but I said: "We're off". I thought I had a great opportunity to make a point to the whole squad that nobody could take anything for granted and that nobody was bigger than the team.'

Realising they had been left behind, panic set in for Devereux and Moriarty with the naughty pair summoning a taxi to ferry them to Wilderspool, the home of Warrington Wolves, where Wales were training. 'We had started warming up when a cab pulled up,' said Griffiths. 'In it were Devs and Moriarty. They were a bit sheepish when they got out and apologised to the whole group. That was the last time anyone was late!'

'After saying sorry to the squad,' confirmed Devereux, 'we got down to prepping for the next game, against Papua New Guinea in the quarter-finals of the World Cup. The last game of professional league both of us had played was about three years earlier and much had changed in the sport, with Wales having new defence and offence drills.

'We trained well all week and I could see that Clive had nurtured a great team spirit in what was a new era for Wales. The squad had Iestyn Harris, Anthony Sullivan and Keiron Cunningham from my era, but there were new, quality additions like Lee Briers, Paul 'Patch' Atcheson and Jason Critchley, who brought much needed Super League experience into the camp.'

The last eight clash with Papua New Guinea was played at Widnes' new Halton Stadium. It was somewhat ironic for Moriarty and Devereux. They had played for years with Widnes at the old Naughton Park, which was old and decrepit. 'The new stadium had come far too late for us,' said Devereux. 'We should have had a stadium like it when we were playing for the club as it would have generated more revenue to enable us to compete with the likes of Wigan, St. Helens and Leeds.

'Match night arrived and me and Muzzy were on the substitutes' bench. PNG were always a very physical side, and when I was sent on by Clive with 20 minutes to go, I was immediately smashed with a high tackle by Stanley Gene.'

Griffiths laughed, before saying: 'Devs and Moriarty found it really hard. The physicality, the ball-in-time play and having less time to recover. I remember Devs taking the ball up and getting a "welcome back to rugby league" hit!'

Devereux chipped in: 'It was a tough second half. We had raced into a 20-2 first half lead but PNG mounted a bit of a fight back in the second. Fortunately, they squandered a few chances and we saw the game out 22-8.'

The victory set up a daunting semi-final against reigning world champions Australia, who had won the previous World Cup, beating England in the final, and were hot favourites for a repeat success.

'They must have thought all they needed to do was turn up at Huddersfield's McAlpine Stadium to beat us and book another final at Wembley,' grinned Devereux, 'but they had failed to take us into account and found things weren't always that easy as we were intent on making our mark on that World Cup.

'We were annoyed by the usual things, like not getting the same recognition as England, and our budget was far inferior to that of England, forcing us to stay at budget hotels and use the basic equipment and kit given to us by the Rugby Football League. There wasn't much to do around the hotel when we weren't training.

'The new generation spent most of their time playing Xbox or PlayStation games and the older ones tended to play cards and drink coffee all day. Wales had bonded well and I could see that there was a real steely determination about this bunch. I knew there was a lot of experience and class in that team, and it was about to introduce itself to the world of league.

'Match night arrived and I couldn't help but think: "What if the Aussies just let rip and tear us apart?" I knew they were well capable of doing that against any country in the world. Selected on the bench, again, I was happy enough but my competitive fire still burned and, deep down, I would have loved to have started. I always found coming off the bench hard as it seemed to take me 10 minutes or so to get up to the speed and awareness of a game. Muzzy started and had been given a massive role in stopping the big Aussie forwards from getting a roll on us.

'There was a smattering of Welsh fans in the crowd and we sang *Hen Wlad fy Nhadau* as one – it was quite emotional. We played the game at a high tempo and, believe it or not, the big Kangaroo pack coughed and spluttered. They had opened the scoring with two unconverted tries, but we knuckled down and registered our first score after 14 minutes, when inside-half Ian Watson went over.'

The game then took off from a Welsh point of view and they moved into the lead when Kris Tassell crossed for a try, converted by Harris. Briers was playing out of his skin and scored another, before adding two drop-goals.

'We were in dreamland,' said Devereux, 'and Australia were stunned as we led 22-8, but our lead wasn't to last. Brad Fitler got a try back and then the Aussies dominated possession and squeezed the life out of us.

'We were still ahead with 23 minutes remaining, but a try from Darren Lockyear ended our dream of pulling off what would have been one of the biggest upsets in sporting history. Clive was beaming as he watched what was unfolding in front of him.'

Australia weren't one of the best teams in rugby league without reason. They didn't panic and regrouped after Bob Fulton, who had been Devereux's coach at Manly, had given them a good rollicking at half-time.

'I played most of the second half,' said Devereux, 'and had some good moments, but myself and Paul were 36 and 37 years old respectively, and we found it so hard to keep getting back up and defending against wave after wave of Australian attacks. They had seized control of possession and turned the screw to pull away.'

The Aussies ran out 46-22 winners in front of what was a disappointing attendance of about 8,000 for a semi-final of a World Cup in league's north of England stronghold. Those that had turned up did make plenty of noise and were treated to a great game.

Briers rightfully received the Man of the Match award, his performance signalling his arrival in the big arena, and he went on to play a pivotal role during many more games for Wales over the next seven or eight years, and for his club at Super League level.

Speaking with pride for the Welsh performance, Griffiths commented: 'It was another epic game and it gave Welsh rugby league huge credibility. We had a 60-point start on the betting coupon and, at the hour-minute mark, we were winning, but the ref, Russell Smith, made what we thought were some dodgy decisions and we didn't touch the ball for the next 10 minutes. Australia took advantage and a winning lead. They had hammered everyone previously but we showed they could be beaten.'

'We may have been beaten,' said Devereux, 'but we had made Wales and ourselves proud.'

22

Rugby Retirement – In Agony

'It was great to welcome Devs to Pontypool Park when I captained Pooler. He was strong, fast, skilful and his Dalek hand-off could put a hole right through you. His achievements in union and league were second to none but, more importantly to me, he's a very humble man who's never forgotten where he's from – a rugby legend and a top bloke.'

Mark Jones

John Devereux doubted whether he would play rugby again after leaving Bridgend in the summer of 2002. It was his club and it had never entered his mind about joining another after leaving the Brewery Field as a player for the last time. Saturday afternoons were spent pottering about the house and on shopping trips and visits to garden centres with Alison, but that changed when he received an unexpected telephone call from an excited Kevin Ellis.

'Devs, I am over in Pontypool,' said Ellis, 'and apart from me and Scooby, who's captain, there's a bunch of kids in the squad. Get over here, the owner Bob Jude has got loads of money and he wants to win the league and get back into the Premiership.'

'It almost sounded too good to be true,' recalled Devereux, 'so, I thought, in for a penny, in for a pound. I was 36 but felt there was plenty of life left in my old legs, and getting back on the pitch certainly beat shopping and gardening!'

He met Jude – who ran a flooring business that was based in the town and handled large commercial contracts with health authorities and other bodies – at the Park Hotel in Cwmbrân. Jude appeared to be a successful businessman but was yet to learn that owning a rugby team in Wales almost certainly meant pouring money down a bottomless pit.

'Bob was a nice enough guy,' said Devereux. 'A bit eccentric but his heart was in the right place. We discussed his ambitions for the club, then he asked me what my personal terms would be to play for Pontypool, and the basics were quickly agreed. He said he would make an upfront payment at the start of the season and another at the end of it. It sounded good. I couldn't complain about the money either as it was the same as I had been on at Bridgend, and we were playing in what was, in reality, the second division of Welsh club rugby.'

With the squad Jude was busy assembling, it seemed it wouldn't be long before Pooler were promoted to the Premiership or, as he would say, back where they belonged. The squad trained three times a week but those living in the Bridgend area – Devereux, Kevin Ellis and John Williams, who was a young full-back from Port Talbot – were allowed to do their own weights sessions locally on a Monday to save having to travel to Pontypool.

Jude had splashed the cash to sign former Wales, Neath and Ebbw Vale enforcer Mark Jones; Kuli Faletau (Taulupe's father), who had played at lock forward for Ebbw Vale and Tonga; Wales international back Byron Hayward, who had starred for Ebbw Vale, Llanelli, Gloucester and a host of other clubs; the powerful wing Lenny Woodard, who had been on Wales' humiliating tour of South Africa in 1998; Wales A international centre Jonathan Hawker; Kevin Ellis; and a second quality scrum-half in Nicky Lloyd.

Pooler were coached by their former hooker, Steve 'Junna' Jones, who had been international and club understudy to Pontypool, Wales and Lions great Bobby Windsor. Junna, who sadly died suddenly at the age of 55 in 2007, was a link with the years when the club dominated the Merit Table and the unofficial Welsh championship. He was popular and didn't pull any punches. To say he was straight with players and the media was an understatement for Junna told it as he saw it.

'He was a good man,' confirmed Devereux, 'and we got on well. Junna's and Scooby's team talks before home games were all fire and brimstone. Scooby's stammer often got the better of him but we knew what he was trying to say: "Get out there, lads and smash the fuckers!" We were the same age and had fought many battles on and off the field. Scooby was a warrior, a hard man who, at times, played with a little bit too much thunder. I guess he only knew one way of playing – what he had been taught at Neath under the 'Ayatollah',

Brian Thomas, during the 1980s. Scooby was a Dr. Jekyll and Mr Hyde character, a quiet man off the field but like a wild animal on it. He struggled with a stutter, but me and the boys always admired Mark's determination to stop it getting the better of him. When Mark won his GB RL cap against France in Perpignan in 1992 he knew he'd have to follow the tradition of singing a song, on stage, at the after-match dinner. The boys were desperate that he'd do okay and, fair play to Scooby, he was up for it. He grabbed the microphone and sang *Two Little Boys*, without missing a beat or a word. He was word perfect. We all cheered and gave him a standing ovation.'

The mutual respect between to two former Wales, Wales RL and GB international teammates was reflected when Scooby commented: 'It was great to welcome Devs to Pontypool Park when I captained Pooler. He was strong, fast, skilful and his Dalek hand-off could put a hole right through you. His achievements in union and league were second to none but, more importantly to me, he's a very humble man who's never forgotten where he's from – a rugby legend and a top bloke.'

Pontypool started the Welsh Championship strongly and Devereux was enjoying himself, until someone decided it was a good idea to arrange a so-called friendly with Premiership big-hitters Neath, away at The Gnoll. The match was to end for Devereux in agony and controversy when he was the victim of a sickening challenge.

'Whoever arranged the fixture should have been put in a padded cell because there wasn't such a thing as a friendly with Neath. We had risen to the challenge and had acquitted ourselves well, but it changed for me when I was 'coat-hangered' by Neath's openside flanker, a Fiji international called Alfie Moceulutu. To put it mildly, he was a bit of a head-hunter. I had watched other games where he had put in big hits but had seen he had often got it wrong and gone high and, sure enough, that's what happened as I was charging through the Neath midfield.

'His swinging forearm caught me flush on the chin and sent me crashing to the deck. Things got worse when he dropped his body weight on my right knee and stood over me shouting: "Get up you shit". If I could, he would have had the full bore from me, but I couldn't as the pain was excruciating. I knew something serious had happened and, sure enough, the anterior cruciate ligament [ACL] had ruptured when he jumped on my leg. Looking back, it was a disgraceful act. Maybe I should have taken legal recourse for compensation but the norm was to say nothing and get on with it.'

A ruptured ACL is a career-threatening injury for a rugby player and Devereux was hobbling on crutches to the clubhouse at The Gnoll when Moceulutu came the other way: 'I had never felt so angry over an incident on the pitch and was going to hit him with one of my best right hooks. I'm not a shithouse but I paused and thought I was in no fit state to start scrapping with anyone while on crutches.'

Devereux went for an MRI scan and Pontypool's club doctor, a retired rheumatologist, viewed the results and told the midfield powerhouse there was no long-term damage and to return to training when the pain eased. Devereux laughs about it now but he didn't at the time because he could hardly walk, let alone run. Over the following weeks, Devereux was urged to begin training. Feeling pressured by the powers that be at the club, he reluctantly agreed to give it a go.

'I was in pain all the time,' he said, 'and my knee was strapped with about £50 of Elastoplast bandage for every training session and game. It got even more farcical when Junna picked me for the bench against Glamorgan Wanderers. Midway through the second half, Junna nudged me and said: "Get on John, go and win it for us". I gave a quiet chuckle and thought: "Oh, how I wish I could, Steve".'

It was the straw that broke the camel's back, so to speak, for Devereux. He decided he needed a second opinion and arranged for another MRI scan – in Cheltenham – that cost him £250, then consulted orthopaedic specialist Dave Pemberton, who had operated on the injuries of numerous rugby players.

Pemberton told John that the first scan he'd had done after his injury showed that the ACL was 98% ruptured, but that the new scan showed it was completely ruptured and he needed an operation to repair the damage.

'I was relieved of sorts but also realistic, being painfully aware that if I needed an ACL reconstruction at 36 and a half, it would be 12 months out of the game and the end of my career. I wasn't keen. Pembo said not all was lost, that he had operated on players and found he didn't need to do a reconstruction because the patient had such strong hamstrings and quad muscles. Fortunately, I did.

'Pembo had a look at the knee under anaesthetic and said it was fairly stable. He opted to take out the ruptured ACL and sow me up.

Within minutes, he was in my room telling me the good news, that the operation had been a success.

'Unfortunately, however, the rehab would not come quick enough for me to play again for Pooler, who went on to win the Championship. I took part in the open-top bus parade through Pontypool that followed but felt bad that I had missed the second half of the season.'

Devereux only had a one-year contract with Pontypool and things were starting to unravel with Jude's flooring company running into financial problems, which had a knock-on effect on the club. Retirement was again beckoning until, lo and behold, his old mate, Ellis, was on the phone again but this time not with one but two offers.

It was the summer of 2003 and Ellis had, by now, left Pooler and joined Maesteg, and he wasn't the only new recruit at The Old Parish. Allan Bateman, the silky Wales and Lions centre who had also starred in league for Wales, Warrington and Cronulla Sharks in Australia's NRL, was already back at his hometown club, and the pair were also in the process of setting up a new amateur rugby league side called Bridgend Blue Bulls. The plan was for the team to play at Bridgend Town Football Club's Coychurch Road ground, where Devereux had watched Steve Fenwick, Tommy David and other former union stars play for the Blue Dragons league team in the early 1980s.

Little did Devereux, Bateman and Ellis know they were to discover two prospects who were to became Wales and world stars at union when the Blue Bulls joined the Mark Jones captained Aberavon Fighting Irish in Port Talbot, Cwmbrân-based Torfaen Tigers, Cynon Valley Cougars, Swansea Valley Miners, Cardiff Demons and Newport Titans in the South Wales RL Conference. The season ran between May and August so did not clash with union.

The Bulls managed to put together a very good squad of rugby union boys all wanting to have a crack at league. They held a few training sessions to go through the basics of league and the recruits quickly picked up the different code. The result was an invincible season in the Welsh Conference, accounting for their main rivals, Cardiff Demons and Aberavon Fighting Irish. It was competitive but one player had stood out.

'Aberavon had a stocky young lad playing for them at hooker with a mop of blond hair. He was about 17, ran strongly with the ball and didn't take a backward step in defence. His name was Richard Hibbard. I was very impressed with him and I heard Super League giants St. Helens were interested in acquiring his services. It never happened but, I reckon, if he had not got into the Ospreys team so quickly, and then Wales, he would have gone to St. Helens as he loved playing league and smashing 10 bells out of the opposition.'

Play-offs at the end of the season saw the top two sides from south Wales play in the British Conference Harry Jepsom Cup. Bridgend beat a few sides and amazingly got to the 2003 final, beating Carlisle in a tough clash at Warrington's Wilderspool ground. It was an incredible achievement and Devereux was delighted to play a part in developing the code, despite the difficulties of fielding a side.

'We played on Sundays and, on some occasions when we were down on numbers, we had to go to some of the houses of boys who had been drinking the previous night and get them out of bed. We were the team everyone – particularly our main rivals, the Fighting Irish – wanted to beat the following season, and the standard of the other teams also improved. We also recruited new players with one rookie really standing out.

'We were a player short for a game so went to the house of a certain Lee Byrne. He was a latecomer to rugby and was playing union for Bridgend Athletic. We dragged him out of bed and he took to league like a duck to water. Scarlets snapped him up and, like Richard, he was to become a superstar with the Ospreys, Clermont Auvergne, Wales and the Lions.'

Bridgend's Blue Bulls again topped the Welsh Conference the following season, 2003-04, and advanced to the last four of the Conference Cup, to face West London Sharks, featuring Wasps and Samoa union hooker Trevor Leota in their ranks.

'A number of us had to play in pre-season union friendlies earlier the same day and our request to have the semi-final put back 24 hours was refused by league bosses. It was a harsh decision. We were knackered when we lined up against Sharks a couple of hours after coming off the union field but were leading until the last quarter, when the wheels fell off as we slipped to defeat.'

Devereux's third and final season as a player with the Blue Bulls was memorable as they only lost once and, yet again, reached the final of the British Conference in 2005, which was held at, of all places, the Brewery Field! It was like having home advantage and helped propel them to clinch the Harry Jepsom Cup with a record 60-10 demolition of Leeds Akkies.

Devereux, who also spent six years, 2006-12, as unpaid Wales RL team manager, was happy to be playing in the centre for both the

Blue Bulls and Maesteg RFC alongside Bateman: 'Allan was a brilliant player and had a great career. We came from similar environments, with him growing up in Maesteg and me just over the mountain in the Garw Valley. Our fathers had been miners and we had played school and youth rugby against each other. I went north in 1989 and he followed a year later, joining Warrington with Rowland Phillips and Kevin Ellis.'

Maesteg RFC – a semi-pro club – were competing in the Championship in 2004 and were determined to push for promotion. Devereux's knee was holding up and he was back more-or-less to his old self: 'I was touching 37, a little slower and heavier than 10 years previously but I still had the hunger and loved the crack with the boys at the club. There was a great team spirit and I enjoyed my time at the Old Parish. Me and Allan were not playing for the money but because we could still play at that level and make a big contribution to the club's ambition of getting into the Premiership.

'We finished in the top three in our first season. It was great. I played all season and stayed fit and injury free. Unfortunately, it was Allan who was to get injured, in guess what, a friendly with Neath! He had rarely been injured in his career but broke his forearm during the game. There wasn't anyone available at The Gnoll to take him to Morriston Hospital, so I volunteered. He was seen by a doctor in A&E and had an operation that night to repair the fracture with a metal plate.

'If I couldn't retire at Bridgend, I suppose Maesteg was the next best place, other than Blaengarw RFC. They were a valley side that had produced many great players over the years, who were frequently snapped up by the likes of Bridgend, Neath and Aberavon.'

Devereux stayed with Maesteg for three seasons, culminating in his finest hour in the club jersey when they faced Premiership big hitters Newport in the quarter-final of the Welsh Cup.

His dodgy knee had been treated again the previous October, by the same consultant, Dave Pemberton, who performed an arthroscopy to flush out some floating cartilage, and he had to manage his time on the park more carefully: 'I had just turned 40 and told our coaches, Leighton O'Connor and Gareth Brown, there wasn't any way my knee would survive all the training sessions and I couldn't manage mid-week and weekend matches on the bounce.'

But there was one big performance left in him: 'I knew my time was running out when we faced Newport at the Old Parish. They were hot favourites but the lads put in a fabulous, gutsy performance and we won. I scored two tries and picked up the Man of the Match award.'

After that high, Maesteg played a midweek match at Ebbw Vale, rearranged from earlier in the season because of an alleged frozen pitch. When a referee had gone to Eugene Cross Park, at 8am, and called off the game, there had been a widespread frost across the Wales but it transpired it was apparently the only game of rugby or football postponed that day, as the strong sun had transformed the icy conditions into almost perfect conditions for autumn rugby.

'Roddy Boobyer, the brother of Ian and Neil, was due to play the rearranged game at Ebbw Vale instead of me, but a bereavement meant I was asked to fill-in. I had a bad feeling about it, and told Leighton in no uncertain terms, but there was no other centre available. It was a wet and windy night, which is the norm for the heads of the valleys, and we lost.

'It was criminal because Ebbw Vale were dreadful that season. Not only did we lose, but my knee blew up and I was in agony after the game. I was done, my knee had won the day and I was now officially retired.'

After dispatching Newport in the Welsh Cup quarter-finals, Maesteg's prize was to play Neath in the semi-finals, with the game to be played on neutral soil at Aberavon. Neath were a fabulous outfit, on a different level, with some of their players being full-time pros, and there was a promising young player, James Hook, playing his first season in senior rugby.

'Ahead of the game I'd been photographed nose-to-nose with a young 'Hooky' for publicity purposes at the Millennium Stadium, with the gleaming cup below us. It took me back to when I was his age and thought: "Oh boy, you have got one hell of a career ahead of you, enjoy the ride, because it will take you places you could only ever dream of and give you a great life, playing rugby for a living." I used to pinch myself sometimes, thinking it was the best job in the world, playing a sport you love, getting paid for it and travelling the world. As I used to say: "It beats working".

'Hooky had a terrific career but should have had many more caps for Wales. Unfortunately, the coaches, Warren Gatland, Rob Howley and Shaun Edwards, were looking for more structure in the way their team played the game, so picked a general in Stephen Jones, who would play to the game-plan and not off the cuff.

'It was wrong, in my opinion, and I would have a James Hook at No.10 in my team every day of the week because you need a playmaker who can run and beat defenders. If you have a 10 who can do that, like Jonathan Davies, James Hook, Dan Carter, Stephen Larkham or Richie Mo'unga, it opens up space for the three-quarters outside them to exploit and prosper.'

Although Devereux had been consigned to the rugby scrapheap, the season ended on a high note as Maesteg won promotion. Unfortunately, its fortunes have plummeted since then and it's tough for him to see a club with its history suffering in the lower leagues of Welsh rugby.

'Professional rugby in Wales is killing the grass roots. There were three feeder clubs in or near Maesteg who supplied players to the senior team – Maesteg Quins, Maesteg Celtic and Nantyffyllon – but none of those teams are feeder clubs for Maesteg anymore. In fact, a few years ago, Maesteg Quins were regularly beating Maesteg. I guess it's how sport changes and no club has a divine right to stay at the top, but it's hard to stomach.'

Epilogue

'If I was to describe John in one sentence, it would be that he's the best provider for his family, loves his dogs, Liverpool FC and drives too fast!'

Alison Devereux

In September 2023, Devereux was inducted into the Welsh Sports Hall of Fame at a ceremony in Cardiff, in the company of many of his friends from his student and rugby-playing days.

'It was a huge shock to get the accolade,' he said, 'and I'm immensely proud to have joined the pantheon of Welsh sporting heroes who have been recognised over the years. When I was invited to the dinner, I didn't have any inkling I was there to be inducted into the prestigious Hall of Fame. Having some of my ex-college butties there with me was a lovely touch from the organisers, as was arranging for Jim Mills to present the award. It was a very special evening. I retired over 17 years ago and have lived another life since then, but that night really put the icing on my rugby career.'

During his days as a world-class rugby player, his career took priority, when club and international commitments had seen him spend large periods away from home, his wife and children, but Devereux clearly now enjoys being able to put his family first, particularly now that he has become a grandfather: 'I love spending time with Alison, my two girls Jessica and Ellen and my little grandson, Beaudie. He's not specifically named after All Blacks star Beauden Barrett, but Jessica liked the name and adapted it. I'm a big family man and I've doted on my two daughters since they day they were born. Although we were living in Widnes, we decided that both our children would be born in Wales. My girls could have played for Wales in any sport had they gone down the sporting route, but that didn't appeal to them and it doesn't bother me. They are my world and make me proud every day.

'Living in Widnes for 10 years, away from our parents was tough on both of us, but especially for Alison who was over three hours away from her mother, Tina, back in Pontycymer, who had to drive over 200 miles to north west England so that she could see her daughter and granddaughters. When I reflect on that commitment and courage she showed I take my hat off to her – *bendigedig* Tina.

'Alison has been so understanding and supportive, particularly when we've had to face big challenges, but we make a great team and I wouldn't have wanted any other life. I've enjoyed every minute of our marriage and we have lived the dream. It's been great, it really has.'

Alison admitted, however, that she wasn't too enamoured with the young John Devereux when they were at school together in the 1970s: 'I first met John when I moved to Pontycymer from Bridgend following my parents' marriage ending. My mum Tina was from the valley and wanted to move back to be near my grandparents, Gina and Watt, who were a massive part of my and my sister, Dawn's, life. I started in Ffaldau Primary School when I was eight and my sister Dawn was four. I remember being very worried waiting outside the headmaster's office with my sister, and when they took her to her new class, I hoped she would have a good first day. It was my turn next and I was taken to my new class. Little did I know that in that class would be a young boy named John Devereux who would have such a huge influence on my life.'

The notorious Devereux physicality and Dalek-like hand-off were in evidence, even at primary school, as Alison discovered to her cost: 'John was always a very sporty boy. He was good at rugby, basketball and football and played all sorts of games in the school yard. One day, during a game of British bulldog, he bumped into me and knocked me over. When I fell to the ground, it hurt so much I thought I'd broken my arm. I didn't really like him much after that.'

As the two school pupils grew older, Alison's culinary skills seem to have played a major part in grabbing the attention of the ever-hungry Devereux: 'A few years later, when we were in comprehensive school, he offered to carry my basket on the bus after every cookery lesson. By the time our 15-minute journey home was over, he had usually demolished the contents.'

Years later, Alison did insist that her soon-to-be husband's move to Widnes took second place to their forthcoming wedding: 'We discussed the offer to turn professional at length and, although I was apprehensive about the move, I knew it was an opportunity we couldn't turn down. My only stipulation that the news was not broadcast until our forthcoming wedding was over. I knew I would miss my mum and nan desperately but I had to be with my husband in our new life together in his new role as a professional rugby league player. We stepped off the plane from our honeymoon on Tuesday and went to Widnes the next day for John to play his first game for the Widnes A team. We then lived in a hotel for eight weeks while our new house was being built.'

'I couldn't have asked for a better father for our daughters, they both have him up there, high on a pedestal. He is a constant supporter to them whether it be advice, if they have car trouble or taken on DIY projects.'

The couple's devotion to each other doesn't mean that Devereux's unerring ability to inadvertently create havoc doesn't occasionally have Alison rolling her eyes in frustration, as she recalled a typical Devs incident when they were in Australia: 'Ken and Barbara, our lovely next-door neighbours in Widnes, came to Sydney in 1993 to visit and stay with us for a few weeks when John was playing for Manly. Ken loved rugby and used to accompany me to the Widnes games on a regular basis, he was the loveliest man you would ever meet. Sadly, he is no longer with us. On the day of the game, Ken and I followed the Manly team bus to the Penrith Panthers game and John was supposed to meet us after the game to navigate the homeward journey. John being John, though, he totally forgot. He didn't come to find us after the game and got on the team bus instead, and left. Poor Ken had to have his wits about him and drive us home, which was a journey of an hour and a half.

'I loved living up north and if the offer from Bridgend hadn't come in, we would probably still be there. We have some great memories and made many friends who we are still in contact with. We made the right decision in moving to Widnes. The club welcomed us with open arms and John's achievements in both union and league make me immensely proud.'

The couple smile warmly, and in unison, when talking about a key part of their life after returning to Wales – holidaying abroad with their extended family, as Devereux explains: 'We had so many very special memories from the summer holidays we spent with my parents and Alison's mother, Tina, over in Portugal. It's our happy place as a family, where we have returned every summer for the last 22 years. They were special times, spent with our two daughters as they grew up. We love the Algarve – the food, the climate and the golf

– but it's more than the place itself, it's the people we've shared our experiences with that's given it a treasured place deep in our hearts.'

Reflecting on the current situation of the game he loves, Devereux is refreshingly honest, saying: 'The rugby union I knew when I played it, pre- and post-league, has changed totally and I'm not sure I would enjoy playing it, the way it's developed. The recent Rugby World Cup quarter-finals were probably the best games of rugby union I have ever seen, but it's simply impossible to play at that level and with that intensity week-in, week-out; the human body cannot not sustain it. I also despair at the state of the game at grassroots level in Wales. The success of the Welsh national team over the last 18 years or so has masked the real problems the game is experiencing, financially and with decreasing player participation. Wherever I go in Wales, I see clubs struggling to field a team, and many having no youth teams. This is the life blood of Welsh rugby and it's drying up.

When asked about the state of rugby league, Devereux commented: 'Very rarely do I watch the Super League, and I really only watch Aussie RL NRL and State of Origin games, because the standard of rugby is exceptional. To all those people who complain about defences dominating rugby, union and league, just need to have a look at the skill levels of those Aussie RL players who work their socks off breaking down their opponent's defences. It's astounding.'

'I've been fortunate to have had a fantastic rugby career and it has given me, Alison and Jessica and Ellen a fabulous way of life. I have travelled the world and rugby has given me and my family financial security. I owe everything to my parents Peter and Valerie, who are sadly no longer with us and I miss them both, so much. They gave me all the love and support, I needed during my formative years growing up in the Garw Valley. I hope I made them proud.

'Some so-called, and self-appointed, experts say the success of a sporting career is measured only by the number of trophies and titles won. In my opinion that's nonsense, normally spouted by those who've never played elite-level sport. I may not have won many trophies, particularly in rugby union, but I played for my country in two-codes, as I did for the union and league Lions. Those caps are my trophies and very few players have all four. For those of us who've competed at the highest level, a successful sporting career is also measured in the memories and friendships that last a lifetime. I've got a personal trophy cabinet full of those wonderful and priceless experiences and I wouldn't swap any of them, ever.

'This book has given me the opportunity to relive so many memories that I had completely forgotten, with the help of scrap books, diaries, videos of games and other people who are less forgetful than me. Playing for Wales from 1986 to 1989 was, and still is, my greatest achievement and proudest moment.

'As the pages turn in my life, I embrace the lessons learnt, cherish the memories and anticipate the unwritten chapters that lie ahead.'

Career Statistics and Honours

	Rugby Union	P	T	G	FG	Total Pts
	School & College					
1970-77	Ffaldau Primary School					
1977-84	Ynysawdre Comprehensive					
1984-87	South Glamorgan Institute of HE	*65				
	Clubs					
1984-89	Bridgend RFC	42	16	0	0	64
1996-99	Sale Sharks	12	0	0	0	0
1999	Worcester Warriors	11	2	0	0	10
1999-02	Bridgend RFC	60	9	0	0	45
2002-03	Pontypool RFC	7	1	0	0	5
2003-06	Maesteg RFC	46	0	0	0	0
		178	**28**	**0**	**0**	**124**
	Representative					
1986-89	Wales	21	4	0	0	20
1986-89	British & Irish Lions	1	0	0	0	0
1986-89	Barbarians	3	0	0	0	0
	Rugby League	P	T	G	FG	T
	Clubs					
1989-97	Widnes	225	125	29	0	538
1993	Manly Sea Eagles	15	2	2	0	12
2003-05	Bridgend Blue Bulls	*21	0	0	0	0
		261	**127**	**31**	**0**	**550**
	Representative					
1991-00	Wales	12	3	1	0	14
1992-94	Great Britain	8	6	0	0	24

*Estimates as no records were available

Club Honours	
Widnes	
1990	Charity Shield winners
1990	Lancashire Cup winners
1990	Premiership winners
1991	Premiership runners up
1992	Regal Trophy winners
1993	Challenge Cup finalists
Bridgend Blue Bulls	
2003	Amateur Conference - British Champions
2005	Amateur Conference - British Champions

International Tours & Honours	
Wales	
1986	Wales Tour of Tonga, Fiji & Western Samoa
1986	Sydney Sevens
1987	Inaugural Rugby World Cup (3rd Place)
1988	Sydney Sevens
1988	Tour of New Zealand (played 2 Test matches)
1989	Sydney Sevens
British & Irish Lions	
1986	v Rest of the World (Cardiff)
1989	Tour of Australia (played 5 matches, on bench for 3rd Test)
Wales RL	
1995	European Rugby League Champions
1995	RL World Cup (semi-finalist)
2000	RL World Cup (semi-finalist)
Great Britain RL	
1990	Tour of Papua New Guinea & New Zealand
1992	RL World Cup Final v Australia
1992	Tour of Papua New Guinea, New Zealand & Australia
1994	Test series v New Zealand (played 3 Tests)

Index

Bryant, David 72, 75, 173
Brynteg Comprehensive School 13
Buchanan, Anthony 58
Burnett, Peter 'Bush' 161-2, 165-6
Byrne, Ged 157
Byrne, Lee 188

C
Caisley, Chris 82, 86
Calder, Finlay 79-80, 84, 87
Callard, Jonathan 16
Campese, David 64-5, 84
Canada (RU) 57, 59
Canberra Raiders RL 121, 126, 178
Cannon, Steve 5
Canterbury RL 102, 106
Cardiff RFC 3-8, 12, 14-5, 18-9, 21-4,
    27, 47, 73, 106, 133, 140, 150, 170,
    172
Cardiff Arms Park 3, 5, 12, 22, 34, 87,
    123, 135
Cardiff Demons RL 187,
Carling, Will 77
Carlisle RL 103, 105, 119, 188
Castleford RL 113, 115
Castres Olympique 174-5
Celtic Crusaders RL 175
Celtic League 174
Celtic Warriors 169, 175
Central Park (Wigan) 108, 119, 122
Challenge Cup (RL) 120-3, 128-9, 149,
    157
Challenge Cup, European (RU) 170
Chalmers, Craig 81, 83-4, 114
Chambers, Tony 153
Charity Shield (RL) 102
Charvet, Denis 34
Chemics, The (see Widnes RL)
Chilcott, Gareth 'Coochie Bear' 81
Clapham, Paul 172
Clarke, Phil 116-7, 139
Clement, Anthony 69
Clohessy, Peter 'The Claw' 175
Codey, David 64
Cohen, Simon 47, 153, 159
Colclough, Maurice 27, 30
Coliseum Promotions 162-6, 171-2
Collins, Richie 55
Connolly, Gary 113, 116, 141
Cordle, Gerald 106
Coventry RFC 27, 163
Cowbridge Comprehensive School 14

Cowie, Neil 136
Coychurch Road (Bridgend) 187
Critchley, Jason 180
Cronulla Sharks RL 187
Crooks, Lee 'Crooksey' 105, 115
Crossan, Keith 57
Cunningham, Keiron 180
Currier, Andy 'Adge' 94, 99, 128, 161
Cusworth, Les 159, 161
Cutler, Steve 65
Cyncoed (see South Glamorgan Institute)
Cynon Valley Cougars RL 187

D
Dacey, Malcolm 38
Dalek 6, 22, 25, 64, 183, 185, 193
Dalton, Andy 61, 73
Davey, Claude 67
Davies, Alan 133
Davies, Carwyn 75
Davies, Gareth 4, 12
Davies, Huw 27, 30, 173
Davies, Huw Llewelyn 43-4
Davies, Jonathan 'Jiffy' 22, 24, 27, 30-3,
    35, 38, 41-4, 57, 62, 64-5, 67, 69-
    70, 73-4, 86, 88-91, 95-9, 101-2,
    104-6, 113, 123-4, 126, 128, 134,
    136-8, 141, 147-8, 150, 162, 191
Davies, Leighton 'Nutty' 4, 18-9, 22-3
Davies, Phil 27, 42, 54
Davies, Simon 22
Davies, Stuart 7, 23
Dawes, John 'Sid' 1-3, 32
Dean, Paul 79
Deans, Bob 71
Deans, Bruce 70
Deans, Colin 80
Devereux, Alison (wife) 50-2, 78, 88, 90-
    1, 96-7, 109, 127, 129-30, 146, 159,
    162, 164-5, 183, 192-5
Devereux, Ceri (sister) 9-10
Devereux, Ellen (daughter) 127, 164,
    192, 195
Devereux, Jessica (daughter) 51, 127,
    130, 164, 192, 195
Devereux, Lynne (sister) 9-10
Devereux, Michael (grandfather) 11
Devereux, Peter (father) 9-10, 21, 36, 63,
    89-90, 195
Devereux, Valerie (mother) 9, 63, 195
Dewsbury RL 152
Diamond, Steve 158

ST DAVID'S PRESS

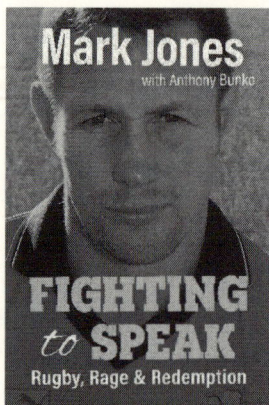

Fighting to Speak
Rugby, Rage and Redemption

Shortlisted for The Sunday Times Rugby Book of the Year (2023)

'I have nothing but the highest respect for Mark. His stammer did not make life easy for him and challenged his mental health, but his immense strength of character saw him beat his demons and win his battles.'   **Jim Mills**

A talented and ferocious player, and one of the acknowledged 'bad-boys' of rugby, Mark Jones' on-field brutality was a direct consequence of the off-field torment he suffered with a debilitating stammer. *Fighting to Speak* reveals the journey of a miner's son with a stutter who succeeded to play rugby at the highest level and defeat his demons.

978-1-904609-018	250pp	£13.99	PB
978-1-904609-025	250pp	£9.99	eBook

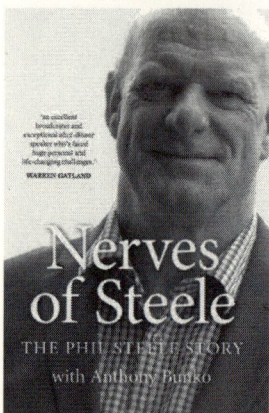

Nerves of Steele
The Phil Steele Story

'I've been lucky enough to get to know Phil during my time as Wales coach. He is an excellent broadcaster who genuinely wants Wales and Welsh players to excel and I respect his friendly and personal approach. I also admire the fact that he has been able to do this while facing personal and life changing challenges.'   **Warren Gatland**

Known to thousands of rugby fans as a knowledgeable, passionate and witty broadcaster, and as an entertaining and popular after-dinner speaker, Phil Steele's confident demeanour and humorous disposition mask a life-long battle against depression and anxiety heightened by heartbreak and tragedy in his personal life.

978-1-902719-50-4	208pp	£13.99	PB
978-1-902719-53-5	208pp	£9.99	eBook

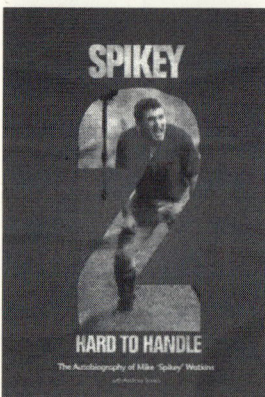

Spikey: 2 Hard to Handle
The Autobiography of Mike 'Spikey' Watkins

'One of the most inspirational leaders that Welsh rugby has ever produced'   **Mike Ruddock**

'No one trained harder, no one played harder...heart of a lion'   **Terry Holmes**

One of the most colourful and controversial characters in Welsh rugby history, Mike 'Spikey' Watkins remains the only player since 1882 to captain Wales on his debut, and win.

978-1-902719-40-5	251pp	£18.99	PB

St David's Press

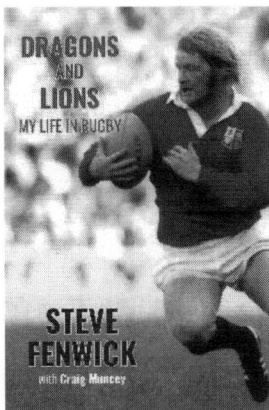

Dragons and Lions
My Life in Rugby

'A player I would go to war with.'　　　　　　　**JPR Williams**

'One of the outstanding centres of the 1970s.'　　　**Willie John McBride**

An icon of Welsh rugby and one of the stars of the great Wales team of the 1970s, Steve Fenwick won four Triple Crowns, two Grand Slams, played in all four Tests of the 1977 Lions tour to New Zealand, and won two Welsh Cups with Bridgend RFC.

Witty and engaging with a very dry sense of humour, in *Dragons and Lions*, his long-awaited autobiography, Steve Fenwick tells the story of the schoolboy from Nantgarw who became one of the most celebrated players in world rugby.

978-1-902719-856	200pp	£13.99	PB
978-1-902719-917	200pp	£9.99	eBook

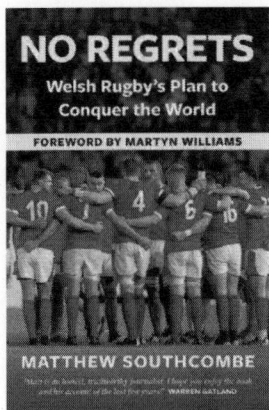

No Regrets
Welsh Rugby's Plan to Conquer the World

'Matt is an honest, trustworthy journalist. I hope you enjoy the book and his account of the last few years!'　　　　**Warren Gatland**

'Having followed Wales' every move over recent years, few journalists are better-placed to chronicle the team's journey over that period of time than Matt.'　　　　　　　**Martyn Williams**

In *No Regrets - Welsh Rugby's Plan to Conquer the World*, acclaimed *Western Mail* rugby correspondent Matthew Southcombe reveals how the masterplan led to the 2017 tour success in Argentina, a clean sweep in the 2018 autumn internationals and, in 2019, a Six Nations Grand Slam, a record 14-game unbeaten run and a World Rugby #1 ranking. Hopes were high, amongst the squad and the nation, as the team headed to Japan with a genuine expectation winning the tournament.

978-1-902719-81-8	176pp	£13.99	PB

White Gold
Swansea RFC 1872-1887

'an incredible insight into the formation of Swansea RFC: its characters, games played and the evolution of the 'Swansea Style'.'
David Richards, Swansea, Wales and British & Irish Lions

Lavishly illustrated with many previously unpublished photographs, **White Gold** has been meticulously researched by club historian David Dow and is the most comprehensive study of the early days of rugby in Swansea ever published.

978-1-904609-07-0	580pp	£75	PB
978-1-904609-08-7	580pp	£38	PB
978-1-904609-09-4	580pp	£25	eBook

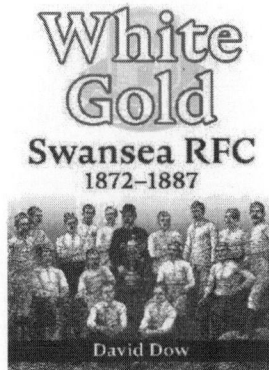

St David's Press

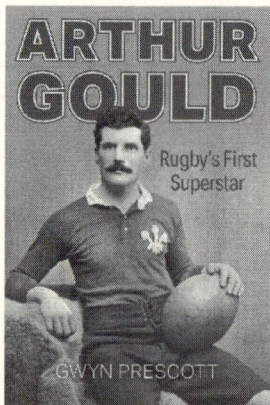

Arthur Gould
Rugby's First Superstar

"Prescott's research is meticulous and he has done Gould and the histories of rugby and Wales itself proud."
Prof Martin Johnes

"Gwyn Prescott has combined impeccable scholarship with an assured readability to produce a terrific book."
Huw Richards

Arthur Gould is the definitive biography of the record-breaking Welsh international player who is widely acknowledged as the first superstar of rugby. Such was his fame and renown, that upon his tragic, early death in 1919, aged just 54, Gould's funeral in Newport was reported as the biggest Wales had ever seen.

978-1-904609-124	254pp	£17.99	PB
978-1-904609-131	254pp	£12.99	eBook

'this rugby spellbound people'
The Birth of Rugby in Cardiff and Wales

"...scrupulously researched [and] well written...Gwyn Prescott has given [rugby in Wales] a history to be proud of."
Huw Richards, scrum.com

"Prescott paints a meticulous picture of Welsh rugby's growth in Victorian Britain"
Rugby World

"...a fascinating piece of research and a major contribution to the history of rugby."
Tony Collins

The Birth of Rugby in Cardiff and Wales is the essential guide to the importance of rugby in Cardiff and to the significance of Cardiff to the development of Welsh rugby in the 19th century.

978-1-902719-43-6	304pp	£16.99	PB

'Call Them to Remembrance'
The Welsh Rugby Internationals
Who Died in the Great War
(Second Edition)

'These pages contain an unexplored and untold tale which, from the deepest anguish of the suffering born of their unquestioning bravery, pierces the heart...This book is [an] acknowledgment of the sacrifice made by 13 Welshmen...Theirs was a sacrifice which needs to be told...Gwyn Prescott, with meticulous and sympathetic attention to detail, tells the story. This narrative is an essential record'.
Gerald Davies, from the Foreword

It is estimated that the First World War claimed the lives of 40,000 Welshmen, all of them heroes whose sacrifice is acknowledged by a grateful nation. *'Call Them to Remembrance'*, which includes over 120 illustrations and maps, tells the stories of 13 fallen heroes who shared the common bond of having worn the famous red jersey of the Welsh international rugby team.

978-1-902719-82-5	180pp	£19.99	PB
978-1-902719-90-0	180pp	£19.99	eBook

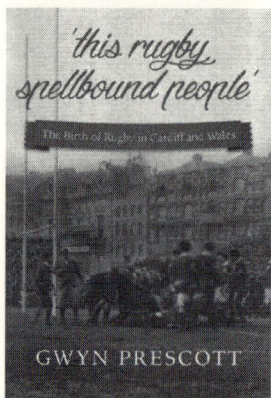

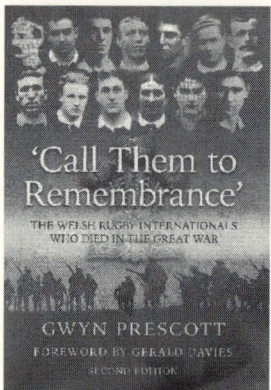

St David's Press

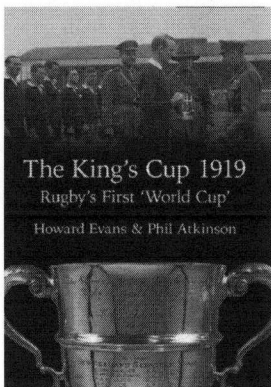

The King's Cup 1919
Rugby's First World Cup

'An intriguing retelling of a significant but largely forgotten chapter of rugby union history, superbly illustrated.' **Huw Richards**

After the Armistice in November 1918 – with the forces of the world's rugby-playing nations and many of their stars still stationed in Britain – and with the public desperate to see competitive rugby played again, an inter-military tournament was organised. *The King's Cup 1919* is the first book to tell the full story of rugby's first 'World Cup' and is essential reading for all rugby enthusiasts and military historians.

978-1-902719-44-3   192pp   £14.99   PB

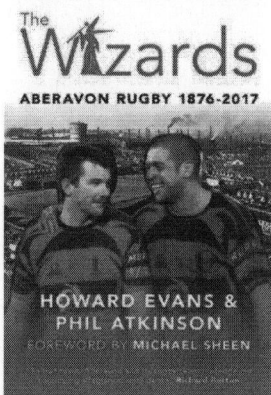

The Wizards
Aberavon Rugby 1876-2017

'I would rather have played rugby for Wales than Hamlet at the Old Vic. To that town, Aberavon and its rugby team, I pledge my continuing allegiance, until death.' **Richard Burton**

One of the traditional powerhouses of Welsh first class rugby, Aberavon RFC has a long, proud and illustrious history, with 50 of its players being capped for Wales, the club winning many league titles and domestic cups, and - with Neath RFC - facing the might of South Africa, Australia and New Zealand. Aberavon RFC is a great rugby club and this is its story.

978-1-902719-66-5   256pp   £19.99   PB

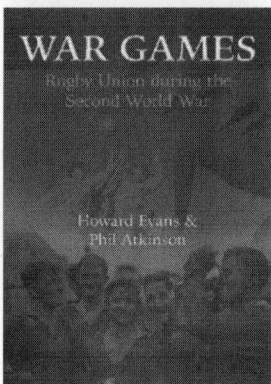

War Games
Rugby Union during the Second World War

Dedicated to 'all those in rugby who did - and who didn't - make it through those troubled times', *War Games* is a comprehensive and highly illustrated commemoration, packed with stories and statistics that for the first time chronicles the history of rugby - the men and the matches, from 'scratch' to international - during the Second World War. Essential and entertaining reading for followers of rugby and military historians alike, respected rugby authors Howard Evans and Phil Atkinson tell the tale - meticulously and with great affection for the game they love - of those men who played for fun but who, on too many occasions, lost more than a rugby game.

978-1-902719-67-2   302pp   £25.00   PB

ST DAVID'S PRESS

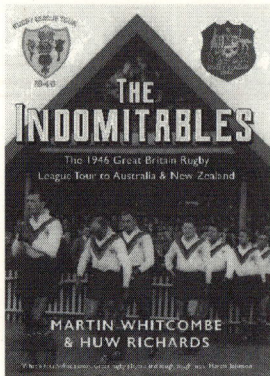

The Indomitables
Rugby League's Greatest Tour
The 1946 'Great Britain' Tour to Australia & New Zealand

'What a tour! What a story! Great rugby players and tough, tough men.'
Martin Johnson

'If you want to know why I and so many other league players wanted, more than anything, to be selected for an Ashes tour - then read this book. It's a sensational story of the greatest team that created the tradition we were all so proud to be part of.'
Andy Gregory

The 1946 Indomitables won the three Test series in Australia with two victories and a draw - an unbeaten record that has never been repeated - and remain Britain's most successful rugby league tourists. Lavishly illustrated with over 300 photographs, *The Indomitables* is the most comprehensive and authoritative account of the 1946 tour that made sporting legends of the 15 Englishmen and 11 Welshmen (including the captain, Gus Risman) who created sporting history and won the respect of the Australian nation.

These were The Indomitables – and this is their sensational story.

| 978-1-902719-702 | 500pp | £28.00 | PB |
| 978-1-902719-924 | 500pp | £25.00 | eBook |

The Indomitable Frank Whitcombe
How a Genial Giant from Cardiff became a Rugby League Legend in Yorkshire and Australia

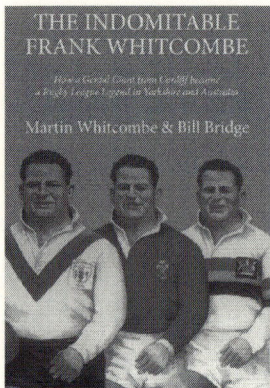

'Frank Whitcombe was a rugby league cult hero in the days before there were cult heroes. An eighteen-stone battle tank of a prop forward, he graduated from Welsh rugby union to become a pillar of the great Bradford pack of the 1940s. In the process, he became the first forward to win the Lance Todd Trophy, a member of the 1946 'Indomitable' Lions touring team to Australasia and had even driven the team bus to Wembley when Bradford won the 1947 Challenge Cup Final. This book is his story - it is essential reading for anyone interested in the history of rugby and the amazing men who made the game.'
Prof. Tony Collins

'Frank Whitcombe became a Welsh international and a Great Britain tourist. He is widely regarded as an all-time great of rugby league.'
Fran Cotton

| 978-1-902719-47-4 | 256pp | £19.99 | PB |
| 978-1-902719-59-7 | 256pp | £9.99 | eBook |